OPEN Modeling with UML

The OPEN Series

Consulting Editor: Brian Henderson-Sellers

Related titles

The Open Process Specification, Ian Graham, Brian Henderson-Sellers and Houman Younessi

Documenting a complete Java application using OPEN, Donald G. Firesmith, Greg Hendley, Scott Krutsch and Marshall Stowe

The OPEN Toolbox of Techniques, Brian Henderson-Sellers, Anthony Simons, Houman Younessi

ACM Press Books

This book is published as part of the ACM Press Books – a collaboration between the Association for Computing Machinery and Addison-Wesley. ACM is the oldest and largest education and scientific society in the information technology field. Through its high quality publications and services, ACM is a major force in advancing the skills and knowledge of IT professionals throughout the world. For further information about ACM contact:

ACM Member Services
1515 Broadway, 17th Floor
New York NY 10036-5701
Phone: +1 212 626 0500
Fax: +1 212 944 1318
Email: *acmhelp@acm.org*

ACM European Service Center
108 Cowley Road
Oxford OX4 1JF
United Kingdom
Phone: +44 1865 382338
Fax: +44 1865 381338
Email: *acm-europe@acm.org*
URL: *http://www.acm.org*

Selected ACM titles:

Software for Use: A Practical Guide to the Models and Methods of Usage Centered Design
Larry L. Constantine and Lucy A.D. Lockwood

The UML User Guide
Grady Booch, James Rumbaugh, Ivar Jacobson

The Unified Software Development Process
Ivar Jacobson, Grady Booch, James Rumbaugh

The UML Reference Manual
James Rumbaugh, Ivar Jacobson, Grady Booch

OPEN Modeling with UML

Brian Henderson-Sellers and Bhuvan Unhelkar

Addison-Wesley

An imprint of Pearson Education

Harlow, England · London · New York · Reading, Massachusetts · San Francisco
Toronto · Don Mills, Ontario · Sydney · Tokyo · Singapore · Hong Kong · Seoul
Taipei · Cape Town · Madrid · Mexico City · Amsterdam · Munich · Paris · Milan

PEARSON EDUCATION LIMITED

Head Office:
Edinburgh Gate
Harlow CM20 2JE
Tel: +44 (0)1279 623623
Fax: +44 (0)1279 431059

London Office:
128 Long Acre, London WC2E 9AN
Tel: +44 (0)20 7447 2000
Fax: +44 (0)20 7240 5771
Website: www.awl.com/cseng/

First published in Great Britain in 2000

ISBN 0-201-67512-9

British Library Cataloguing in Publication Data
A CIP catalogue record for this book can be obtained from the British Library

Library of Congress Cataloging in Publication Data
Applied for.

Acknowledgements
The publishers would like to thank Derek Renouf of Adaptive Arts Pty Limited for permission to use the OPEN logo.

10 9 8 7 6 5 4 3 2 1

Typeset by MRules
Printed and bound in the United States of America.

The Publishers' policy is to use paper manufactured from sustainable forests.

To Ann

– Brian Henderson-Sellers

Asha: For her unconditional support

– Bhuvan Unhelkar

Acknowledgements

We would like to thank Alistair Cockburn for permission to reproduce figures 2.41 and 2.42 from *Writing Effective Use Case* (in preparation), Addison-Wesley.

We would like to thank OMG for permission to adapt figures 2.3, 2.4, 2.6, 2.10, 2.21, 2.31, 2.34, from OMG (1999) *UML Modeling Language Specification, Version 1.3*, June 1999; and figures 2.9, 2.17, 2.20 from OMG (1997) *UML Notation. Version 1.1*, 15 September 1997.

Figures 2.40, 3.45–3.51 are adapted from S. Lilly (1999) 'Use case pitfalls: top 10 problems from real projects using use cases', in *Proc. TOOLS 30* (ed. D. Firesmith *et al.*) the IEEE Computer Society Press

Figures 1.4, 3.1, 4.4, 5.1, 5.4, 5.7, 5.8, 5.9, 5.27–5.29 are adapted from B. Unhelkar, (1999), After the *Y2K Fireworks. Business and Technology Strategies*, CRC Press. Figure 3.52 is from B. Henderson-Sellers *et al.* (1998) *The Open Toolbox of Techniques*, Addison-Wesley.

Trademark Notice

Contents

Foreword

In 1996, in concert with a good friend and one of the world's great methodologists (Ivar Jacobson), I pulled together a meeting that a scant two years before would have been impossible. In a room in San José, California, at an Object Management Group (OMG) Technical Meeting, were to be found nearly all of the world's methodologists or their representatives. They had come not necessarily to agree on an object-oriented methodology (although within a year or so they would do so), but rather to agree to agree; that day, the object-oriented analysis and design community agreed that the time had come for standardization in their field, and that the open, neutral OMG process would be the fastest, surest route to achieve such a standard.

In September 1997, the OMG adopted its first methodology standard, the Unified Modeling Language. Twenty-one companies took part in the effort to create a single, standardized analysis and design notation and metamethodology. Over the succeeding years, the UML standard has successfully unified the previously highly fragmented object-oriented analysis and design market-place (as well as the tremendously fragmented academic outlook on analysis and design). This is a success story for the analysis and design community, as well as for the OMG itself (which leveraged this novel experience to begin standardization in over a dozen other fields, from genetic modeling and air-traffic control to manufacturing, healthcare and financial standards). The OMG had successfully drawn the community together to agree a single, worldwide standard, with even higher industry consensus than had been achieved with OMG's successful CORBA systems integration platform standard.

Since 1997, the OMG has expanded the UML standard in several important directions. The Meta-Object Facility (MOF) provides a UML-based approach to storing and sharing models of all kinds, including software repositories and data dictionaries. The Common Warehouse Metamodel (CWM), nearly complete at this writing, provides a set of unifying principles to finally pull together the myriad corporate databases into a single picture of an organization's operations. Leveraging the immensely popular new Extensible Markup Language (XML), the OMG published an XML Model Interchange (XMI) language for sharing repository data between far-flung corners of an enterprise (and more importantly, between enterprises in a business-to-business context).

What more could anyone want? UML, MOF and XMI have revolutionized the modeling world, integrating software development threads across the spectrum of requirements modeling, systems analysis and design. Could the OMG countenance opening Pandora's Box one more time to see what might come next?

In fact, the OMG is going in several directions with UML-based technology at this writing. Besides the comprehensive, multidatabase CWM, the OMG is revising the UML specification, planning on a version 2.0 based on vigorous feedback from the user and vendor communities. But still missing is a major component of the analysis and design market-place: standardization of process.

In the beginning, as it were, software development was simple. Everyone understood the waterfall that led from user need, to requirements capture, to systems design to implementation. Everyone also knew that this simple model, while easy to understand, was not actually the model software architects followed (feedback was a bit more inherent than the waterfall admitted!), but at seemingly minor perturbations of this model (such as the quite popular iterative waterfall model), it seemed close enough for everyday development.

The nascence of the Unified Modeling Language, however, propelled the need for standardization of development process to the fore. And as I write this, the confusion that reigned in the methodology market-place four years ago is deeply embedded in the psyche of process modelers everywhere. Over the next year or two the OMG will address this lack of standardization with some solution, developed publicly under the OMG public, neutral, open standards process.

The book in your hands presents a major contender for this Process Crown. Henderson-Sellers was one of the architects of UML, and remains prominent in the revision and management of the UML standard as it rolls forward based on user and vendor experience. Unhelkar brings to bear his own direct practical experience from consulting and training using these ideas. Their ideas about process are therefore pertinent, and as you read this tome not only will you find a well-defined and well-honed methodology for managing your own software development processes, but you will also pick up a strong sense for the power of a standardized metamethod and how it can be integrative in your organization. Clear explanations of fundamentially difficult concepts make this book a major contribution to the literature and to future standardization in this arena; I hope that you will find yourself motivated to make your own contribution to international standards for analysis and design processes!

RICHARD MARK SOLEY, PH.D.
CHAIRMAN AND CEO
Object Management Group, Inc.
March, 2000

Preface

Purpose of this book

Austin, Texas, October, 1995. We were both there to listen to the jagged and ragged singing of one of the three Amigos of the Unified Modeling Language as its precursor, the Unified Method, was announced on an eventful evening. The UML has come a long way since then, and a large number of IT professionals[1] have worked towards smoothing the edges of this now very popular modeling language. With the acceptance of the UML by the Object Management Group in 1997, it is now a public domain modeling language that is available to anyone and everyone who wishes to follow a disciplined and standard approach to modeling systems and applications in the new millennium. It is thus a 'necessary' part of any software activity but, needless to say, not 'sufficient'. Insufficiencies of the UML arise from the fact that it is a pure modeling language, nothing more. It contains no elements of process that would guide software development from 'start to finish'. Being only a modeling language, it also does not take responsibility for data issues, migration issues, component integration issues, nor for the higher-level process and project management issues. As the IT world moves forward in the new millennium, a dearth is felt by most IT professionals of a 'process' that would not only provide the control and guidance needed for varied software development situations, but of a 'process environment' that would lend itself to 'tailoring' – a customization process that would enable the development process to be tailored to precisely fit the individual organization's development environment. While there is a lot of process material that discusses 'new' software development, there is a dearth of discussion on processes that help in 'customizing' software packages and/or provide help in 'integrating' newly developed components with existing legacy software. These are some of the areas that are addressed in this work through OPEN.

So, what is OPEN?

OPEN stands for Object-oriented Process, Environment and Notation. It is a 'third generation' methodological approach that has been very successfully used in practice, as well as for teaching about object-oriented methods and even basic object-oriented concepts around the world, for several years. In this book, however, we present OPEN at an introductory level for industry. Having read this book, you will no doubt want to find out further, more detailed, information. This can be found in other titles in the OPEN book series. We have written two full books to describe all the detail (Graham *et al.*, 1997a; Henderson-Sellers *et al.*, 1998). These contain the information on how to use OPEN on real projects once you have mastered the introductory level concepts described in *this* book. There is also a detailed case study example in the book (see Bibliography) of Firesmith *et al.* (1998). In contrast to those earlier books, therefore, this book will initiate interest and provide

1 Including one of the authors (BH-S)

support in the use of a process-based development effort. It will be found useful both for industry users and also at a university Master's level.

Summary of the book

The book is primarily written around a pair of case studies. The first (Chapter 4) is a relatively simple one showing how to use OPEN in a responsibility-driven style of development, and the second, in Chapter 5, focuses on the use of OPEN in a use-case-driven software project. This choice of case studies illustrates our belief that to learn about good software design, you must observe, study and then replicate (with fine tuning, of course) existing development material. This is best exemplified by a case study.

However, since this is an introductory level book, we precede these two case studies by some ground-laying material. In Chapter 1 we give a brief overview of the OPEN process and an appropriate modeling language: UML (the Unified Modeling Language of the Object Management Group). These two topics (UML and OPEN) are then examined in the next two chapters in more detail.

In Chapter 2 we describe the key elements of the UML. We must stress here that, while UML is a modeling language and thus contains both a metamodel and a notation, it is primarily the notational element that we will introduce here. The metamodel is implicit in the rules we give you about how to build models and how to document them using the notation and the recommended diagram types. We will also use it, as and when required, in the context of the OPEN process (Chapters 3–5). This contrasts with, for instance, one of the first books on UML (see Bibliography) by Fowler and Scott (*UML Distilled*) which only addressed notation, but still found it necessary to invent fractions of process (e.g. the four phases of development) in order to explain the notation. Similarly, in a recent book by Quatrani, the focus is on modeling with the ROSE™ tool – although there is a stronger process element than in *UML Distilled*. Please note that we have no issues in using any CASE tool in order to show the use of notations and diagramming technique. In fact, we have used evaluation versions of three different CASE tools to draw UML diagrams in the last three chapters in this book. However, our focus here is on the use of process rather than notation. This means that we are in no danger of omitting important methodological process steps and, at the same time, we introduce only commonly used notational elements.

In Chapter 3, we examine the support in OPEN for modeling. OPEN contains a number of Activities, Tasks and Techniques, many of which are focused on modeling. Indeed, this book only deals with modeling. So, in this chapter, we select those elements of OPEN which support modeling and discuss, particularly, its modeling Tasks and Techniques. These give you the tools and the process by which to build software. The work product or artefact resulting from the process can then be documented using the chosen modeling language of UML. OO methodologies in general (and OPEN is no exception) are often more extensive than their traditional (structured) counterparts, since they reflect an increasing sophistication in our use of modeling techniques. Companies are building increasingly sophisticated software and find that their use of object technology permits this. They can take on challenges and establish their competitive edge in ways that they could only dream about 10 or 20 years ago. Using a good, process-focused methodology is only one element in making those dreams come true. Skills of people, an organizational fit (between culture and process) and a determination to succeed all facilitate the road to success. Object technology (and increasingly OO-based component technology) provides a bridge between technical success and management success.

Finally we would note that using OPEN on a commercial project requires access to the full methodology as well as a modeling language. In other words, a significant number of the OPEN project management tasks and techniques will be needed, as well as detailed iterations of the activities of requirements engineering and deployment. Due consideration of quality and reuse will also be required. Some of these activities and related issues are alluded to in Chapter 5 as well as demonstrated, albeit briefly, in the Appendix. Training and mentoring on the process, modeling language and tools is also necessary and is offered by relevant and rapidly maturing third-party organizations. (See www.open.org.au for details.)

Literary audience

This book is targeted at an introductory industrial level or a senior academic level. It will be of prime interest to methodologists, project managers, process managers and quality assurance professionals who are responsible for implementing software development processes or managing development thereof, in their respective organizations. Students of component-based software development who, on completion of their C++ or Java courses, have realized that languages are not enough for industrial software development, will quickly find that this book answers many of their questions on 'practical component development'. Thus, this book can be used as a two-day course in an industrial setting, or as part of a one-semester course in an academic environment. Finally, it will be of interest to anyone and everyone involved in modeling software components, who are practising the UML standard, and who wish to start following a process in order to correctly model their requirements and systems, so that they produce 'business value' to the sponsors of their projects.

Mapping to a workshop

It is envisaged that this book will provide invaluable process and modeling-related information to a wide range of audiences. As mentioned before, the material in this book may be used in a two-day industrial training setting or as a course in a university environment. Here, we briefly outline how a two-day workshop can be conducted in conjunction with this book. Please note that the two case studies in this book can be expanded and discussed in detail if more time is available. For instance, if the workshops are conducted with the help of a CASE tool, then the workshop outline provided here will need three or more days to complete. On the other hand, if less time is available only one of two case studies may be used.

Mapping of the chapters in this book to a two-day workshop

Day	*Session*	*Presentation and discussion workshop topic*	*Relevant chapters*	*Comments*
1	8:30–10:00	**The UML – basics; The necessity and *in*sufficiency of the UML**	Chapter 2	All basic UML notations are described, together with their importance; the need for a process is highlighted – especially its acute need to complement industrial usage of the UML.
	10:30–12:00	**The OPEN process – basics; How OPEN complements the UML**	Chapter 1	Basic concepts of OPEN – how it is a 'process environment'. Its relevance in component integration, Internet-based development, etc., focusing on OPEN's 'tailorability'. Together with UML, a complete IT environment.
	1:30–3:00	**The OPEN artefacts – Activities, Tasks and Techniques**	Chapter 3	Some of the OPEN artefacts – especially the ones relevant to tothe case study in Chapter 4 – are discussed in detail as a preparation for the first case study.
	3:30–5:00	**Case study 1 – Library management system**	Chapter 4	This session highlights the use of OPEN and UML in a responsibility-driven design approach. Participants are expected to use material from the previous session and attempt the process and designs.
2	8:30–10:00	**The OPEN artefacts – Activities, Tasks and Techniques**	Chapter 3	Remaining OPEN artefacts are discussed in greater detail, especially those required for a use-case-driven approach as shown in Chapter 5. Also,

Day	*Session*	*Presentation and discussion workshop topic*	*Relevant chapters*	*Comments*
2 *(cont)*				OPEN artefacts *not discussed* in the book are highlighted.
	10:30–12:00	**Case study 2 – Small Business Loan System**	Chapter 5	Discuss the problem statement; Attempt at 'tailoring' the OPEN lifecycle. Create Project Plan, Requirements Model.
	1:30–3:00	**Case study 2 – Small Business Loan System**	Chapter 5	Complete the Activities of Analysis and Design, Evaluation.
	3:30–5:00	**Summary and conclusions**	All chapters	Use discussion topics at the end of each chapters; Review and summary; Further readings, etc.

Semantics

The authors firmly believe in gender-neutral language. *Person* is therefore used wherever possible. Quotes and other references have been left untouched.

Terms like *programmer* and *manager*, unless otherwise mentioned, represent roles performed by actors. These terms don't tie down real people like you and us who, in a short span of time, can jump from the role of a programmer to a manager to a director and back. Thus, when we say 'a programmer has to implement these designs', it implies the *role* of a programmer which might be filled by a person today who, in five (or two) years' time, might be performing the role of a manager with significantly different responsibilities.

We throughout the text refers not only to the authors, but also includes the reader. Occasionally, *we* refers to the general IT community of which the authors are members. Thus, a statement like '*we* need to follow a process' implies all in the IT community need to follow a process.

Acknowledgements

It is in the nature of things that the sum of parts has something more to it than a mere arithmetic sum. This is especially true of explaining the concept of OPEN with

UML, as has been attempted here in this book. We are grateful to a number of individuals who, having written eminent work in this same area, found it worthwhile to give their time and effort in commenting on our drafts. Other friends contributed to the drawing and supplying of some of the figures, reading our work and passing constructive criticisms. We wish to thank them all, and mention some of them in particular. They are, in alphabetical order of first names, Alistair Cockburn, Anneke Kleppe, Christopher Biltoft, David Hazlewood, Errol Thompson, Levi Martinovich, Paresh Shal or Rahul Mohod, Rob Rist, Shreekanth Sindia, Sid Mishra, Sunil Vadnerkar and Susan Lilly, to name but a few.

SriPrabhat (S.D.) Pradhan, CEO, Tata Technologies India Limited, has been very supportive of this work and sees its immense value in promoting software process discipline in the phenomenal and still rapidly growing software industry in India. 'The new millennium in India can do well with a simple and lucidly written work like this', he says – and we thank him sincerely for his comments.

We also wish to thank our respective families in their support during our effort. BH-S: To Ann for her continued support of my book-writing efforts. BU: Thanks to my wife Asha, daughter Sonki Priyadarshini and son Keshav Raja, as well as my extended family Girish and Chinar Mamdapur, for all their moral support.

Finally, this work acknowledges all trademarks of respective organizations, whose names and/or tools have been used in this book. Specifically, we acknowledge the trademarks of Adaptive-Arts (for SimplyObjects™), Computer Associates (for ParadigmPlus™ and Process Continuum™) and Rational (for ROSE™).

Critiques

It will only reflect a healthy state of affairs within the IT world if this work receives its due share of criticism. We believe that all criticisms have an underlying rationale and that they should all be accepted in a positive and constructive vein. All comments on this work, both positive and negative, *will* be accepted positively. Thus, to all our prospective critics, whose criticisms will not only enrich our own knowledge and understanding of the subject discussed in this book, but also add to the general wealth of knowledge available to the IT community, we wish to say a big *thank you* in advance.

BRIAN HENDERSON-SELLERS &
BHUVAN UNHELKAR
Sydney, January, 2000

List of acronyms

BOM: Business Object Model
BTW: By The Way
CASE: Computer-Aided/Assisted Software Engineering
CIRT: Class, Instance, Role or Type
CMM: Capability Maturity Model
CORBA: Common Object Request Broker Architecture
COTS: Commerical Off The Shelf (software)
CRC: Class, Responsibility, Collaborator
CRUD: Create, Read, Update, Delete
DFD: Data Flow Diagram
ER: Entity Relationship
GUI: Graphical User Interface
IIP: Iterative, Incremental, Parallel
ISO: International Standards Organization
MOF: Meta Object Facility
OCL: Object Constraint Language
OMG: Object Management Group
OML: OPEN Modeling Language
OMT: Object Modeling Technique
OO: Object-oriented
OOA: Object-oriented analysis
OOD: Object-oriented design
OOP: Object-oriented programming
OPEN: Object-oriented Process, Environment and Notation
OT: Object Technology
OTUG: Object Technology User Group
PSP: Personal Software Process
QA: Quality Assurance
RDBMS: Relational Data Base Management System
RDD: Responsibility-Driven Design
RTF: Revisionary Task Force
RUP: Rational Unified Process
SEI: Software Engineering Institute
SEP: Software Engineering Process
SOM: System Object Model
STD: State Transition Diagram

SVDPI: Subject-Verb-Direct_object-Preposition-Indirect_object
TBD: To Be Decided
UML: Unified Modeling Language
VDM: Vienna Development Method
V&V: Verification and Validation
WP: Whole–Part
XP: eXtreme Programming

Introduction to OPEN

Abstract

In this chapter, we discuss the key elements of the Object-oriented Process, Environment and Notation, otherwise known as OPEN. OPEN is the premier third-generation, public domain methodology for software development, focusing on the use of object technology. It is really a framework in that it can be tailored to individual demands brought about by existing team skills, organizational process maturity, project size and so on. Indeed, it is this tailorability that is a key asset of the framework approach, permitting and sustaining organizations, and teams within those organizations, to be sure that their version (or instantiation) of OPEN is exactly what they require. Key elements of the OPEN process framework are Activities, Tasks, and Techniques and Work Products. These Work Products are often in the form of or supplemented by graphical diagrams. These can be drawn using your preferred notation. Here, we introduce and use the Object Management Group's UML (Unified Modeling Language) standard for the notation.

What is OPEN?

OPEN is a *third-generation, full lifecycle, process-focused, methodological approach* that is especially suited for component-based, object-oriented and Internet-based software developments as well as for business modeling and systems modeling. It can be *tailored* for use on large mission-critical systems, customizing packages and small applications developments, as well as integrating with legacy code. OPEN stands for Object-oriented Process, Environment and Notation and it is in the public domain. It has been tailored and used by many organizations worldwide in developing industrial-strength software.

OPEN is a complete process environment, in that it includes everything needed for software construction within a business environment. It covers technical aspects such as modeling and metrics, project management aspects such as team and organizational roles, and business decision-making aspects, as well as sociological aspects such as usability. In this book we concentrate on the more technical aspects of object-oriented *modeling*.

OPEN is a methodological approach with a focus on object-oriented (OO) development

Methods, often called methodologies, have been around a long time; but it is only since about 1990 or so that they have been available to support object-oriented development. An object-oriented method relies on the notions of abstraction, strict modularization, information hiding and polymorphism. Requirements, design and code all use the same model of the 'object' (Figure 1.1) which encapsulates together state and behaviour with a tightly controlled interface. While the initial emphasis is always on the 'what', not the 'how', within the development lifecycle (requirements), this is followed by the 'how' (detailed design and coding).

With this more holistic view of modeling and software design, it is beneficial to ask about the high-level responsibilities that an object has: responsibilities for doing, for knowing and for enforcing. In later design and coding, these are translated into first, operations (in the interface) and then methods (internal code details) of the classes. Whilst using a responsibility-focused approach is found useful, object-oriented software can also be specified and developed using a data-driven approach or a use-case-driven approach, depending on the particular problem and problem domain (Figure 1.2). We will illustrate how to apply both a responsibility-driven (Chapter 4) and a use-case-driven (Chapter 5) approach in this book.

We should also expand a little on the statement that OPEN is suited for component-based and Internet-based development. Development in the new

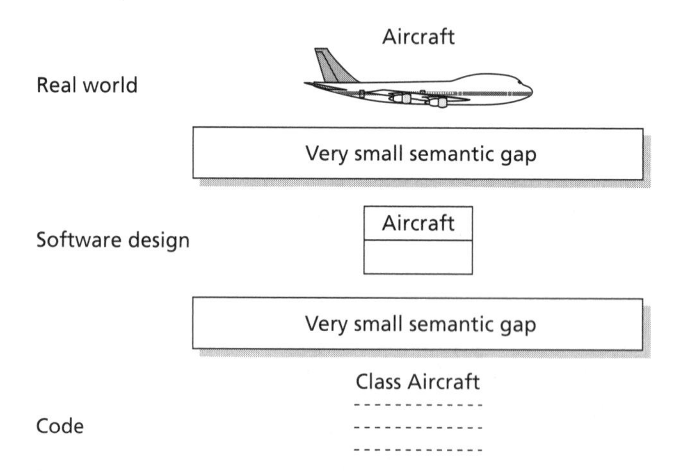

Figure 1.1 When translating the real-world problem to the software design and then to the code, the same concept of 'object is used – although the representation is different, the underlying modularity and granularity of the object concept remain unchanged.

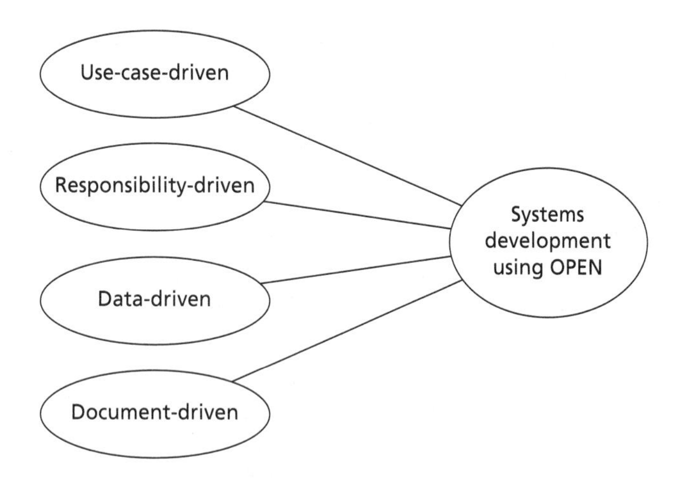

Figure 1.2 Systems development using OPEN may be use-case-driven, responsibility-driven, data-driven or document-driven.

millennium will incorporate distributed architectures almost by default. With the advent of the Internet and industrial-strength middleware to support distributed architectures, a good method(ology) has the responsibility of providing the detailed process of architecting and designing fully encapsulated components that can be deployed over a company's network or on the web. OPEN provides detailed support for such applications, as will be illustrated, in part, in Chapter 5.

OPEN supports the full software lifecycle

Software can be considered to have a lifecycle from cradle to grave. The need for software can arise when business problems need solution. So the first step (the cradle) occurs when a business problem is identified. This is a problem that must be clearly enunciated. And although a software solution is not mandated at this stage, for those problems that *do* lead to a software solution, the requirements engineering activity, which focuses on elucidating the business problem, is clearly a vital part of the software lifecycle. Business decision making, requirements engineering and systems analysis are all 'early lifecycle' activities. OPEN includes specific elements (called tasks and techniques) which are useful in these early stages – and which are lacking in other contemporary approaches to OO development. In the real world, if technology (here object technology, or OT) is to be relevant to commercial environments, an OO method *must* consider these early lifecycle issues and not just assume that the lifecycle begins with the handing over of a clearly and uniquely defined requirements definition to the software developer.

Similarly, a method should cover the late lifecycle activities. Whilst most are good at program design and coding, they tend to tail off in their coverage of issues such as deployment, user training and future enhancements/maintenance. It is just as important that a method addresses these issues, perhaps using testing metrics to do fault detection and usability studies to evaluate customer acceptance of the delivered product, for instance.

OPEN is a process-focused methodological approach.
Process is the key to good software development practices. It imposes order and rigour. A process, of any sort, tells you how to take certain steps in order to accomplish a specific task or goal – to get something done. Taking steps involves ordering those into some sequence because we live in a temporal universe and, as individuals, do not live concurrent lives. A process offers a repeatable and manageable underpinning to software development when something goes wrong; it can be identified, corrected and avoided on future occasions. It has been called 'documented decision making' and equated to workflow description.

Processes may be in an individual's head or may be written down as an organizational (or international) standard to be followed on each project. They may be large or small, 'authoritarian' or flexible. Sophisticated processes are highly compatible with measurement and using those measurements to manage, control and adapt the process. In this book we use the OPEN process framework which is tailorable (see Section 1.2) to all of these situations.

Indeed, one of the prime purposes of developing OPEN was to provide a useful and usable 'standard' software development *process framework*. OPEN has many elements: process, modeling, management, measurement and so on. There are three levels of process in OPEN: the business-focused 'product lifecycle', the Software Engineering Process (SEP) and the modeling process (Figure 1.3). The modeling process assists with identifying how things change with time and what work products should be created and when. It is a central part of the method, which is objective (i.e. independent of people) and can be written down. The modeling process is just one component of the method.

The second process element of OPEN is the Software Engineering Process or SEP which brings together the methodological element in the context of one or more individuals in the team (the third or sociological element), as well as taking into account organizational culture and organizational standards and the technology available (Figure 1.4). This is the sociological aspect of the process and, in a sense, is the 'real' process because if this fails so does the project and ultimately the product. The third process element is outside the software domain. It describes how a business works by identifying three, essentially linear, stages (Figure 1.5): evaluation of the business problem or opportunity, an embedded software engineering process stage (discussed in detail in Section 1.2) and deployment to the client. Thus this OO process bridges between the business requirements and business processes (the 'product lifecycle') and the software solution (the 'process lifecycle'), OPEN being the only OO third-generation method to do this. In addition, it can be seen that there are strong similarities in Figure 1.5 between the growth period (initial development) and subsequent enhancement or maintenance periods. OPEN has traditionally viewed maintenance as a series of enhancements conforming to the business-level stages, as shown here. Instead, it could be said that rather than maintenance being viewed as a special case of development, it is more realistic, particularly in a business-focused COBOL environment, to view the initial development as a special case of the more prevalent Enhancements (maintenance 'phase').

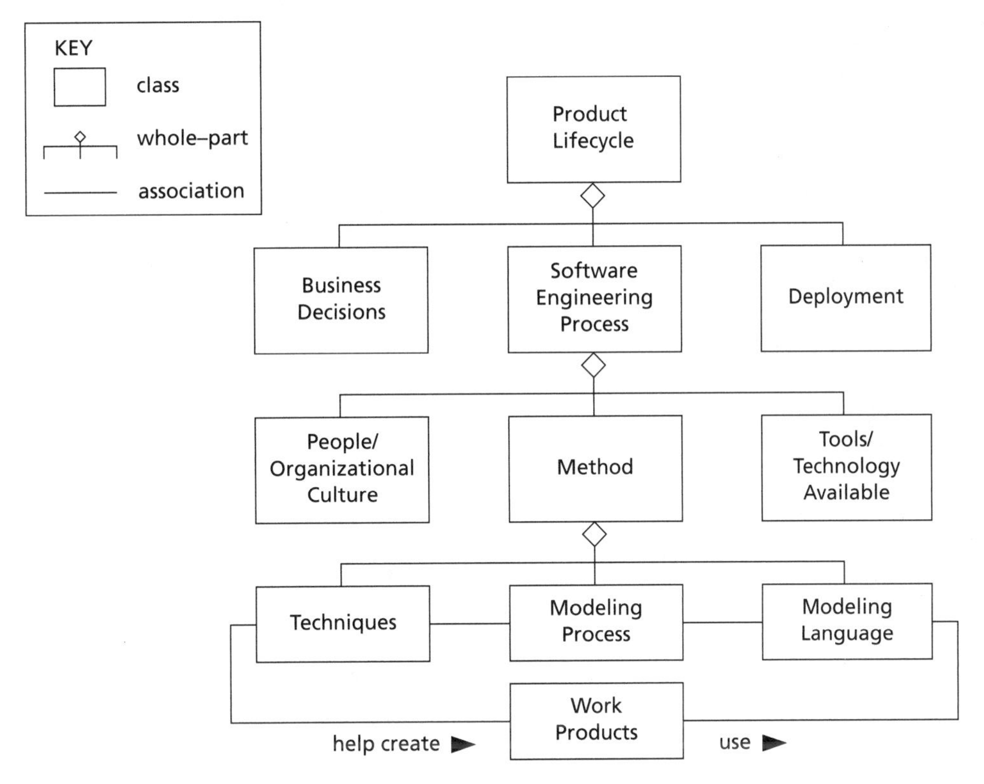

Figure 1.3 A software engineering process encompasses methodology, people/organizational culture, and the tools and technology available. In turn, methodology consists primarily of lifecycle process, techniques and representation.

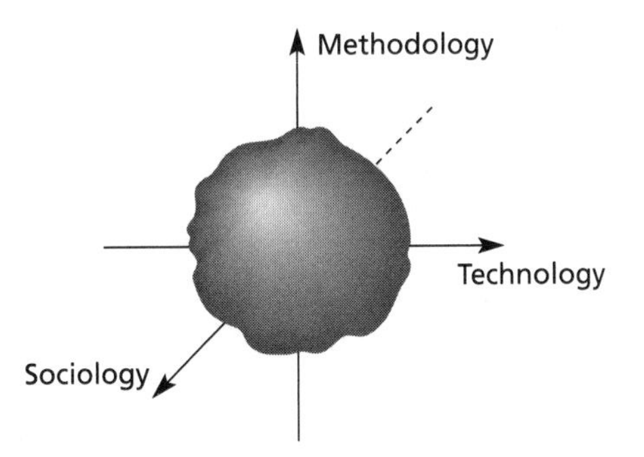

Figure 1.4 Methodology, organizational culture/sociology and technology can also be viewed as three orthogonal dimensions which describe, respectively, the 'how', 'who' and 'what' of the process (after Unhelkar, 1999; © CRC Press).

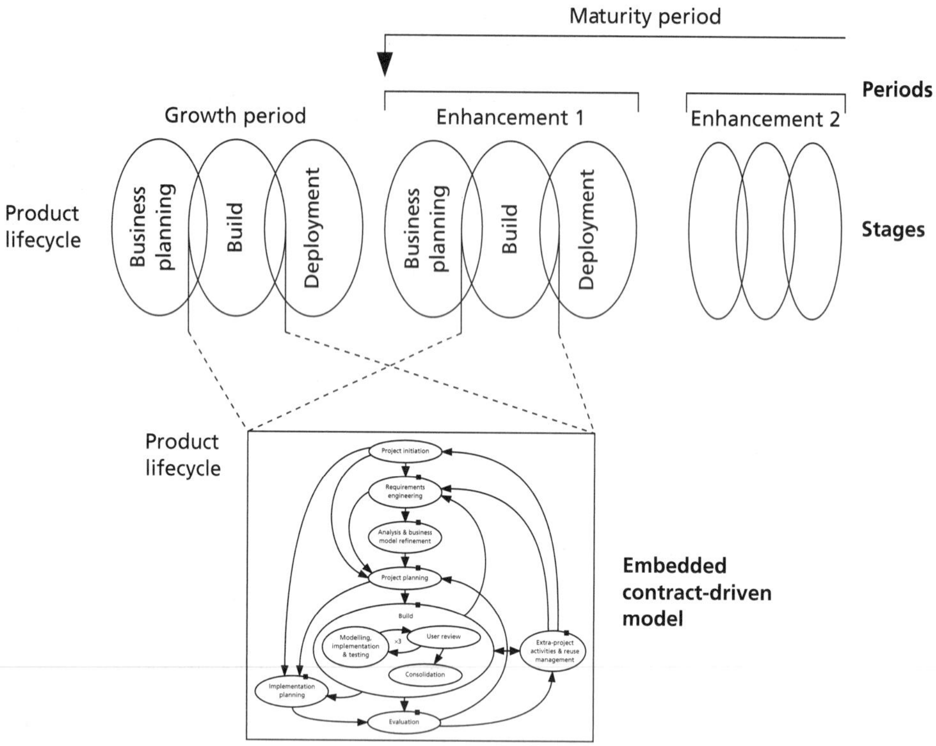

Figure 1.5 Product and process lifecycle with embedded contract-driven lifecycle model, derived originally from the MOSES lifecycle architecture.

Whilst a modeling process can be codified, it relies on real people to make it effective. Different people have different skills sets and varying experience. The organizational culture also has a bearing here; for example, using a process that is very authoritarian in an organization that is very collegiate can be a disaster. Similarly, the effect of available technology is evident. If the project mandates a high degree of traceability and version control then a tool that does code generation and reverse engineering may be called for – using a drawing tool that only supports data flow diagrams makes it difficult to design with an OO mindset.

There is thus a myriad of variables in any software development project: tools, programming languages, people, processes, quality goals, size and so on. It is not possible to use a one-size-fits-all SEP. Larger projects require more project management; smaller projects can compress the timescales of requirements analysis/design/code into days or even hours without the need for detailed project management. University projects have needs for intensive activities interspersed with relative lull. Thus a single, 'out-of-the-box', pre-tailored process is inadequate. What is needed is a process framework that establishes the overall architecture of the process while still permitting choice at the detailed level. Making those choices and constructing one specific OPEN-compliant process is called process tailoring or process engineering. It permits *one* process framework to be instantiated to create *several* project-specific and tailored processes (Section 1.2). Thus, OPEN is more than just a process – it is a complete process environment.

In an OO development environment, many of the traditional process and associated project management techniques are applicable. However, there is one major constraint that can alter this. This is the recognition by all OO developers, consultants and mentors that the process lifecycle for an OO development must be

(a) iterative (reworking of existing products),

(b) incremental (creating pieces of new products), and

(c) parallel (working concurrently on several parts of the system).

In contrast, the traditional waterfall lifecycle dictates that you follow a number of steps (often called phases) sequentially and once any given step is completed it is never returned to. In an iterative, incremental and parallel (IIP) lifecycle, there is often some sequentiality but, after steps are completed, they *are* often returned to, both for a further iteration (rework of existing products) and for further increments (addition of new product). This type of development is thus 'circular' (Figure 1.6) – although this is no excuse for poorly executed rapid prototyping and/or hacking. Iterations and increments need to be carefully planned and executed and need to go across *all* lifecycle stages (user requirements' elicitation, analysis, design, code and test).

Iterations involve returning to earlier parts of the lifecycle in order to improve on what we created previously based on knowledge gained in 'later' lifecycle phases. Cockburn (1999) defines iteration as: 'Iterative development is a scheduling and staging strategy supporting predicted rework of portions of the system'.

In contrast, 'Incremental development is a scheduling and staging strategy allowing portions of the system to be developed at different times or rates, and integrated as they are completed' (Cockburn, 1999). Incremental delivery (right-hand side of Figure 1.6) is linked with the iterative approach to some degree in that an OO development should deliver products to the users incrementally, possibly every few weeks, each increment being a *portion* of the final product. Incremental delivery

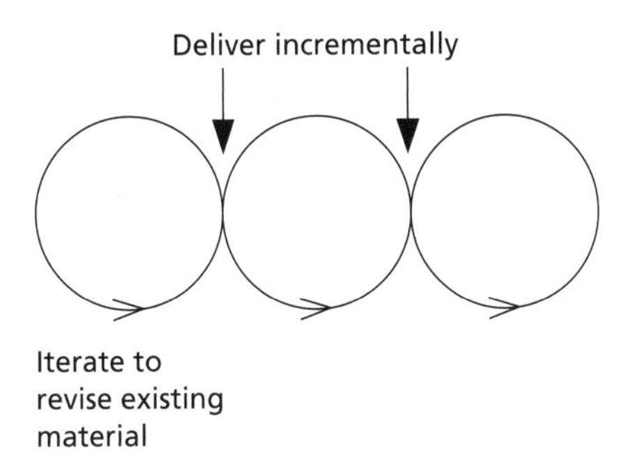

Figure 1.6 Iterations and increments

keeps the customer in the loop, ensuring that they always have in their possession a delivered and running version that is, at worst, a few weeks old. They can thus give immediate feedback rather than waiting for a one-time delivery of the full system perhaps as much as two years after they first made the request for its development.

Finally, OO supports a parallel lifecycle in that the full software system awaiting development can be easily broken down into packages or subsystems. Because of the high degree of modularity supportable in an OO development, it is relatively easy to ensure that these several packages can be developed essentially independently of each other. It is also worth noting here that even non-OO projects may benefit from a carefully tailored iterative and incremental lifecycle derived from OPEN.

1.2 Why is OPEN a tailorable process framework?

The beauty of the OPEN process is that it is not a straitjacket that lays down the law on what you shall and shall not do. OPEN is a *process framework* or environment that can be tailored by individual organizations in a way that suits them.

Whilst a dream some years ago, the 'Holy Grail' of a universally applicable software development process has proved, and will continue to be, unattainable. Projects to build aircraft navigation software, nuclear reactor control systems, a small web applet, a core banking application, CAT scan software, a theatre booking system and so on are so very different in size, safety criticality and timescale to market, and highly likely to be built in environments with such different organizational maturity (say, in terms of CMM[1] levels), personal skills sets and quality aims, that the thought of a one-size-fits-all process is laughable. However, if instead of a process we have a library of modularized process elements (components), we can construct a whole swag of processes from the one component library in such a way that each is 100% suitable for the particular environmental and project demands.

Large projects, for example, may need 'high ceremony' processes – ideally suited for hierarchical and bureaucratic organizational cultures. Process documentation is extensive and the process is formal and comprehensive. OPEN provides all the elements to support such a 'high ceremony' organization.

Small projects need 'low ceremony' processes. For example, while these should include a planning activity, it might take only a few hours rather than the several months of a large project. Timescales are shorter, formal tracking less important than product delivery – particularly when the critical success factor is 'time-to-market' and the web product lifetime is envisaged to be only a few months. OPEN can readily be tailored by selection of a minimalist subset of components from the Process Library to support rapid web development, open source developments and can even be tailored to be compatible with XP (eXtreme Programming).

1 The Capability Maturity Model (Figure 1.7) of the Software Engineering Institute (SEI) in the USA.

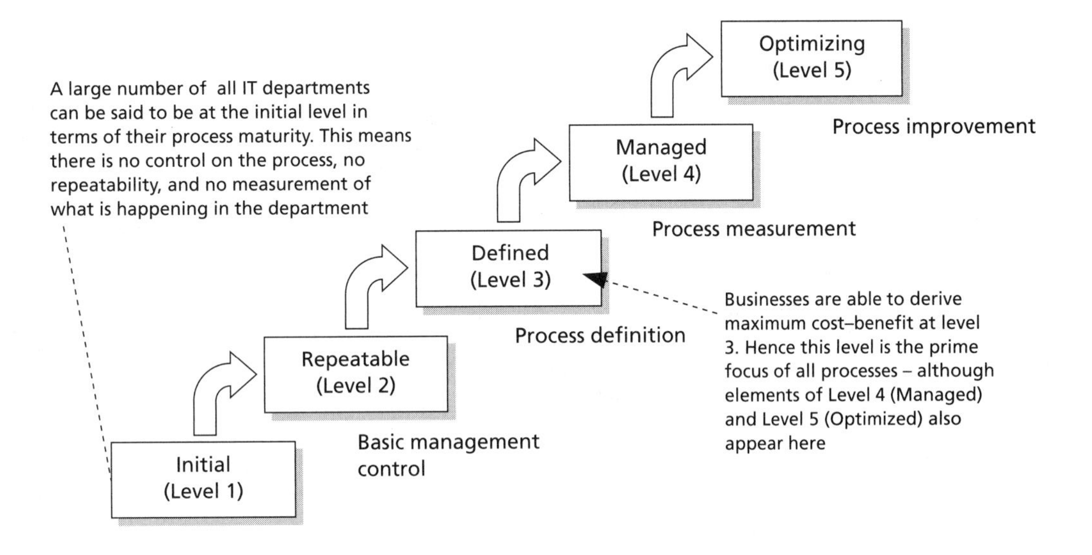

Figure 1.7 SEI's CMM: Process maturity

A process framework is really a model defined at the metalevel. OPEN's metamodel/framework is shown in Figure 1.8. The overall process itself consists of a number of Activities. Activities are granular descriptors of a collection of heterogeneous jobs that need to be done. These can be decomposed into a number of Tasks, each of which corresponds to a homogeneous job that can be done in a short time and which is readily ascertained as being either complete or in progress (i.e. incomplete). However, since Tasks have to be done by someone (or some thing, such as another piece of software), it is useful to introduce a metaclass called Task Performance, which consists of a Task and its Producer. Thus, in the OPEN metamodel (Figure 1.8) we say that an Activity consists of several Task Performances. A Workflow is then a number of Activities, most simply shown, as here, as a sequenced collection of Task Performances.

In order to fulfil the Tasks, the Task Performance is supported by the user, a person or team playing a specific role in the development, of one or more OPEN Techniques, each of which contributes part or all of a Work Product. Work Products are usually finalized at the end of Activities, so a link from Activity to Work Product is apposite. Overall, then, we can see that the SEP consists explicitly of Activities, Work Products, Techniques and Producers and implicitly of Tasks. Sequencing is undertaken by attaching Assertions to each Task. These assertions describe the contracts of the objectified Activities and Tasks in the lifecycle. Used in this way, the lifecycle itself can best be described by a contract-driven model – based, in part, on the older fountain lifecycle model. In the same spirit, since Work Products evolve over time, they also form a sequence (often given version numbers). Thus we can attach a state machine to the Work Products in order to assess their current state (complete, partially complete, etc.).

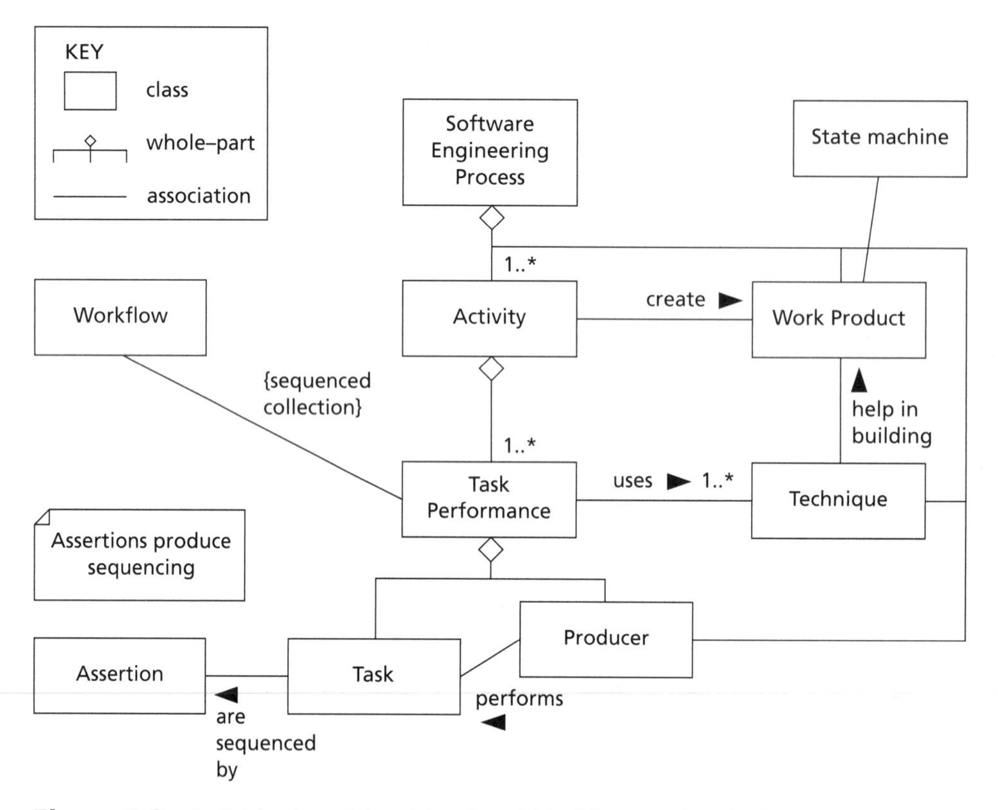

Figure 1.8 Activities (possibly with subactivities) have tasks which are realized by the use of one or more Techniques

The framework (or metamodel as in Figure 1.8) sets out how elements are connected at a high abstraction level but does not delve into any specifics. Details are added when the framework is instantiated in a particular context. The person doing this instantiation (often the process engineer or chief methodologist of the organization) then has flexibility to choose, for example, Activities which relate to the current specifics, e.g. problem domain, team size and skills, timeframe and quality level required. While this requires effort on behalf of the software development team/organization, the end product is *exactly* what is required. It is a 'personal' process, created from the OPEN 'standard' framework (Figure 1.9).

Tailoring requires choosing a set of specific Activities, as well as the way Activities are typically interlinked together with appropriate Tasks complemented by compatible and effective Techniques. The repository of all the elements from which to choose and tailor your own OPEN-compliant method is in the full texts on OPEN (see Bibliography). Here, we explain how the pieces fit together in general terms (in this section) and then explain further by means of two illustrated examples (Chapters 4 and 5) which form the core of the book.

As we have seen, the overall architecture of OPEN is that of a number of Activities

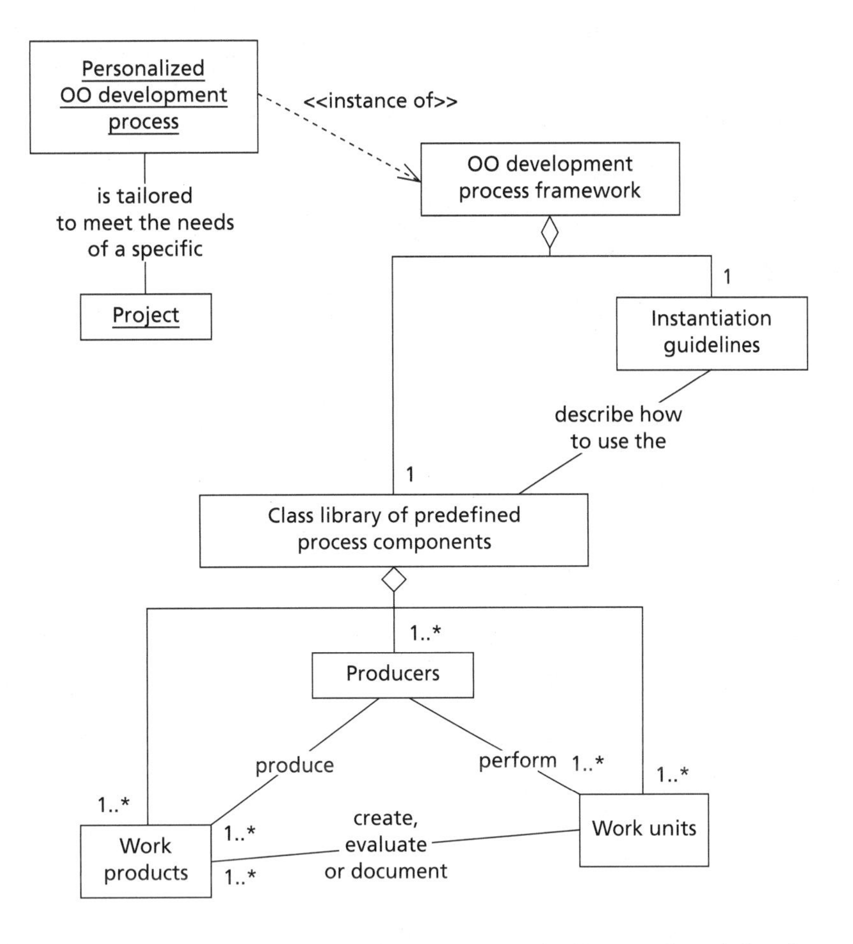

Figure 1.9 The OPEN process framework consists of a library of predefined components plus instantiation guidelines. ***Your*** tailored version of OPEN is one particular instantiation of this framework in which specific elements of the library have been selected (redrawn from Firesmith and Henderson-Sellers, 1999).

(Figure 1.10) which are connected together in a flexible and tailorable way to form an OPEN process which is one specific instantiation from the OPEN process framework (Figure 1.9). The way in which these Activities are put together will lead to slightly different versions or instantiations. Each Activity is represented by an object in the process description (Figure 1.11) and these are connected together by lines in this diagrammatic representation indicating potential transitions that the process user can make (in Figure 1.11, the example shown is most pertinent to MIS domains). The development proceeds as suggested by these lines but only when the post-conditions of the current Activity have been met. These should be specified clearly and should include testing criteria, document delivery, model-building criteria, etc. Once these have been satisfied, then the development team may move on to another

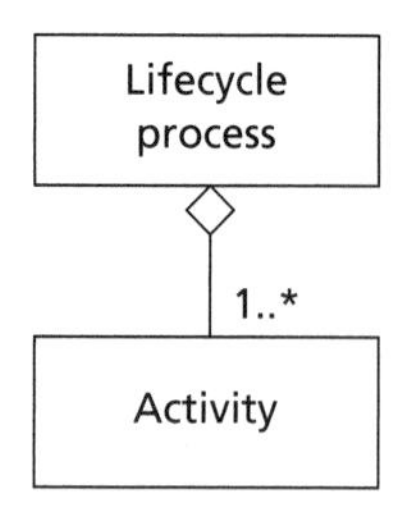

Figure 1.10 The Lifecycle Process consists of several Activities.

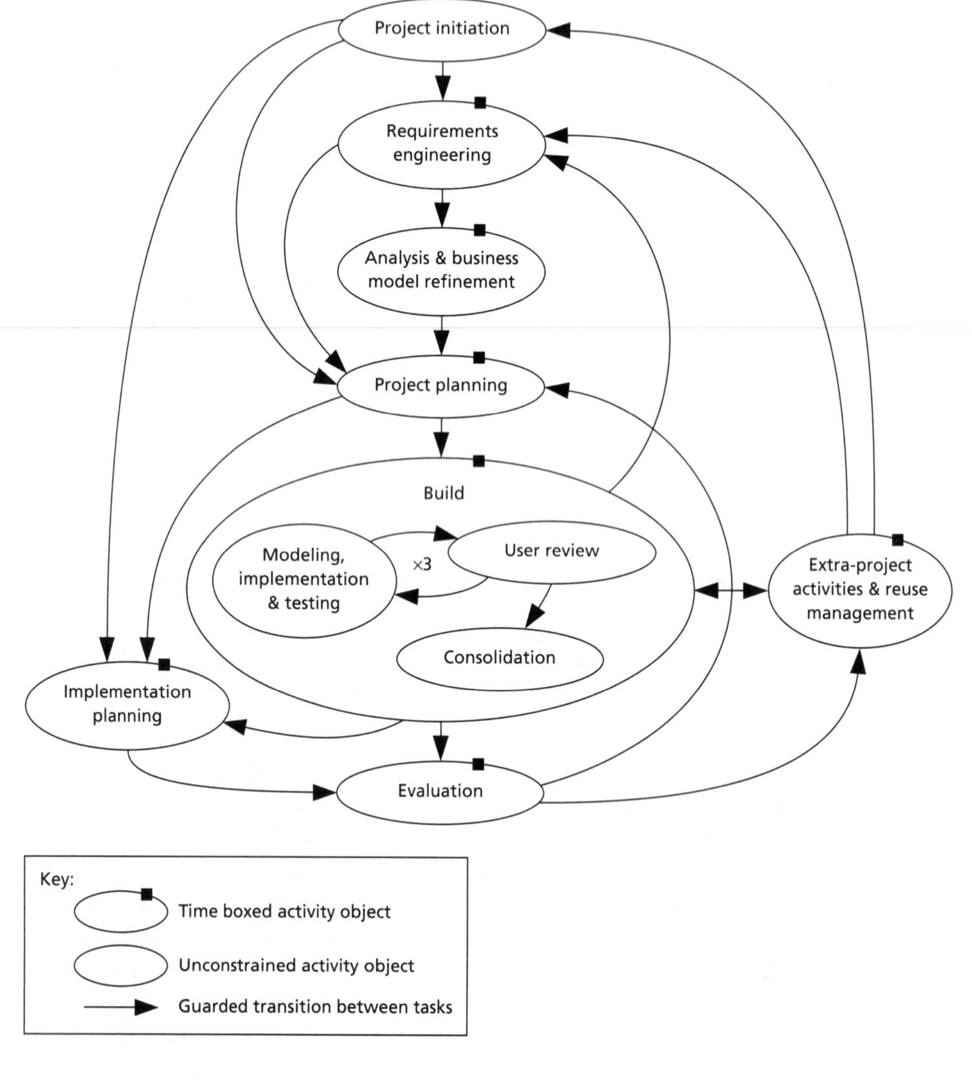

Figure 1.11 The contract-driven lifecycle for multiple projects in an MIS domain

Activity – again assuming that the pre-conditions of that next Activity have been achieved. These might be that certain Work Products have been created, that a certain percentage of the system has been designed, that certain signoffs have been made, and so on.

Activities in OPEN are coarse granular descriptions of what needs to be done. They are the equivalent of phases in a waterfall process, though in our process they are iterative and incremental. Furthermore, as Activities lose the temporal sequencing implication of phases, sequencing rules need to be explicitly included. In OPEN, when using a contract-driven lifecycle, these are added as pre- and post-conditions (Figure 1.8) on the Tasks. This applies the programming by contract ideas to the very description of the process and results in a process that is itself object-oriented.

An important Activity with regard to modeling (the topic of this book) is the Build Activity.[2] This is a technical, highly iterative activity. The Build Activity may have several subactivities. Typically three may be described in an MIS domain (although there are many other possibilities for appropriate subactivities, particularly in different domains like building real-time control systems):

- Evolutionary development or OOA/OOD/OOP together with verification and validation (V&V). This is the seamless analysis, design and code cycle as exemplified, for instance, in the fountain model. In the contract-driven lifecycle (e.g. Figure 1.11), it is often called 'Modeling, implementation and testing'.
- User review. A planned iteration (usually around three overall) between the development team and the users. In other words, the end users are intimately involved with the software development and have several opportunities to give the development team feedback and to trial interim releases as they are incrementally delivered through these planned iterations.
- Consolidation is a user+developer finalization after all the formal reviews have been satisfactorily accomplished.

In this book, we focus mainly on OPEN's support for OOA/D/P of the Evolutionary Development Subactivity.

While Activities are generally large-scale descriptions of what is to be done, they tend to focus on long-term objectives and are often difficult to manage because of their potential duration. To *manage* the 'what', a finer discrimination is needed – the Task. A Task is the smallest unit of work, which can be evaluated as either complete or not complete. Tasks are thus smaller scale 'jobs to be done' associated with each of the activities in the lifecycle. The authors of OPEN listed 30 tasks that could usefully be identified within most software engineering processes. Those relevant to OOA/D/P (and hence this book) are listed in Table 1.1.

The Activities and Tasks of OPEN say what is to be done. They do not suggest any ways of accomplishing them. This is the role of the OPEN Techniques of which there are over 150. These Techniques, documented separately and in detail in *The OPEN*

2 The scope of older methodologies, such as OMT, was basically that of this Build Activity.

Table 1.1 OPEN Tasks relevant to the Build Activity (in alphabetical order)

1. Code
2. Construct the object model
3. Evaluate quality
4. Identify CIRTs
5. Map roles on to classes
6. Test
7. Write manual(s) and prepare other documentation

Toolbox of Techniques (see Bibliography), bring together all the well-tested OO techniques that have been used worldwide for the past decades. They are tools and the users of the process are able to choose the one most likely to be successful for their particular Task.

Since Techniques are just ways of doing things, they can be thought of as the 'tools of the trade'. Just as the tools of the trade of a plumber include hammers, screwdrivers and wrenches, the tools of an object technologist include knowledge about the use of, for instance, CRC card modeling, aggregation modeling and OO team building. Similarly, the value of a plumber is the knowledge and experience in choosing which of the screwdrivers and wrenches are needed to solve any particular problem. Just so for the object technologist who needs to be able to choose the best OO technique to accomplish the specific OPEN Task being worked on. Choosing the correct technique is largely a matter of experience, combined with relevant training and, possibly, availability of tools.

OPEN represents these links between Technique and Task by a many-to-many fuzzy relationship represented as a two-dimensional matrix (Figure 1.12). This matrix represents the reality that it is not just one Technique that is useful for each Task. Any chosen Technique may in fact be useful to help fulfil several Tasks. Conversely, any chosen Task is likely to need the use of more than just the one Technique. In part, this many-to-many linkage applies because there are, in fact, many 'alternatives' in OPEN's toolbox. For example, there are several techniques for finding objects. Some OO software developers start by a textual analysis, some use simulation, some use CRC cards and yet others prefer a use-case-driven beginning to a software project. It is your choice. Perhaps after you have seen some examples, in the remainder of this book, you will acquire some further insights as to what techniques best suit the tasks of your organization.

Activities performed iteratively by means of a set of tasks result in Work Products (Figure 1.13). Work Products are the documents, including software, that are produced either for internal inspection or for external evaluation and final delivery/use. Those Work Products that are handed over to external clients may be called deliverables. Since (almost) any Work Product can thus act as a

Techniques \ Tasks	A	B	C	D	E	.	.
1	M	D	F	F	F	.	
2	D	D	F	F	D	.	
3	D	D	O	O	D	.	
4	F	O	O	O	F	.	
5	F	M	O	D	F	.	
6	R	R	M	R	O	.	
7	D	R	F	M	O	.	
8	D	F	M	D	D	.	
9	R	R	D	R	R	.	
10	O	D	O	O	R	.	
11	F	M	O	F	D	.	
.	.	.	.	.	.	.	.
.							

For each Task/Technique combination, one of the five levels of probability (from Always to Never) is chosen as appropriate

5 levels of possibility
M = mandatory
R = recommended
O = optional
D = discouraged
F = forbidden

Figure 1.12 A core element of OPEN is a two-dimensional relationship between Tasks and Techniques. Each Task may require one or several Techniques in order to accomplish the stated goal of the Task; and Techniques may be applicable to several Tasks. For each combination of Task and Technique, an assessment can be made of the likelihood of the occurrence of that combination. Some combinations can be identified as mandatory (M), others as recommended (R), some as optional (O); some are discouraged (D) but may be used with care, and other combinations are strictly forbidden (F). Filling in the matrix values is an important part of the lifecycle tailoring Task in OPEN (redrawn from Graham *et al.*, 1997a).

deliverable, there is no utility in creating a separate class of Deliverable in the metamodel. Work Products may be textual or graphical (using UML). In OPEN, these artefacts are created as part of the post-condition of the Activities. However, since the lifecycle is iterative and incremental, often the delivery is only partial (but planned that way). Delivery may be to other members of the team, to the manager or to an external party, such as the end-user/customer. It needs to be made clear to the recipient of each Work Product just what proportion of the final delivery is being made in such an incremental lifecycle. Thus Work Products are built up over several iterations but linked to the Activities. They are not created by the Activities directly but rather by the Techniques used to realize the tasks of the Activity (Figure 1.8). Any one Work Product can therefore be the result of the application of several Techniques spread over several iterations.

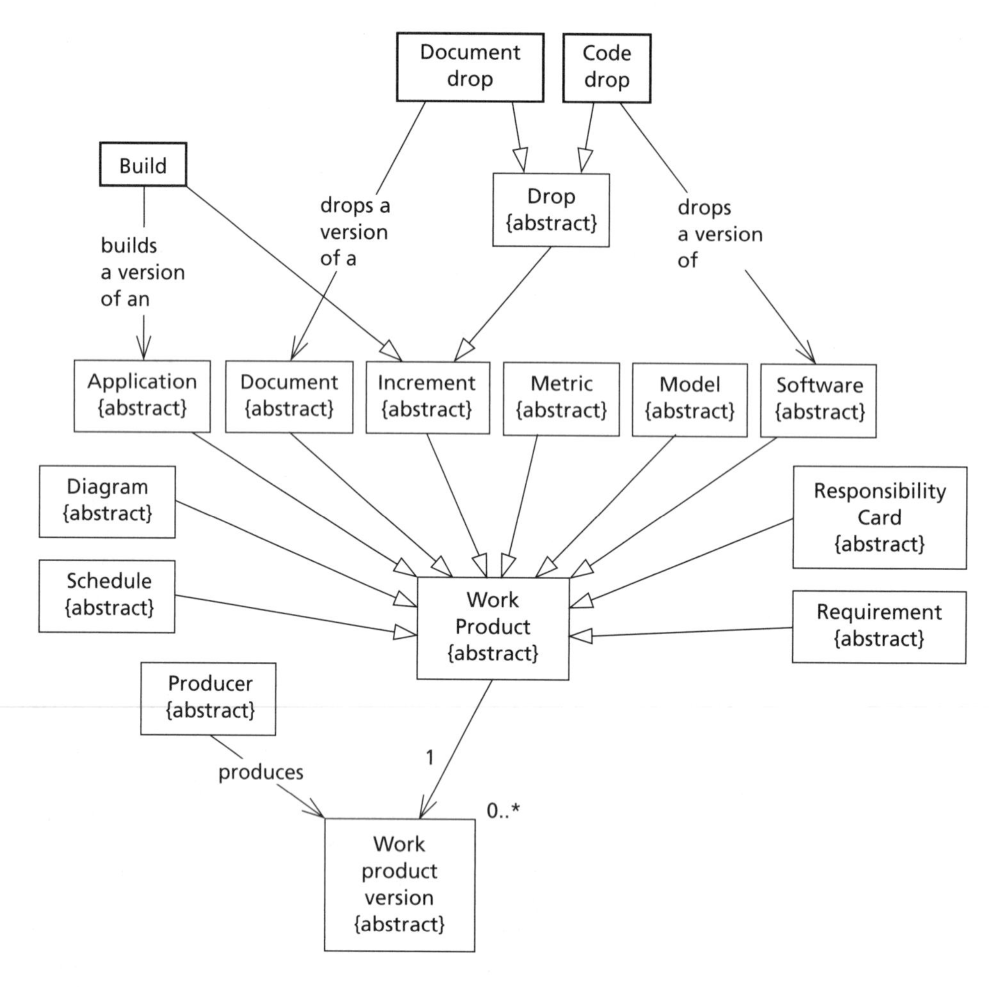

Figure 1.13 There are a number of Work Products available in OPEN. Some of these are linked to specific styles of usage, e.g. internal 'drops' and deliveries to external clients (redrawn from Firesmith and Henderson-Sellers, 1999).

1.3 What is UML?

The part of a method (Figure 1.3) that then allows you, the developer, to deliver documentation and other artefacts, including the final code, must include a modeling language. A modeling language consists of a metamodel plus a notation (Figure 1.14). The metamodel is essentially the set of rules that say what you can and cannot do with the language elements, which are themselves represented graphically or textually. Together the metamodel and notation will be the tools you use to depict the results of modeling and coding as you build software.

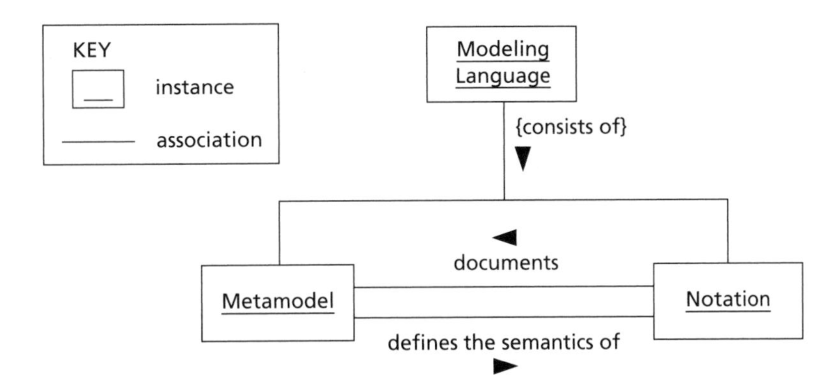

Figure 1.14 A modeling language consists of a metamodel plus a notation.

Understanding of the metamodel is the realm of methodologists and CASE[3] tool builders; software developers do not generally need to see the metamodel itself. If the methodologists get the metamodel right and the CASE tool vendors implement it correctly, then you have access to fine and flexible tools that increase the quality and productivity of the software produced.

One well-known modeling language is the Unified Modeling Language, or UML for short (described in Chapter 2), which was endorsed by the Object Management Group in late 1997. UML continues to be refined and the latest version, as used here, is 1.3. UML tends to be more pragmatic than some other modeling languages and more aligned with hybrid approaches such as C++, Java and relational databases. UML will be used throughout this book in order to express our requirements model and all other OO diagrams. In fact, we've already used it in the majority of diagrams in this chapter.

The UML is comprehensive. It offers support for a wide variety of domains and interests. It supports important parts of the lifecycle. Thus, when learning the UML, you need to be aware that certain constructs and notations are only helpful in detailed design while others are useful in requirements analysis. However, being primarily a modeling language, UML needs to be used together with an effective process, such as OPEN. UML, on its own, is not able to (and was never meant to) relate to the various pieces of the lifecycle. For example, while sequence diagrams and class diagrams are expressed using UML notations, questions such as whether sequence diagrams should be drawn before or after class diagrams must remain unanswered by UML, since processes are not considered in it. In OPEN, we consider questions precisely like these.

As we noted above, in this book we will follow the application of the OPEN process to two case study examples (Chapters 4 and 5) using the UML notational elements described in full in Chapter 2 together with the OPEN Techniques of Chapter 3.

3 CASE stands for Computer-Aided/Assisted Software Engineering.

There are six major types of diagram in UML (Table 1.2), although both interaction diagrams and implementation diagrams have two subtypes. These are well interconnected, as they should be, so that altering elements in one diagram should be reflected in automatic updating in all the connected diagrams. This interconnectedness stresses the fact that each diagram does *not* represent an orthogonal model of the system; rather, each diagram is but one view of a *single* model. The static viewpoint seen in the class diagram is complemented by the functional (use cases) and dynamic (state, interaction and activity) viewpoints of the remaining diagrams. Specific implementation issues (primarily of the software/hardware interface) are depicted in the implementation diagrams.

Table 1.2 Diagram types in UML

1.	Class diagram (with object diagram as option)
2.	Use case diagram
3.	Statechart diagram
4.	Interaction diagram (collaboration and sequence)
5.	Activity diagram
6.	Implementation diagrams (component and deployment)

1.4 Tying it all together: OPEN with UML

OPEN is a methodological or process framework. It needs to be instantiated and tailored to particular problems, projects (domain and size) and organizations. The Activities need to be described and selected along with appropriate OPEN Techniques creating a SEP (Software Engineering Process) fully customized to your specific requirements (Figure 1.15). This tailoring is undertaken, using a matrix, as described in Section 1.2. The tailoring of the process by fine-tuning this matrix is one of the strengths of OPEN, which makes it suitable for a wide range of project types. This is why we call OPEN a methodological *framework* rather than a method.

OPEN is process-focused. It can be used with any one of a number of available notations. Four of these were discussed in an earlier book (Henderson-Sellers *et al.*, 1998). In this present book, one of these, the UML, is chosen as the vehicle to graphically display the results of the OPEN process, i.e. its work products. These range from use case diagrams to class diagrams to state diagrams. We choose only to use a subset of the UML notation. The most relevant and useful elements of the UML notation are discussed in the next chapter (Chapter 2).

For large projects, most of the OPEN elements will be needed with significant contribution from those focusing on project management. For smaller projects, the SEP will be a 'cut-down' version and the whole process more informal. Both will

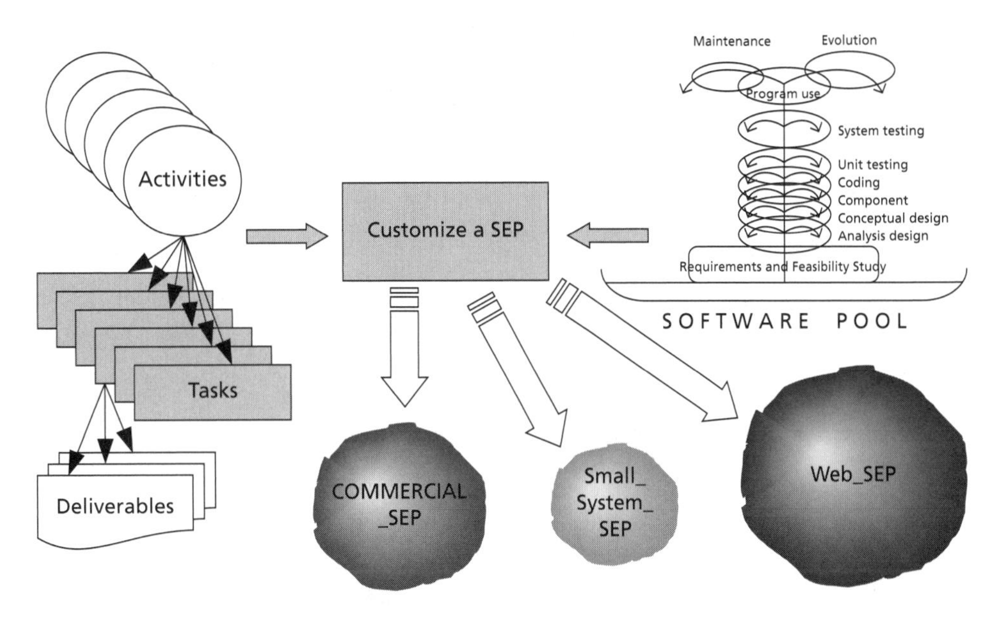

Figure 1.15 Tailoring industry-specific or company-specific SEPs, here using the foundain lifecycle model as an alternative to the contract-driven lifecycle used earlier.

use UML as the notation. For really small developments, perhaps two people developing a web application in a couple of weeks, the UML will be the dominant influence with only a very lightweight process being used, perhaps a personal one held in the developer's brain. Whether this can or should be viewed as a simplistic version of OPEN or not is a moot point. In reality, such a lightweight process is likely to consist of a number of techniques with which to use specific UML diagrams, such as use cases, class diagrams and perhaps sequence diagrams, for example, together with some rough ordering of the tasks associated with building these diagrams. In Chapters 4 and 5 our case study examples fall into the 'middleweight' class, although the one in Chapter 5 is specifically aimed at a web application.

Summary of Key Points

- OPEN is a third-generation object-oriented methodological framework constructed out of Activities, Tasks, Techniques and Work Products. It is tailorable to very specific demands of a project and is supported in its diagrammatic work products by a notation.
- UML is chosen here as the notation to document the OPEN work products. UML (Unified Modeling Language) is the language derived under the auspices of the Object Management Group and adopted as a standard in 1997 (as Version 1.1). It is continually being revised and upgraded. The current (late 1999/early 2000) version is UML Version 1.3 and it is this version that we use in this book.

Discussion Topics

- What is the importance of 'tailorability' in a process and how does OPEN satisfy it?
- Why is it important to use a standardized notation like UML?

Notes

OPEN, together with UML, is adopted by a number of organizations. COTAR, Myriad, iOpsis, Interactive Objects Software, etc., support it. In previous incarnations it was also used by, for example,

- (MOSES) Dow Jones, FourFront,
- (SOMA) Chase Manhattan Bank, Swiss Bank.

2 The modeling language to be used: UML

Abstract

In this chapter we discuss the key elements of the Unified Modeling Language (UML) of the Object Management Group. We do not describe it in full detail since it is an extensive and, in part, highly sophisticated and complex language. In practice, about 20% of the UML will cover about 80% of common eventualities. It is this 20% that we document and explore here.

2.1 History of UML

The Unified Modeling Language (UML) consists, as do all other modeling languages, of (i) a metamodel and (ii) a notation. There is also a language to add constraints – the OCL or Object Constraint Language.

A metamodel is a set of rules and constraints on the elements of the model (i.e. the metatypes and metarelationships) that underpin the ways in which these elements are brought together in the modeling language (i.e. their semantics, syntax and usage). The notation is used to visualize the results of bringing together these elements in the design and documentation of a software system. Thus, any model we build is actually created by using the knowledge encapsulated within the metamodel and documented using the notation (Figure 2.1).

UML has gone through several versions since its inception around late 1995. During that time it has grown in size and complexity. In this chapter, we will therefore not attempt a full description but include only those elements of UML that readers will need in their understanding of the case studies in this book (for example, we offer no discussion on activity diagrams). We will use UML Version 1.3; there will be a Version 1.4 which will include minor corrections and then the next major release will be 2.0 some time in the next few years. (We should also note that in Version 1.3 there are still some areas where the metamodel is generally

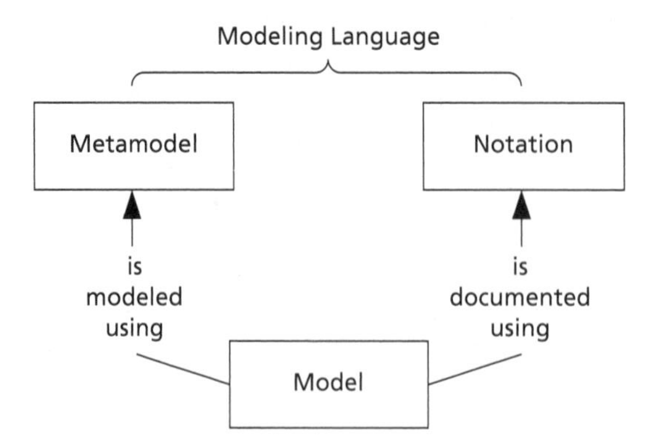

Figure 2.1 A model is described using the rules of a metamodel and documented using a notation.

considered to be sub-optimal. We wish to point out some of these areas not only for the sake of 'correctness' but also because these are the changes one would expect in future versions of the UML.)

The UML documentation divides up the metamodel into a number of different packages. A package is a means by which to group model elements together and is shown, in UML, by a tabbed rectangle (Figure 2.2). Using UML to describe itself, Figure 2.3 shows how the foundation classes are the most important such that the two packages of behavioural elements and model management are dependent upon the foundation metaclasses. (A dependency relationship is shown in UML by a dashed arrow.)

Within these main packages are other packages and interdependencies (Figure 2.4). The most important packages in the metamodel are probably the core package which describes concepts and relationships particularly for the class diagram. The use cases package includes detailed description of all concepts needed for the use case diagram, and similarly the collaborations package and the state machines package. These are the main packages to be discussed here.

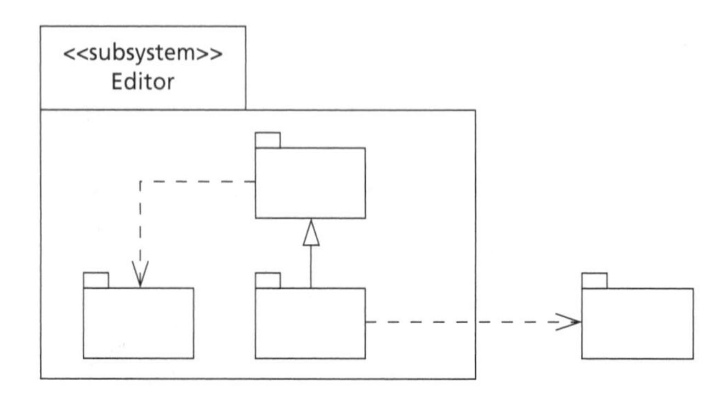

Figure 2.2 UML package notation

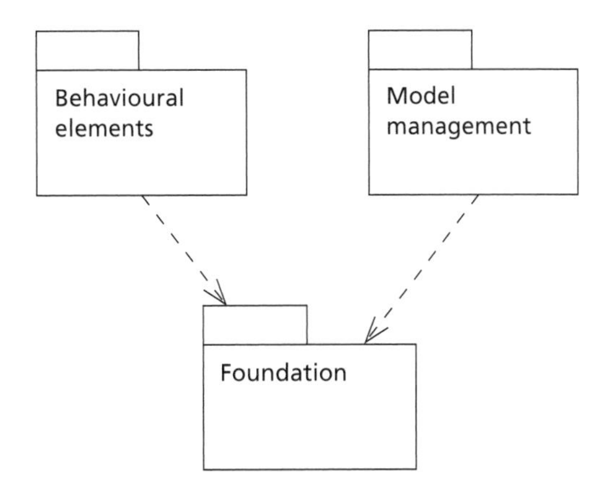

Figure 2.3 UML package structure (© OMG, 1999a)

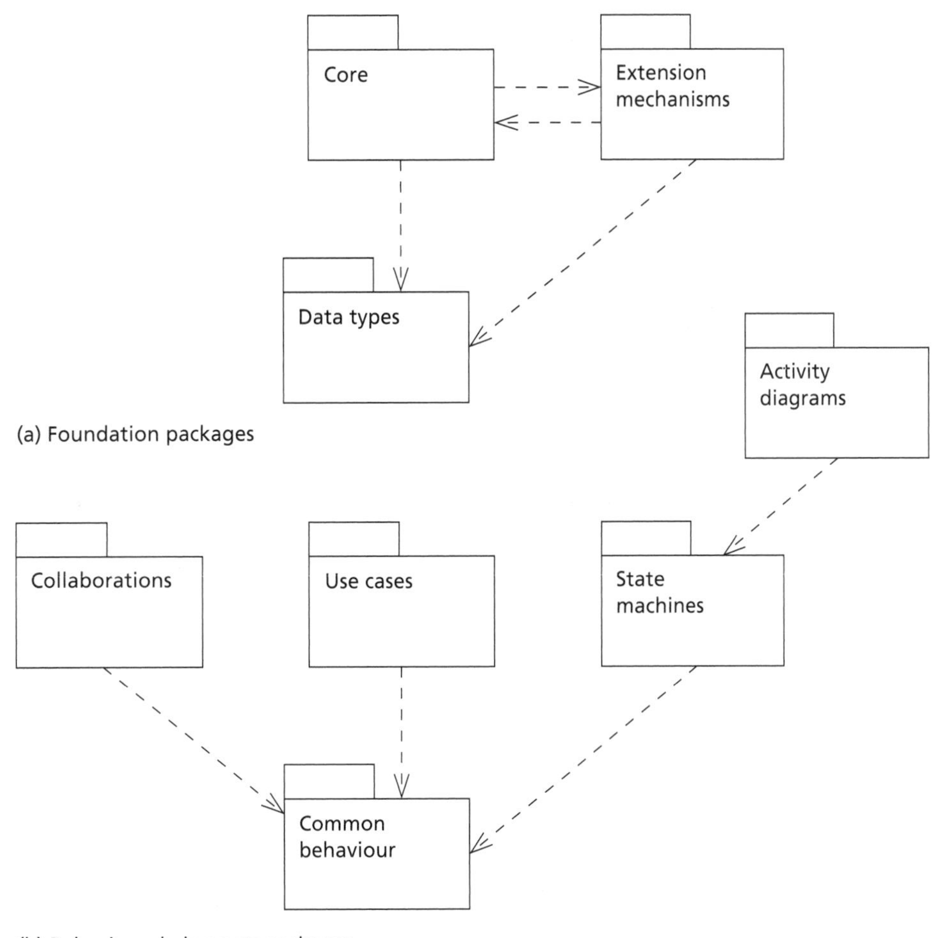

Figure 2.4 Detailed UML package structure (© OMG, 1999a)

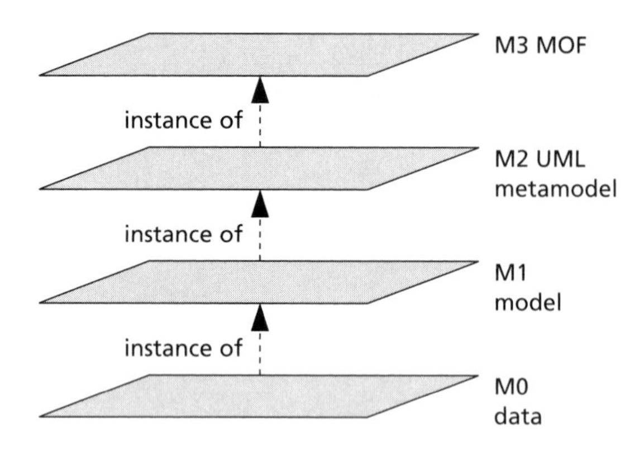

Figure 2.5 Four-layer architecture of UML

The architecture of UML is a four-layer one (Figure 2.5). At the bottom level are instances, typically objects, which represent the 'data' in a system. Design is usually undertaken at the M1 or model level. Software designers use UML's notation in order to represent classes, use cases, states, etc., at this M1 level. This is the level of object-oriented analysis and design techniques and methodologies. Indeed, most developers will not even be aware of and may, perhaps, not need to know the higher levels. As noted above, however, UML is a metamodel plus notation. The metamodel is at level M2. So, to understand UML properly we need at least to be aware of this M2 or metalevel model. This is also the level of interest to CASE tool developers. Since the metamodel (M2 level) describes all the rules of what is and is not valid in a UML (Level M1) model/diagram, we need to describe elements of the metamodel here. Finally, the metamodel itself can be modeled which leads to the metametamodel at the M3 level. In the OMG parlance this is called the MOF (standing for the Meta Object Facility). The UML metamodel is then designed to be an instance of the MOF in the same way that any given OO model is an instance of the metamodel and a set of collaborating objects is an instance directly derivable from the metamodel. Thus the connections between the Mn levels is always that of instantiation (Figure 2.5).

It should be noted that the UML uses a loose meta-modeling style in that it permits cross Mn level connections, such as instantiation, to be shown on the same diagram. Rigorous metamodeling would disallow this. It is still being argued which approach is better in creating a standard OO modeling language. However, it is pointed out that, at present, the loose metamodeling can lead to some inconsistencies, such as in the way instances are notated at different levels. In addition, while the four levels are described initially in the UML documentation,[1] the focus in the bulk of the description is in fact on levels M1 and M2. Here we shall follow this and in fact focus on level M1 with some initial discussion of level M2.

1 The reference for the standard UML is the OMG documents (OMG, 1999a). All other articles and books are derivative and may or may not correctly represent the standard.

2.2 Static architectural elements

Figure 2.6 shows the static architectural model for UML Version 1.3 in which there are five major metalevel concepts, collectively called classifier.[2] A classifier is an element which declares a collection of features with a name unique within the Namespace enclosing the said classifier. The five classifiers in the core package are:

- a *class*, which describes a set of objects sharing a collection of features, thus describing both its state and its behaviour. A class may also realize zero or more interfaces;
- an *interface*, which is 'a declaration of a collection of operations that may be used for defining a service offered by an instance'. In other words, it represents operations but no attributes, associations or methods;
- a *datatype*, which is a type whose values have no identity but are simply pure values. All operations of a datatype are pure functions (they can access but not change values);
- a *node*, which is 'a run-time physical object that represents a computational resource and upon which components may be deployed';
- a *component*, which is 'a physical, replaceable part of the system that packages implementation and provides the realization of a set of interfaces'.

(Node and component were not present in UML Version 1.1.)

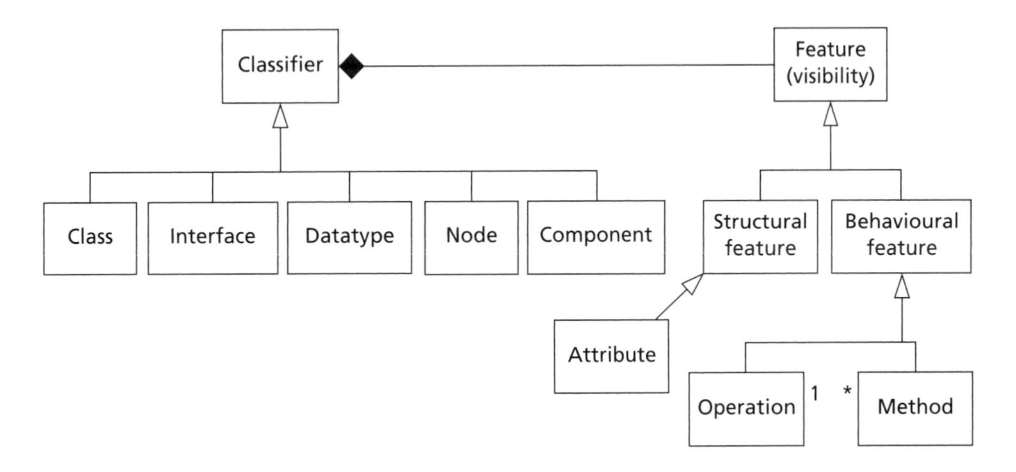

Figure 2.6 Main structural elements of the UML metamodel. The notation is UML in which the white arrowhead is an is-a-kind-of inheritance and the black diamond (the symbol for composite aggregation) is said to represent here a (meta)relationship in which 'a Classifier *declares a collection of* features' (OMG, 1999a, but our italics).

2 We follow OMG/UML convention and use an initial capital letter for metaclass names.

Classifiers have features[3] which have an associated visibility. Features may be structural or behavioural. On the structural branch, the only subtype is the attribute. The behavioural branch has both operations and methods as subtypes, where operations (which are external i.e. visible in the interface) are implemented by methods (which are internal, i.e. hidden inside the class and *not* visible in the interface).

While class and classifier are full metalevel concepts (metaclasses), there are other relevant stereotypes[4] of class. These are «type» and «implementation class» (Figure 2.7), where the implementation class is said to *realize* the type. The implementation class of Figure 2.7 describes how a class is implemented, whereas type has only attributes, operations and associations in comparison with the metaclass Interface which has only operations. One problem with this model is that the generalization inheritance shown in Figure 2.7, as implied by the use of a stereotype, is in fact implementation inheritance, since the subtype here (type) is *less* than its supertype (class) – a type does not have methods in the way that a class does. If generalization inheritance were being used correctly, then we would be able to say that 'a type is a special kind of class'. Thus the type metaclass (shown as such in Figure 2.7) subtracts from its 'parent' – recognized many years ago by Brachman (1985) as a bad modeling strategy.

At this point, we should foreshadow some of the other areas of the static metamodel of Figure 2.6 which are weak in the context of support for OPEN Techniques: these weaknesses relate to roles, responsibilities and assertions.

UML supports two interpretations of the word 'role'. In static diagrams, role names can be added to association ends. OPEN does not encourage this usage, since

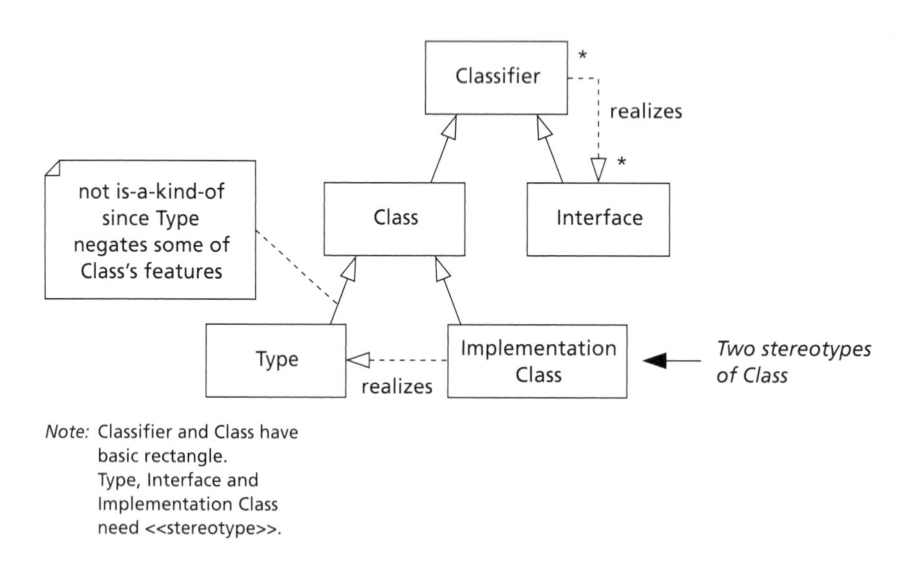

Figure 2.7 Relationships between UML metaclasses of classifier, class and interface and the two stereotypes of class: type and implementation class

3 But see discussion on composition (black diamond notation) in Section 2.5.

4 See Section 2.4 for details of stereotypes.

it is either tautological (Figure 2.8) or redundant. The much stronger interpretation of role is the dynamic one (as in OOram) in which objects take an additional, contextually dependent secondary classification. These are only supported in UML in collaboration diagrams. OPEN, on the other hand, advocates the use of OOram-like roles not only in terms of the objects interacting in a collaboration diagram, but also in the static modeling as exemplified by a UML class diagram.[5] We thus currently need to make an extension to the UML metamodel by adding a stereotype for role. The «role» stereotype can be used in OPEN, on either objects or classes. (See later discussion in Section 3.11.)

Responsibilities represent knowledge maintained by an object, actions performable by an object or the associated business rules. Each responsibility groups together one or more services offered in the object's (class's) interface into a higher level abstraction that can be named. They convey the high level 'purpose' of the object/class. They are represented by a stereotyped comment in UML Version 1.3.[6] This means they consist of an annotation with no semantic force. Responsibilities in OPEN are used much more significantly than a mere comment, more along the lines of the way they were introduced in the 1990 OO method RDD (Wirfs-Brock *et al.*, 1990). Since responsibilities are eventually (in OPEN) realized in terms of class features, in UML we need to manually[7] introduce a dependency link from the responsibility to the class together with a dependency from the responsibility to individual elements such as attributes and operations in order to model responsibilities in UML when using OPEN.

Responsibilities are related to contracts which provide the context for and rules governing the interaction of two objects. Contracts are specified using assertions – pre-conditions, post-conditions and invariants. In UML, these are represented by adding stereotyped Constraints to operations and classifiers.

Each of the elements in the UML metamodel can be represented by its own specific notation. The basic icon for both class and type is a rectangle with three

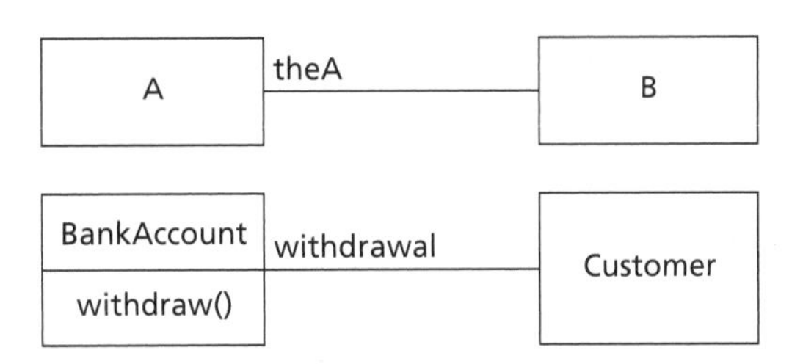

Figure 2.8 Examples of the use of roles as labels on AssociationEnds in the UML

5 It is encouraging to see a statement such as 'In UML, a role is itself a classifier' (Jacobson *et al.*, 1999, p. 76). Whilst not true in terms of the current UML metamodel, it may foretell the future.

6 This is a change from Version 1.1 in which they were a tagged value.

7 According to discussions with Grady Booch.

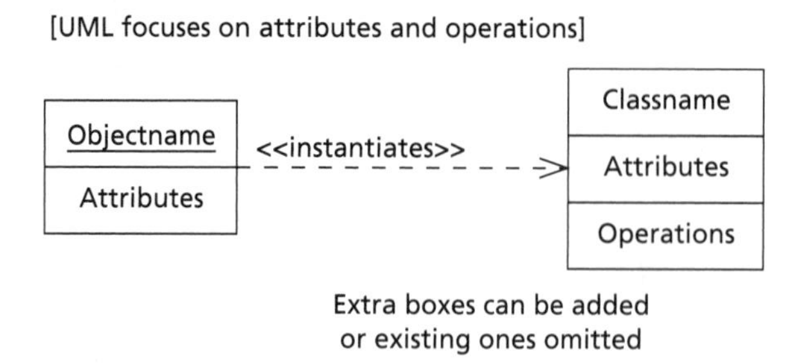

Figure 2.9 UML notation for object, class and interface (derived from OMG, 1997)

parts: name, attributes and operations (Figure 2.9), differentiating between class and type being accomplished by use of a stereotype (see Section 2.4). A class, as seen here, has both attributes and operations, while only the name and attributes are shown for an object (e.g. Rumbaugh *et al.*, 1999, p. 361) which is, of course, an instance of a class. Operations are not shown 'because they are the same for all objects of a class'. Since both use a rectangular symbol, they are differentiated by means of the object name being underlined. Consequently, if all boxes are present, objects have two compartments and classes three; although in many cases one or more of these boxes may be suppressed. Alternatively, extra boxes may be added to document, for example, assertions, responsibilities or exceptions.

While the three-box representation of classes is the most normal (default), there are other options. The default and two alternatives are shown in Figure 2.10. For early requirements analysis, just a box with a name may be useful (attributes and operations both suppressed). In analysis/early design, we might want to show attributes and operations but suppress details such as initializing values and visibility. A full description, invaluable for implementation level diagrams, is shown on the right-hand side of Figure 2.10. Here, visibility annotations of +, #, – are used for public, protected and private attributes and operations. Remember that it is always good practice to make all attributes private, although one might wish to represent 'logical attributes' in some way. This can be done either by using a public visibility on the attribute (a little dangerous since it might be interpreted incorrectly) or by attaching the property query to an appropriate operation (rather than using an attribute at all). The UML standard stresses that the absence of a visibility marker indicates that the visibility is not shown, not that it is undefined or public. Attributes (like almost all other elements in UML) can also be grouped or classified with stereotypes.

Interfaces are metatypes in the M2 model. However, they still need a stereotype (predefined in UML) for their notation (Figure 2.11). Interfaces can be shown either in this way (as a stereotype) or, alternatively, using the 'lollipop' notation as shown here (Figure 2.12).

Style guidelines are given in the UML documentation. We suggest that you either adopt these recommendations or ensure you have an equally tightly scoped set of

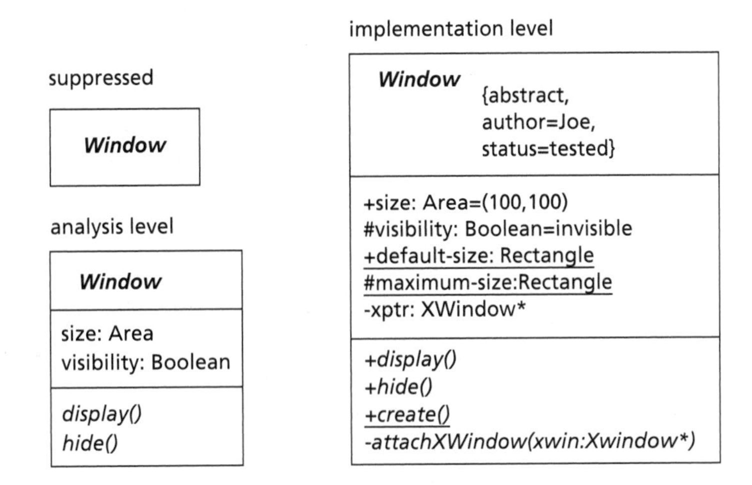

Figure 2.10 Three styles of UML notations for the abstract class Window (© OMG, 1999a)

your own. In other words, based on our experience we strongly urge that you *do* have style guidelines for your company.

It is suggested in the OMG documents describing the UML that:

- class names be bold and centred;
- class names for abstract classes be bold, italic and centred;
- stereotype names be plain font enclosed in guillemets which are placed above the class name and centred;
- class names begin with an upper case letter;
- attributes and operation names are left justified in a plain font. If they are abstract, then an italic font should be used instead. Names should commence with a lower case letter;
- both attributes and operations can also be classified with stereotypes.

These are the main elements for building a static diagram to describe the application. Known as a class diagram, it shows classes (and possibly objects and

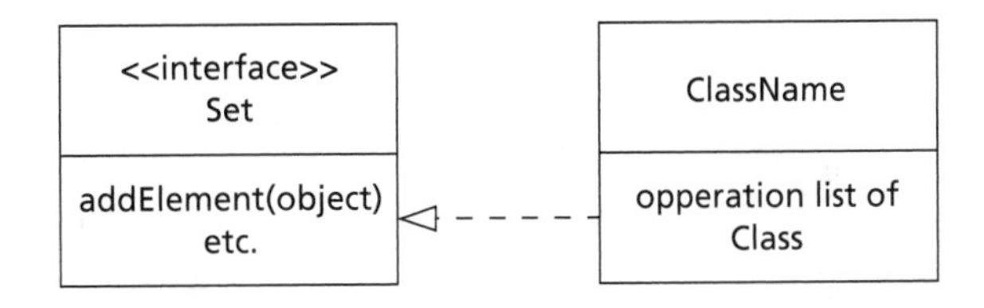

Figure 2.11 UML Interface notation

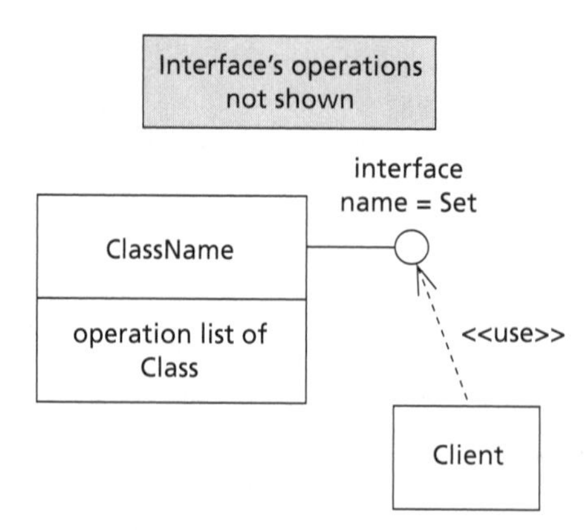

Figure 2.12 Alternative 'lollipop' style of notation for interface

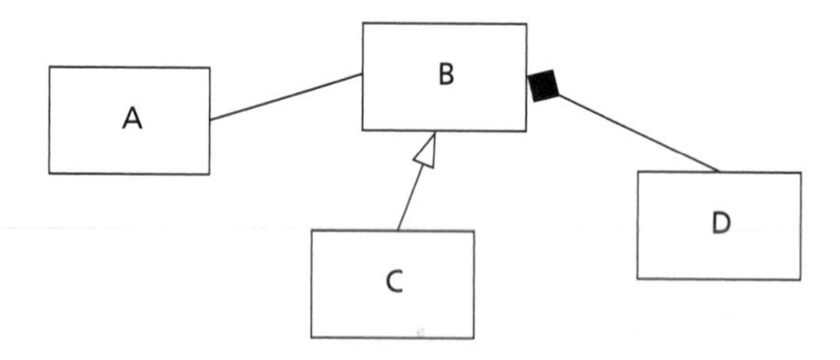

Figure 2.13 UML class diagram

packages) and how they interconnect. Of course, to understand a class diagram (such as that shown in Figure 2.13) properly, we also need to be able to understand the notations for the various relationships (details are in Section 2.5). In this simple example (of Figure 2.13), there are four classes: A, B, C and D. Classes A and B have an association relationship between them, C is a subtype of B which in turn has D as a part. Although shown in terms of classes, a class diagram is really a surrogate for how individual objects interrelate, in much the same way that an entity relationship diagram actually describes entity sets as indicative of how individual entities are structured.

2.3 Architectural diagram types

Within UML there are many different diagram types (Table 1.2). In older OO modeling languages, there were often doubts as to how, or indeed if, such diagrams fit together. However, it is important to realize that the different diagrams just give different *views* on a single system. Hence, changing the name of, say, an operation in one diagram should be reflected in a similar change in all diagrams in which this particular modeling element exists.

Figure 2.14 shows how these different diagram types of the UML link together. The main architectural diagram is the class diagram (static structure diagram). It describes the nature of classes, objects and their features such as attributes and operations. It also shows relationships such as inheritance, association and aggregation.

Objects (as opposed to classes) can appear in a variant of the class diagram – the object diagram – and can also appear in a collaboration and/or a sequence diagram, both of which are types of interaction diagram. Messages shown on interaction diagrams link to events in the statechart diagrams, some subtypes of which in turn link back to operations in the static structure diagram. A statechart diagram is drawn for each class[8] with interesting state transitions. Another version of a statechart diagram is the activity diagram which is part of UML but is not used in OPEN. Thus, while class diagrams show the static structure of a system using, primarily, classes, the

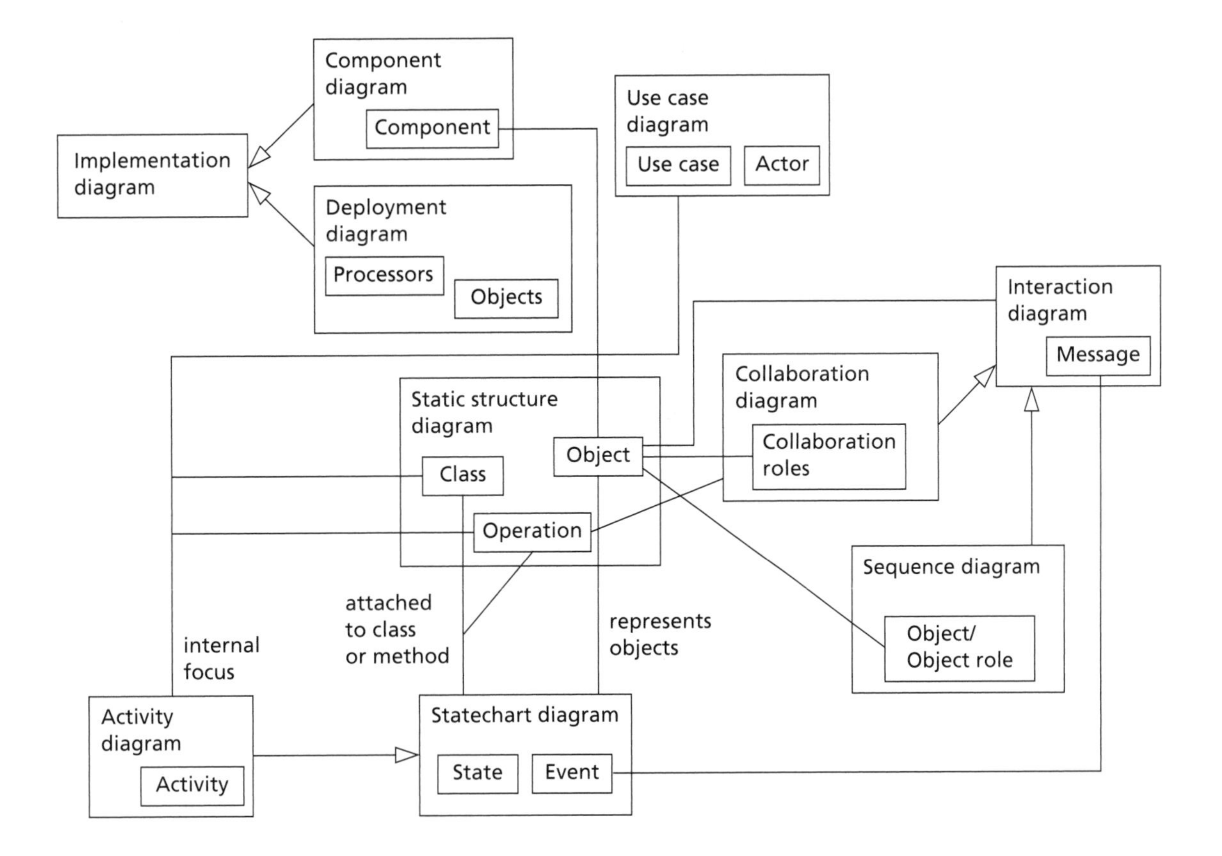

Figure 2.14 UML diagram connectivity (redrawn from Henderson-Sellers, 1998b)

8 Strictly here we use class as a surrogate for the objects belonging to the class since it is objects, not classes, that possess a state.

dynamics for individual instances of classes (objects) are seen in statechart diagrams and interactions between objects detailed in one of the two kinds of interaction diagram. These diagrams are typically used to show sequencing of messages when an instance of one class is asked to perform one specific operation, which often leads to delegation or subcontracting which in turn involves other objects that are then added to these diagrams. Activity diagrams (a type of UML diagram not discussed in this OPEN with UML book) can be used to show larger-scale control flow (but not in a clearly object-oriented fashion) as well as for the non-object-oriented design of the internal details of individual methods within each class, if needed.

A functional view of the system is found in the use case diagram of UML which can also link to sequence diagrams (but not shown in the metamodel) and activity diagrams. Finally, two implementation diagrams – component diagrams (Figure 2.15) and deployment diagrams (Figure 2.16) – complete the suite. These describe systems considerations and hardware platforms respectively, but because they deal with actual development and deployment of the system (as against its modeling), we do not discuss them further.

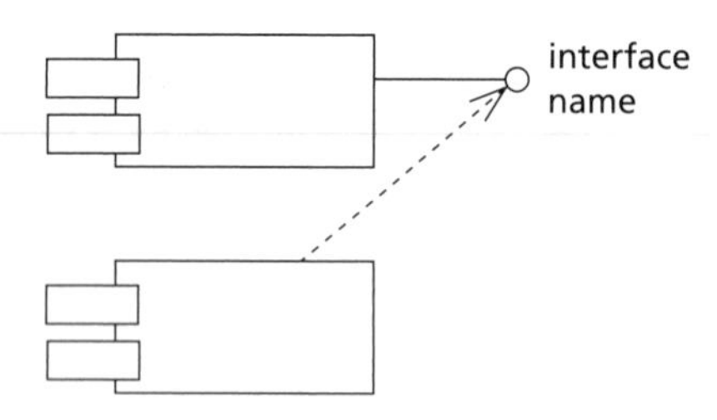

Figure 2.15 UML component diagram

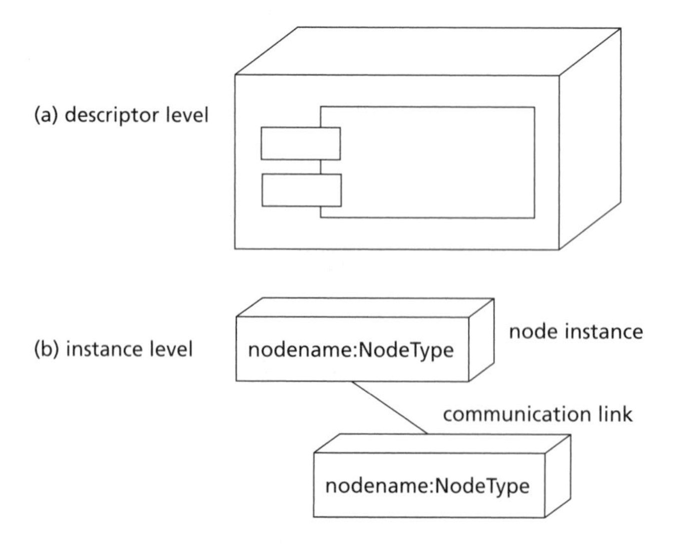

Figure 2.16 UML deployment diagram

2.4 Stereotypes

Stereotypes are user-defined class specializations at the M1 level where they are used for specializing a number of artefacts/elements such as classes, attributes, operations, relationships, packages, etc. They provide the capability for the *user* to create explicit refinements to the artefacts used at the modeling level and can also be viewed as implicit refinements to the metalevel or M2 level – they create virtual submetatypes in the M2 model. For example, in Figure 2.17, we see that instances of this particular Computer Mouse class are also instances of a class of type Control, i.e. this icon describes only the subset of Computer Mouse objects which are also Control objects (see also Figures 2.18 and 2.19 which show how stereotypes are related to partitions and metasubtypes respectively). The stereotype name, in guillemets, is placed above the class name. Stereotypes can similarly be used for relationships (Figure 2.20) – the name is placed above the relationship symbol. Indeed, many of the relationships in UML have predefined stereotypes (Table 2.1). In UML, all the stereotypes (column 3 in Table 2.1) are indicated by a keyword in guillemets. In addition, some but not all of the metaclasses (columns 1 and 2) also use guillemets, while others, e.g. dependency and generalization, have their own symbol.

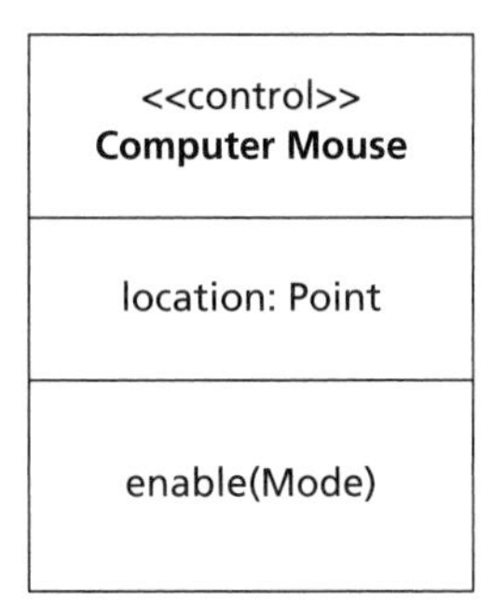

Figure 2.17 Stereotypes in UML

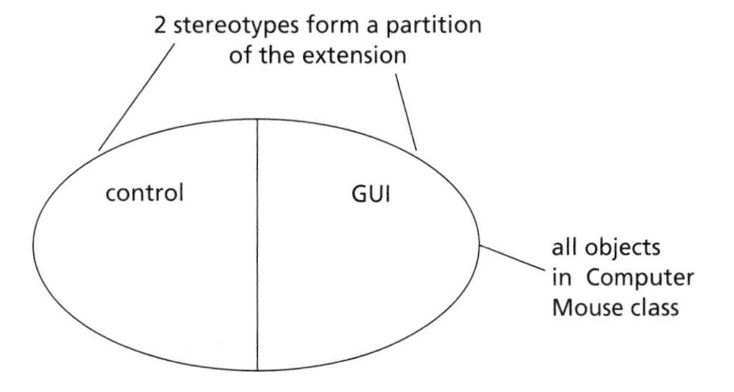

Figure 2.18 Describing stereotypes by use of partitions

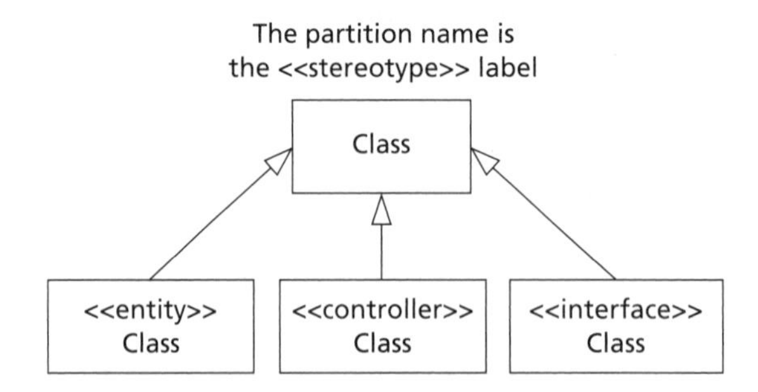

Figure 2.19 Depicting stereotypes using subtypes

Figure 2.20 An example of a stereotyped relationship (© OMG, 1997)

Figure 2.7 showed at the metalevel how classes could be stereotyped into types and implementation classes. Here, in Figure 2.21 we show the associated notation for one such example. HashTableSet, which is an implementation class, realizes[9] Set, which is a type. (This is the M1 analogue of the M2 relationship in Figure 2.7 in which we see that the metaclass implementation class realizes the metaclass type.)

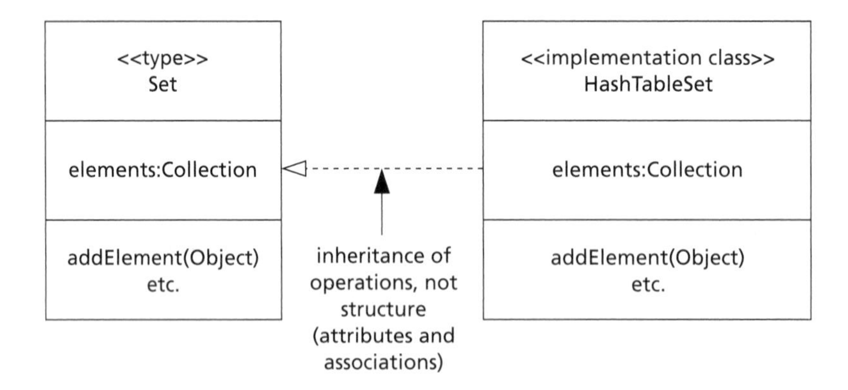

Figure 2.21 UML classes can be stereotyped as types of implementation classes (derived from OMG, 1999a)

9 A dashed generalization arrow – see Section 2.5.

10 An extension is a version of UML which has additional stereotypes, tagged values and constraints (at the M1 level) compared to the basic UML, as defined in the OMG documents. A variant of UML makes additions and changes to the metamodel (M2 level) itself.

Table 2.1 Relationships and their stereotypes

Subtypes of relationship in the metamodel	Subtypes in the metamodel (of the subtypes in the first column)	Stereotypes
dependency	abstraction	«derive»
		«realize»
		«refine»
		«trace»
	«bind»	
	permission	«access»
		«friend»
		«import»
	«use»	«call»
		«instantiate»
		«create»
		«send»
flow		«become»
		«copy»
generalization		«implementation»
association		
«extend»		
«include»		

While we have shown here the expression of stereotypes as names in guillemets, the UML documents show two specific examples of UML extensions[10] (the same could apply to UML variants) in which new symbols are introduced. The two examples given there are for the Objectory Process and for Business Object Modeling in which new icons for Control objects, for instance, are introduced. If you prefer this kind of approach, then the UML variant known as OML (Henderson-Sellers *et al.*, 1999) may be useful to you, in which the above stereotypes (for type, class, implementation, etc.) are all given their own symbols (Figure 2.22). We also find many CASE tool vendors using different notations instead of the stereotype, which may occasionally lead to confusion if the notations are not properly defined and understood.

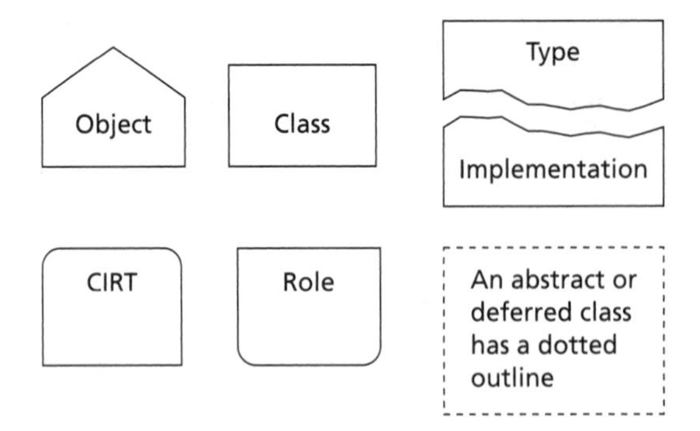

Figure 2.22 In the OML variant of UML, stereotypes of classifiers have their own icons. Class, Type and Implementation have direct analogues in Figure 2.6. Role is a stereotype. CIRT (= Class, Instance, Role or Type) is approximately related to Classifier in that it is a supertype of Type, Implementation, Object (Instance) and Role. However, in the OML variant it is a concrete, not an abstract, metaclass. This permits the modeler more flexibility, since he or she can use the CIRT symbol when undecided as to whether a class, instance, role or type/interface is most appropriate. It is thus useful in analysis rather than design.

2.5 Relationships

There are a number of relationships available in UML for modeling inter-class connectivity (Figure 2.23). The main ones for class diagrams are generalization, dependency and association. Extend and include are the two use case relationships introduced in Version 1.3.[11] Links are instances of associations, and transitions are found only in state models. Of the relationships (shown in Figure 2.23), only association is generalizable; and neither the instance-level link nor the class-level transition are relationships but are direct subtypes of ModelElement.[12]

A further relationship is that of realization which relates the implementation to the specification. The specification describes the 'what', not the 'how'. Adding the 'how' is realization. It is said, in UML, to be an indication of the inheritance of behaviour without the inheritance of structure (as noted earlier on Figure 2.21).

There has been much discussion about these different relationships – whether dependency and association should be subtypes, the one of the other; what is the meaning of the two varieties of aggregation, themselves created as constrained forms of association (no separate metatype). In 1998, a connection was sought between dependency and association by members of the OTUG email discussion group, whereas members of the OPEN Consortium published papers (Henderson-

11 These replace «extends» and «uses» in Version 1.1.

12 This is an area of the metamodel that we foresee could change in future releases.

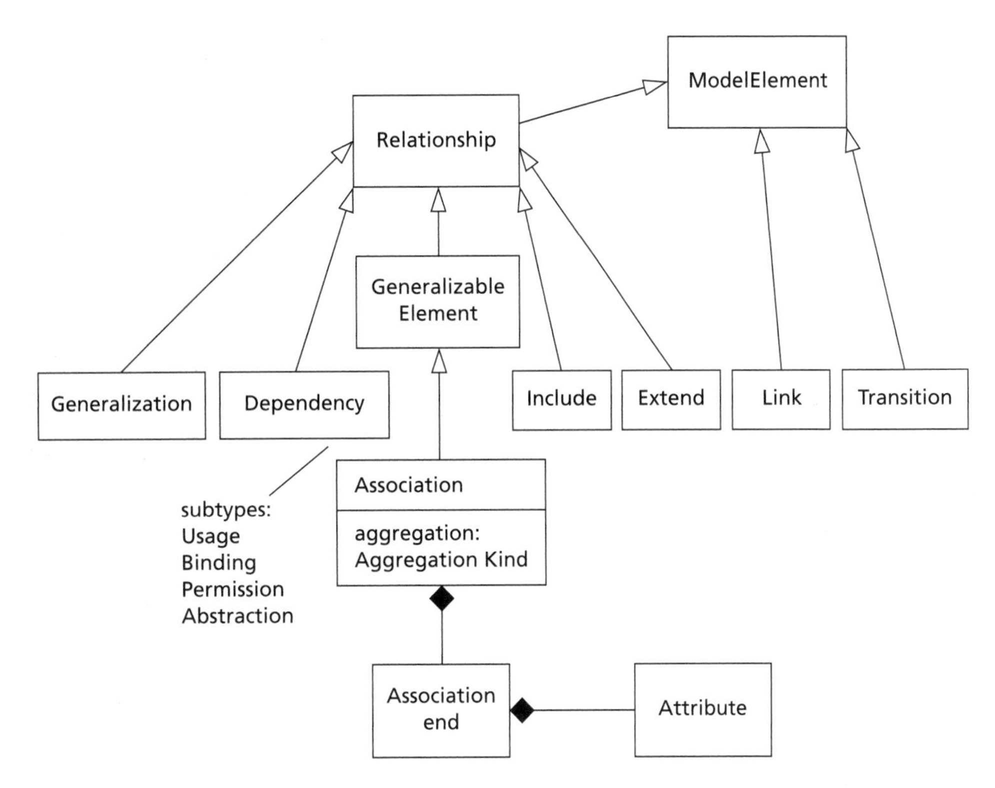

Figure 2.23 UML relationship metamodel

Sellers, 1998a) suggesting that perhaps dependencies reflected the dynamic side of a referential relationship in contrast to the static descriptor of the association (Figure 2.24).

The dependency relationship in UML is said to describe the connection between two classes wherein a change to the 'supplier' class leads to the need to make a change in the 'client' class. It is really a generic term to collect together a large number of other relationships which are thus shown as stereotypes of dependency (see Table 2.1). Dependency is a unidirectional relationship, in comparison with the traditional bidirectionality of association.[13] In 1998, UML authors were describing dependency as an entity which in a different view might be an association (Rumbaugh, 1998). Some ambiguity thus remains about these various relationships, especially composition, which can be shown to be self-contradictory (Henderson-Sellers and Barbier, 1999). This confusion about the meaning of the black ('composition') and white ('shared aggregation') diamond in UML Version 1.3 has led to many avoiding their use altogether[14] and to the problem being added to the agenda for the 2.0 revision (OMG, 1999b).

13 But see previous recommendation for use of associations in OPEN.

14 See further discussion in Section 3.8 on the WP relationships, and how to use them in OPEN.

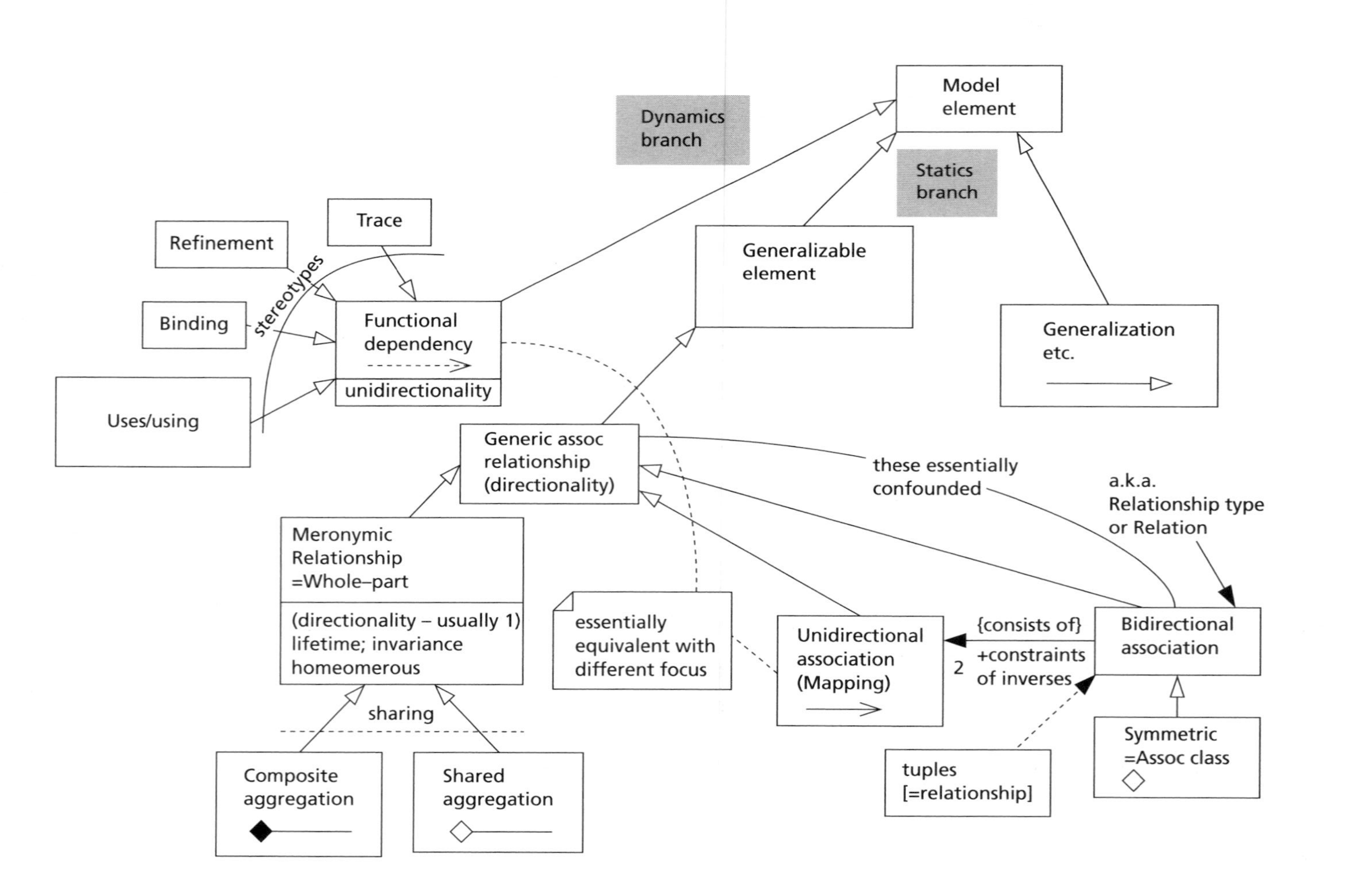

Figure 2.24 Converged metamodel for relationships, as proposed by Henderson-Sellers (1998a)

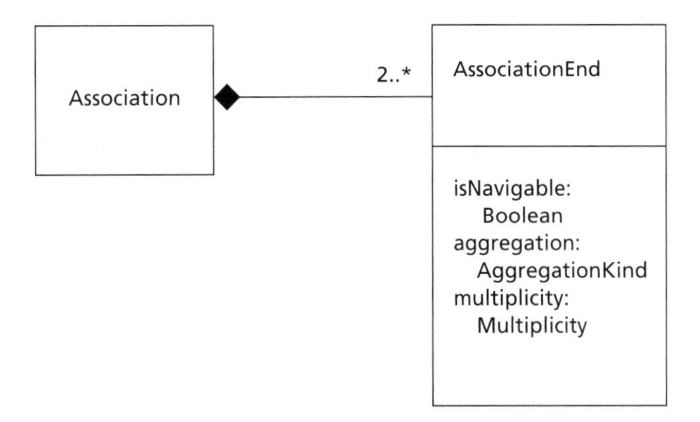

Figure 2.25 Metamodel fragment of AssociationEnd showing the key metaattributes

There is no separate metatype in the UML for whole–part relationships (for example, in Figure 2.23); rather UML's aggregation and composition (white and black diamond notation respectively) are created from an association by choosing one of the three values of the metaattribute AggregationKind of the metatype AssociationEnd. Values of this attribute can be either none, aggregate or composite. In UML, all associations have two or more ends (Figure 2.25). These AssociationEnds actually play quite a large role in UML since, as well as attributes for 'aggregation', they have many other metalevel attributes. In particular, here is where navigability and multiplicity information is stored.

2.5.1 Notation

There are three presentation options for relationships in UML:

1. Show all arrows – no arrow therefore implies no navigation.
2. Suppress all arrows.
3. Suppress two-way arrows.

The UML notation for association is a line. OPEN users are encouraged to use Option 1 and show an arrowhead since in OPEN associations are, by default, unidirectional. Option 3 (an option often seen in other UML books) takes bidirectionality as a default. The problem here is that bidirectionality thwarts reuse and has been shown (Graham *et al.*, 1997b) to violate encapsulation/information hiding – a basic tenet of the object-oriented approach. An association may also have an (optional) name as well as the navigation arrowhead we encourage (Figure 2.26).

In the UML metamodel, as noted above, there is no explicit metaclass for the aggregation relationship, the semantics of aggregation being specified entirely by setting attribute values on the AssociationEnd metaclass. Despite this, in the notation,

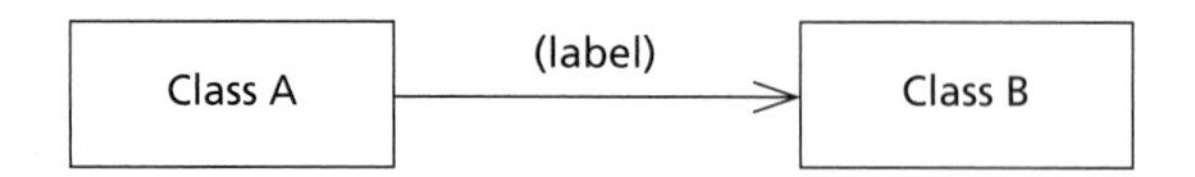

Figure 2.26 UML association notation

aggregation does have its own notation: a white diamond denotes so-called shared aggregation and a black diamond is used for composite aggregation, also known as composition. Both diamonds are drawn on the 'aggregate' end of these whole–part relationships (e.g. Figure 2.27). An alternative representation for composition using nested icons is shown in Figure 2.28.

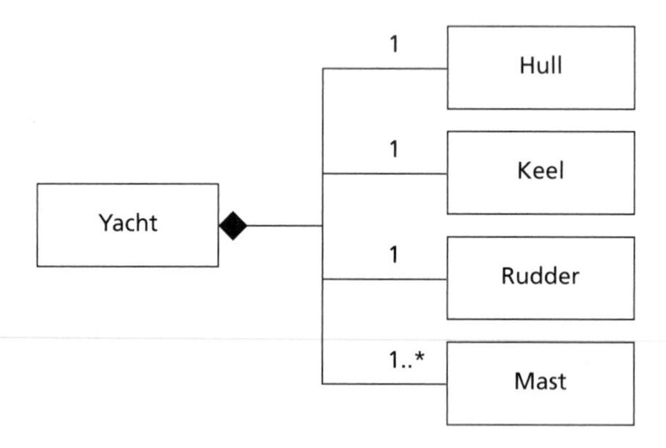

Figure 2.27 UML composition notation

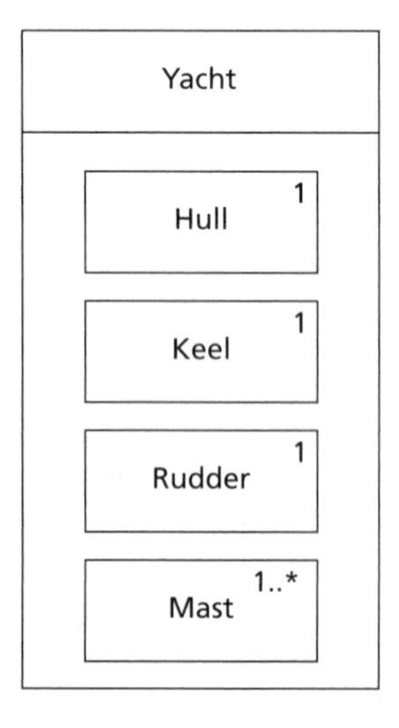

Figure 2.28 An alternative UML notation for composition (as a nested set of icons)

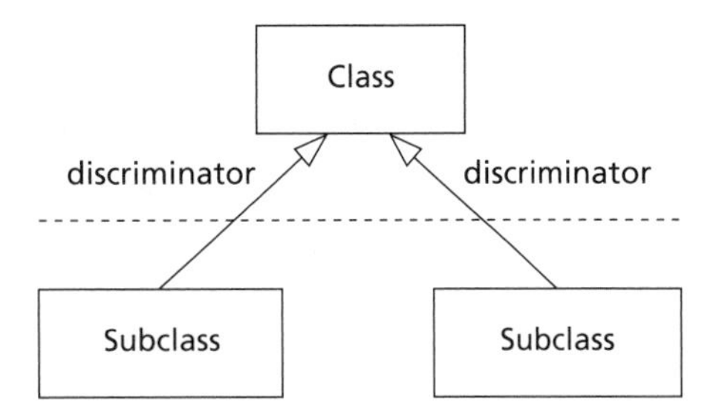

Figure 2.29 UML notation for generalization and discriminators

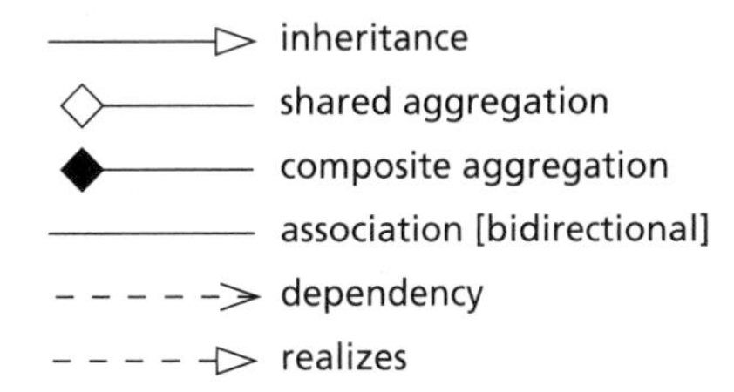

Figure 2.30 Summary of relationship notation for UML (arrow option 3)

The notation for the generalization relationship is a line with a white[15] headed arrow (Figure 2.29). This arrow style indicates that the relationship is a generalization/specialization form of inheritance in which there is type substitutability. In other words, the subclass is in fact a subtype and the question 'Can I say the subclass is a kind of the superclass?' receives a positive answer. When multiple partitioning (leading to the subsets shown) is in use, there is also the need for a discriminant which is a label attached to the members of that particular partition. Thus multiple partitions can be readily annotated.

All dependencies in UML are shown by a dotted arrow with an open arrowhead. A particularly useful one is «use» which represents a fairly common client–server relationship in the object model.

Realization depicts the fact that an implementation realizes its specification. Although it is a kind of dependency (i.e. a subtype) (Table 2.1), its notation is not the dependency dashed arrow but a dashed generalization arrow.

Figure 2.30 summarizes the notations for these various UML relationships.

2.5.2 Further uses of associations

Associations are treated as generalizable elements which permits models such as that shown in Figure 2.31 in which an association called Chair-of is a specialization (subset) of the Member-of association. Another use of associations is to express two

15 Originally black in Version 0.9.

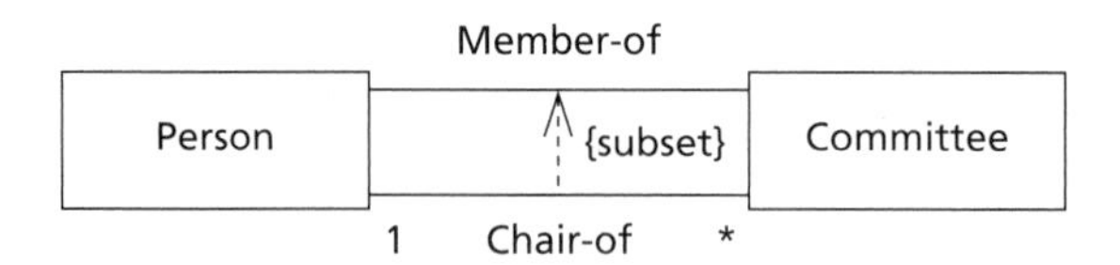

Figure 2.31 Using an association in a generalized context (© OMG, 1999a)

alternatives. This uses the *or* constraint as shown in Figure 2.32, although this often suggests a missing class (lower part of Figure 2.32).

We may also have an association relationship which is additionally considered to be a class, e.g. marriage. In UML, an association class is used which inherits (in the metamodel) from class and association and is the equivalent of a link table in a corresponding relational design. It can be depicted as a class icon attached with a dotted line to the relationship line (Figure 2.33). In using associations in OPEN, however, we recommend that a relationship that needs to be turned into a class should *simply be turned into a class*, i.e. its metatype is changed from Relation to Class. It is then shown graphically like any other class – by a rectangular icon. In other words, there is little or no need to use an association class when using OPEN.

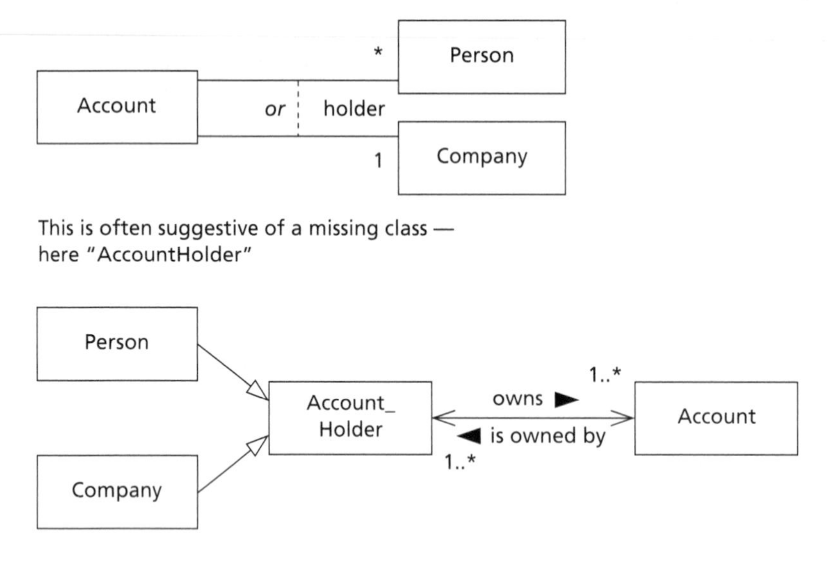

Figure 2.32 An 'or' association

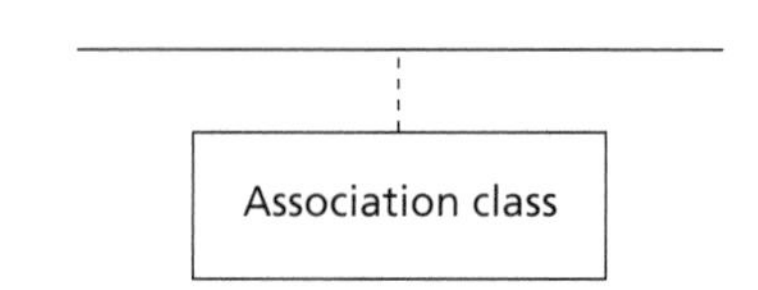

Figure 2.33 UML notation for an association class

2.6 Use cases

A use case, or more strictly a use case class (Kruchten, 1999, p. 97) describes the functionality of a software system as used by a user playing a role (called an actor in UML) in order to realize some goal. Use cases are thus not strictly object-oriented but can be used equally as part of an OO process or as a precursor to top-down functional decomposition. Of late, they are becoming a popular way of capturing requirements for any type of project, as well as for modeling business processes. However, Cockburn (2000) notes that business use cases tend to be written in a whitebox style, a style which includes internal actors, whereas for modeling software (as opposed to business modeling) a blackbox style of use case is used.

UML metamodels a use case as if it were itself an 'object' (Figure 2.34), i.e. it is represented by a metaclass analogous to that for classes – they are both subtypes of Classifier in the metamodel. If a use case is at the class-level, then a use case instance, or scenario, is at the object-level. Consequently, a use case is said to be composed of attributes and operations; it has association ends and can have interface(s) and instances.

Use cases can be linked together by a generalization relationship (see below) or by one of the two dependency relationships: include and extend (expressed as stereotypes (Figure 2.35)). These relationships replace the two contentious ones[16] of Version 1.1: «Use» and «extend» (although the unexpected connection[17] to AssociationEnd remains). The «extends» relationship describes how a use case representing additional functionality, often describing an anomalous situation or an

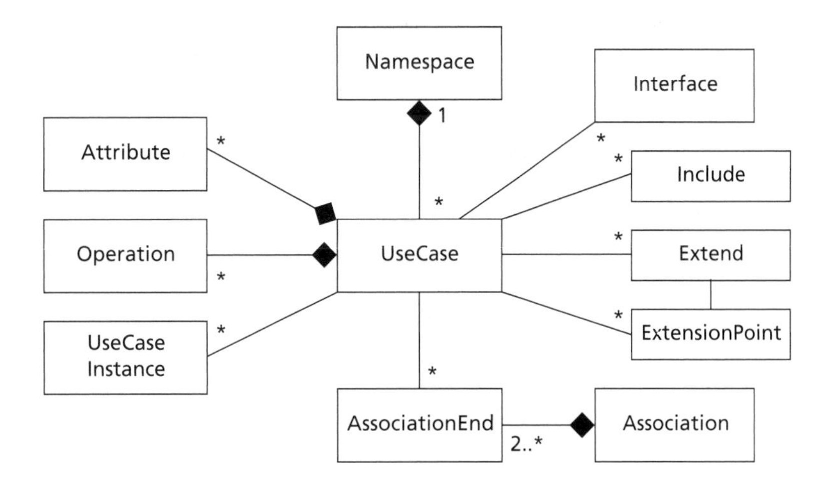

Figure 2.34 UML metamodel for use cases (© OMG, 1999a)

16 Although even Version 1.3's «extend» appears still to be contentious (Cockburn, 2000).

17 Since you cannot have an association relationship between two use cases, only between a use case and an actor.

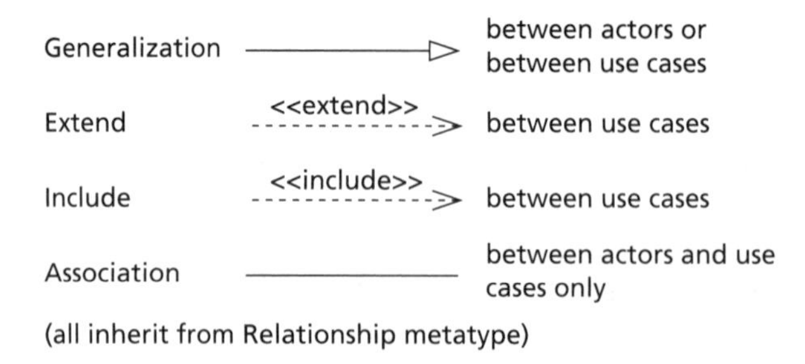

Figure 2.35 Use case relationships in UML Version 1.3

exception, beyond that provided in the base use case, is incorporated. The extending use case may thus be thought of as representing an 'option'. The «include» relationship permits a use case to represent functionality that might need to be included in more than one use case. This relationship represents a mandatory situation. Thus, for example (Figure 2.36), the base use case of Buy Train Ticket can be extended, in certain circumstances, by functionality expressing what to do when the Buy Train Ticket gets stuck (in this case, the bill being used to pay is rejected by the train ticket dispensing machine because it is folded). This is the use case Return Folded Bill which is inserted into the base case at the appropriate place – the so-called extension point. The Return Folded Bill use case is activated only occasionally, i.e. *not* on every execution of the base use case (here Buy Train Ticket). To illustrate «include», consider the case (Figure 2.37) when the Buy Plane Ticket use case and the Make Theatre Booking use case need to access and utilize the capabilities of the Print Receipt use case. Thus the Print Receipt use case is included in every execution of both the Buy Plane Ticket and Make Theatre Booking use cases.

UML also permits a generalization relationship between use cases to be specified – Use cases and actors in the metamodel are both subclasses of classifier and are therefore both generalizable. The 'parent' use case could then be 'abstract', and may be appropriate in describing a very high level of abstract interaction. In most practical use case modeling, generalization of use cases often makes little sense.

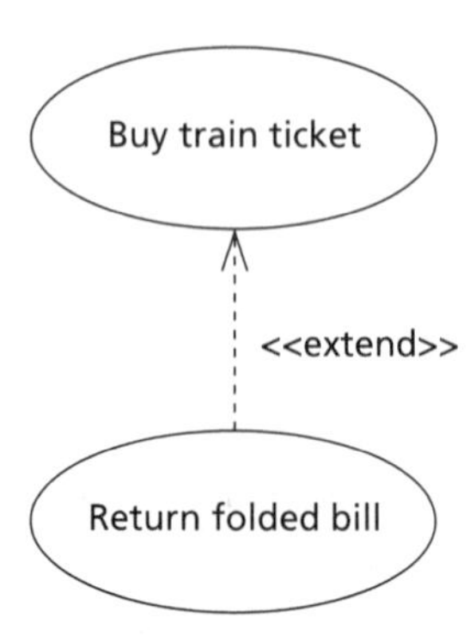

Figure 2.36 Example use case showing use of «extend»

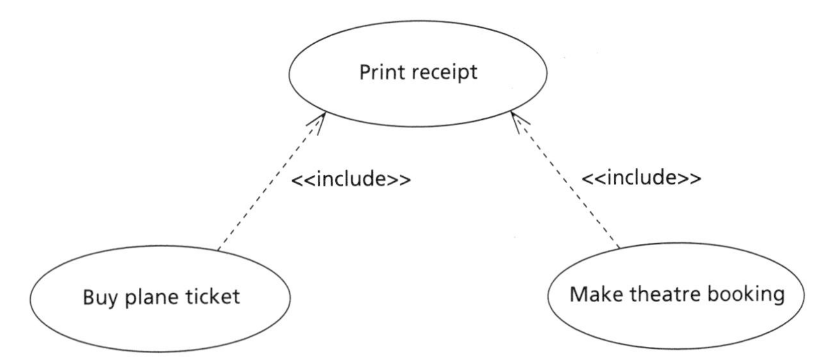

Figure 2.37 Example use case showing use of «include»

Another notation relevant to use cases is that for actors (Figure 2.38). An actor is a role played by a person or thing which is *external* to the software system. The actor interacts with the system. Actors are used in use case diagrams. A use case diagram (Figure 2.39) is a graph of actors, which are external to the software system, plus a set of use cases enclosed by a system boundary. It should be noted that, although this boundary line is optional in the UML standard, most use case experts suggest that its omission can lead to problems and, if the drawing does not support this, a visual arrangement with an imaginary box (Figure 2.40) provides a better format. Actors are externals[18] which use the functionality of the system. This functionality is represented by the ellipses within the system, the system itself being represented by the rectangle.

Actors are also generalizable. However, this, coupled with the generalizability of use cases, could readily lead to an example such as that shown in Figure 2.41. Here, a Senior Agent is a special kind (subtype) of Sales Clerk and the use case to Close a big deal is a good subtype of the Close a deal use case. The problem is that in now adding the actor–goal pairing (actor to use case relationship) we have introduced

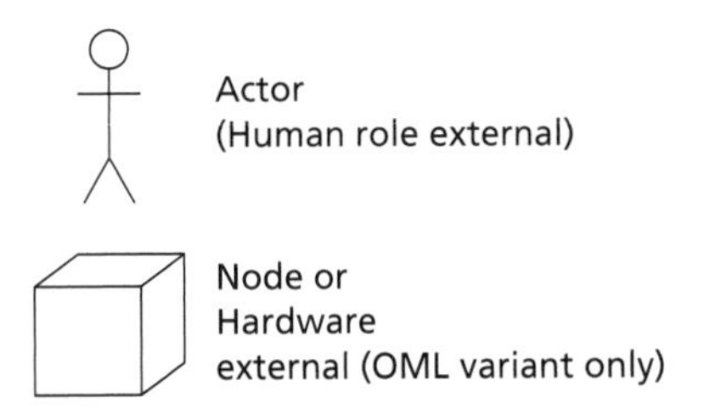

Figure 2.38 Externals and actors

18 In UML, all types of externals are denoted by the stick figure symbol for actor. In the OML variant of the UML, other kinds of external, such as hardware external and software external, are identified and the stick figure reserved for wetware (people) externals. An actor can also be represented in UML by a class 'box' and the stereotype «actor».

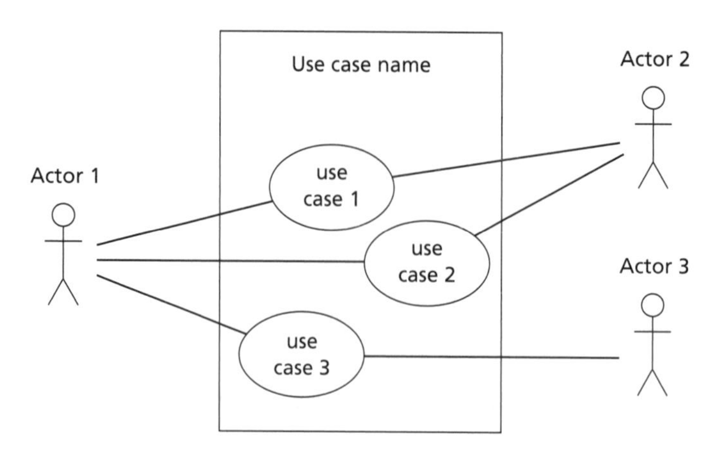

Figure 2.39 Example use case diagram

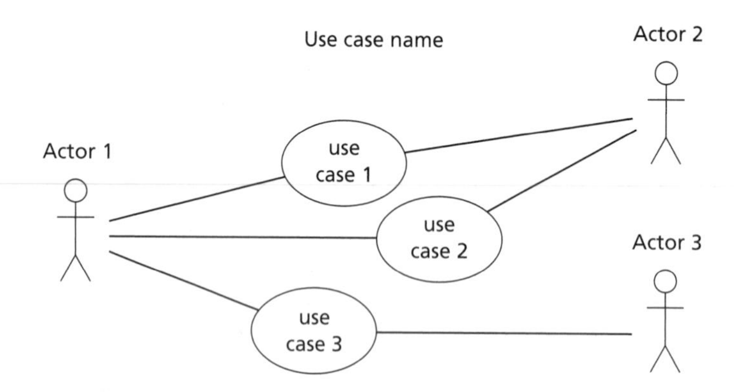

Figure 2.40 Use case diagram arranged so that it is clear which items are external and which internal to the software system (after Lilly, 1999, © IEEE, 1999)

unwanted semantics. What we wanted to say was that a Sales Clerk could close a deal but it needed a more senior (more specialized) Senior Agent to close a big deal. Unfortunately, because of the pre-identified inheritance (generalization relationships[19] between (i) Senior Agent and Sales Clerk and (ii) Close a big deal and Close a deal, we also have represented in this diagram the ability for a Sales clerk to Close a big deal since this can polymorphically substitute for the 'parent' use case of Close a deal. A revised, and correct, version of Figure 2.41 is given in Figure 2.42.

Focusing on an individual use case, the most usual way of describing it is free text or, perhaps better, using a template[20] (Figure 2.43) to add some semi-formal

19 By the way (BTW), Cockburn (2000) also notes that there isn't actually an agreed semantics for generalization/specialization (i.e. subtyping) when applied to use cases.

20 Slightly different versions have been given by various authors (e.g. Rumbaugh, 1994; Cockburn, 1997b; Jaaksi, 1997). More recently Cockburn (2000) suggests the need for *two* templates: the first a 'casual' low ceremony one and the second a 'fully dressed' one for high ceremony projects.

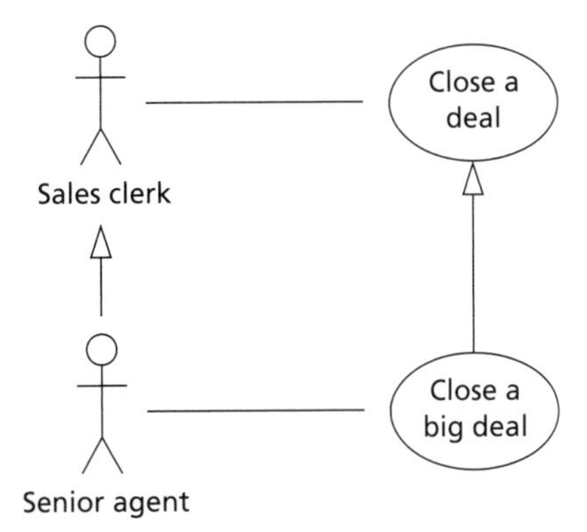

Figure 2.41 Using generalization in both actors and use cases concurrently may lead to incorrect semantics (after Cockburn, 2000; © Addison-Wesley)

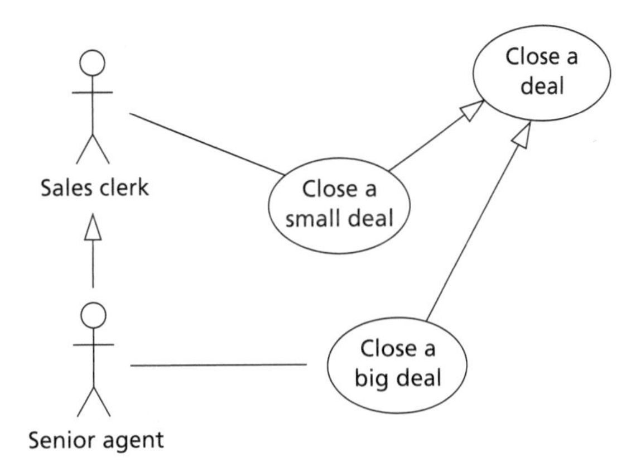

Figure 2.42 Redrawing of Figure 2.41 eliminates the problem encountered (after Cockburn, 2000; © Addison-Wesley)

System under discussion:	<name>
Use case name:	<name>
Version number:	<#>
Summary:	<one sentence description>
Actors:	<name list>
Goal:	
Pre-conditions:	
Main Success Path:	<#n> <description of step n>
Extensions/Alternatives/ Exceptions/Variations:	<#n> <z> <description of extension z relating to main use case path step n
Post-conditions	

Figure 2.43 Simplified template for describing a use case

structure to the text. Here we see the main elements.[21] They set out the context and then describe the steps in the use case – first following the Main Success Path and then looking at alternatives. Pre- and post-conditions for using the use case need also to be specified clearly.

2.7 Interaction diagrams

In UML, interaction diagrams show the dynamic aspect of the system – the passing of messages. They are either sequence diagrams or collaboration diagrams (Figure 2.44). Both show essentially the same information but display it in a different visual fashion. Sequence diagrams emphasize the temporal element and collaboration diagrams emphasize the structural features.

Interaction diagrams show objects (not classes)[22] and the way in which messages are passed between the objects. In a collaboration diagram (Figure 2.45), the objects are visualized in a similar fashion to a class diagram, but here a sequence of message passes is superimposed *together with* an indication of their ordering (1.1, 1.2, etc.). This sequence of messages effects the answer to a single request, as indicated (here the request action()). When shown as a sequence diagram (Figure 2.46), each object is rearranged in a linear fashion across the top of the page and a timeline for that object is drawn vertically downwards.[23] Horizontal arrows are drawn for each message passing. Different arrowhead styles are available to denote synchronous and asynchronous messages if desired. Thickening of a temporal line indicates when the individual object is active (i.e. the object is either receiving a message, executing an

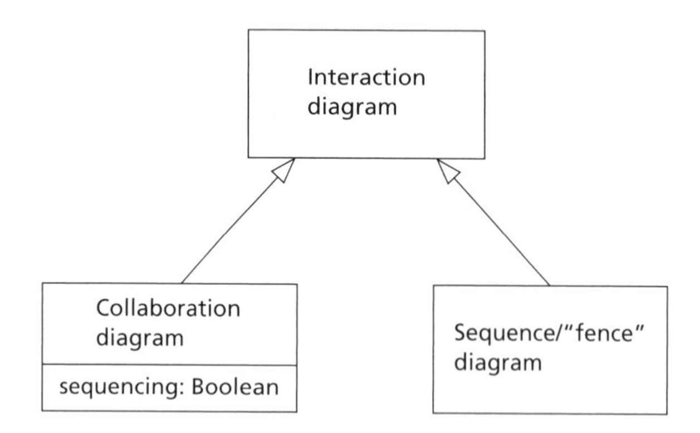

Figure 2.44 Interaction Diagrams are either collaboration diagrams or sequence diagrams

21 More can be added – for a more extensive template, see Section 5.6.4.

22 Although anonymous objects can also be used and are represented by the class name prefixed by a colon (and underlined), e.g. :Account.

23 It is possible to draw a sequence diagram with horizontal timelines but this is unusual.

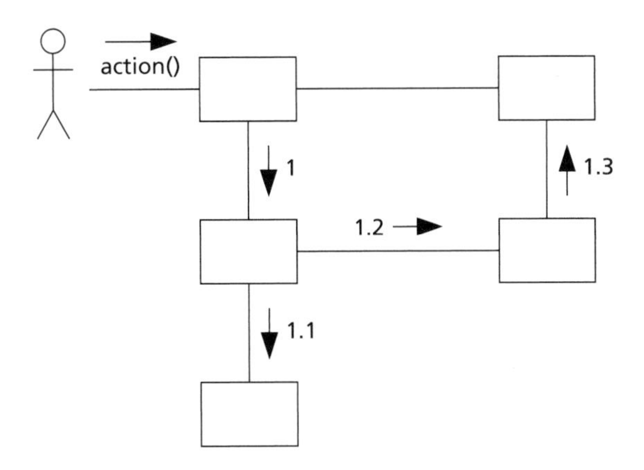

Figure 2.45 Example collaboration diagram

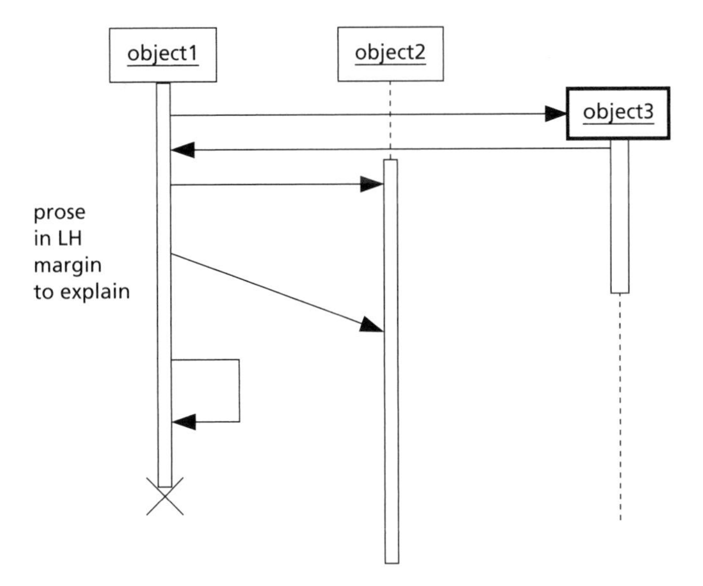

Figure 2.46 Example sequence diagram

operation or sending a message). An arrow going directly to an object box (as for object 3) indicates the actual object creation caused by that incoming message. Object destruction is shown by a large cross. Internal message sends are shown as arrows turning back to the lifeline; whereas a slanting arrow indicates a message that is not instantaneous, taking a finite amount of time to execute. Prose may also be added in the left-hand margin to explain the control flow logic.

2.8 Statechart diagrams

The UML State Machine Model is derived from Harel's statecharts. It uses traditional state modeling based on traditional concepts (e.g. events). The Version 1.3 metamodel is shown in Figure 2.47 in which we see that the StateMachine consists of states and transitions. Events are triggers and should be interpreted as either messages or exceptions. An event occurs at a point in time and may cause a state change. Transition models this change of state and has guard(s) which evaluate whether a state change occurs following the trigger (event). In other words, the same event may or may not cause a state change depending upon whether or not the guard condition is satisfied.

In state transition modeling, states are represented by rounded rectangles and transitions between states by regular arrows (Figure 2.48). States can be nested and the initial and final states have their own notation: a dot and a 'bullseye'. The dotted line in Figure 2.48 indicates two parallel states. Each statechart explains the state changes of a single class, i.e. it describes how each and every object in that class may change its state.

In practice, statechart diagrams are drawn only for the most important or complex objects. Objects that change their states based on a complex series of conditions should have a corresponding statechart diagram.

In a simple way, though, a statechart diagram is a pictorial representation of different values of a 'flag' associated with an object, or for that matter with a record in a relational table.

In UML, there is a notation ('H' inside a circle) to represent the fact that an object can remember its previous state. Thus, when it transitions back to the superstate it

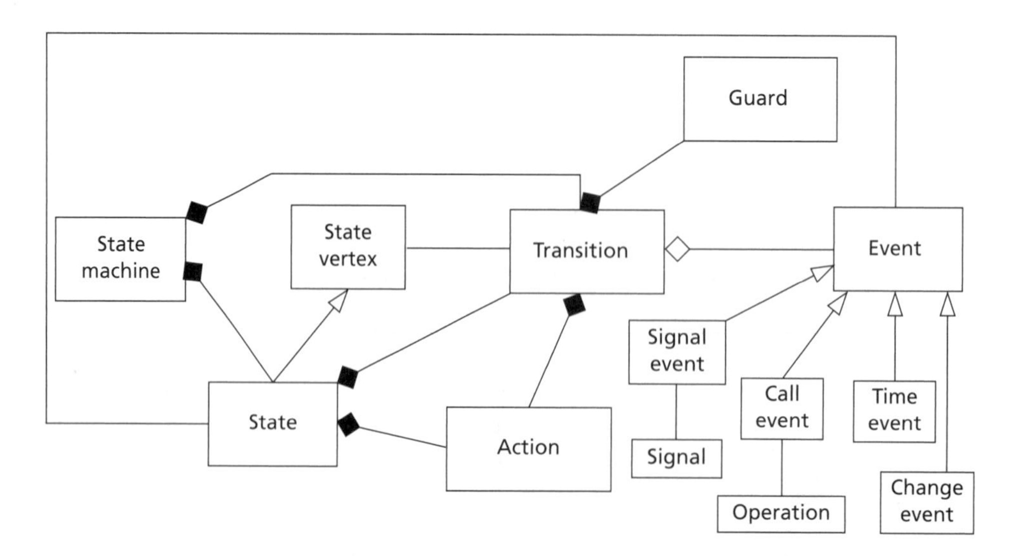

Figure 2.47 UML state model metamodel

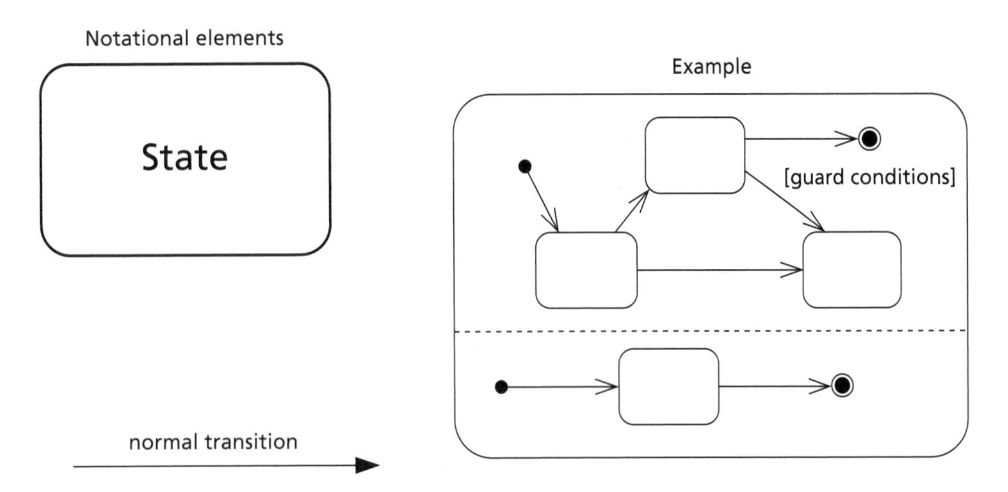

Figure 2.48 Statechart notation in UML

enters the correct substate. This is called a history state and is one of the kinds of available Pseudostates, themselves a submetatype of StateVertex. In addition to history, UML also permits the sending of events between communicating state machines.

Summary of Key Points

- The current version of UML (Version 1.3) is large and only a subset is described here.
- UML has diagrams and metamodels for all aspects, static and dynamic, of object-oriented systems.

Discussion Topics

- How are dependency relationships and associations connected?
- Is there any value in striving to identify good semantics for whole–part relationships, especially when their implementation in most programming languages will be the same as for an association, i.e. a reference?
- How important is it for (a) developers and (b) management to understand the metamodel component of the UML?
- How should OCL be best used?

Bibliographic Notes

The first version of the UML was 0.8. This was, at that time, supported only by Rational and a small number of partners. By the time it had reached 1.0, it was submitted to the Object Management Group as part of their standardization process for a metamodel and optional notation. Following the submission of this and a number of other proposals, a converged modeling language, also known as the Unified Modeling Language, emerged in mid- to late 1997. Version 1.1 was ratified by the OMG in September 1997. Further development by a Revisionary Task Force (RTF) of the OMG led to the submission to the OMG Board in late 1999 of Version 1.3 and, at the same time, plans were made for Versions 1.4 and 2.0. A Request for Information or RFI for UML V2.0 was issued in mid-1999 with a submission date of 17 December 1999 and the anticipation that an RFP (Request For Proposal) might emerge in mid-2000. None of these versions has been published other than through a document of the Object Management Group (available electronically from their web site). Many derivative books have been published but all run the risk of misinterpreting or omitting important parts of the UML. The only definitive and reliable source of the UML remains the OMG document (Version 1.3 was made available in June 1999).

3 OPEN's Modeling Tasks and Techniques Explained

Abstract

In this chapter we describe the Tasks and Techniques of OPEN which pertain to the modeling domain. These are described very roughly in the order in which they might occur.

3.1 Introduction

Having set the overall scene for the OPEN process in Chapter 1, and explained the elements of the Unified Modeling Language in Chapter 2, we now focus on those Tasks and Techniques of OPEN that support object-oriented modeling. Most of these Tasks/Techniques form a major element of the Build Activity of Figure 1.11. These are the technical elements needed for software construction using an object-oriented approach and, in particular, the OPEN process. Many important modeling Tasks/Techniques also come into play in the earlier activities of the OPEN process. For example, use cases often play an important role in Requirements Engineering.

We focus here on the modeling activities, Tasks and Techniques since it is these that produce work products that are able to be documented in UML. Thus other Tasks and Techniques, while important to the overall process, are deemed outside the scope of this modeling-focused 'OPEN with UML' book. These modeling Tasks and Techniques are also shown 'in practice' in Chapters 4 and 5. It is also worth noting that a mere discussion of the Tasks and Techniques is not good enough for practical software engineering. We also need to put these Tasks and Techniques in some sequence, and also decide on the iterations to be performed using these Tasks and Techniques. This sequencing and the necessary iterations form part of the 'tailoring' element of the process and are discussed in the case studies in Chapters 4 and 5.

In engineering the requirements of the end user and translating them into software development, we create many models – or more accurately many partial

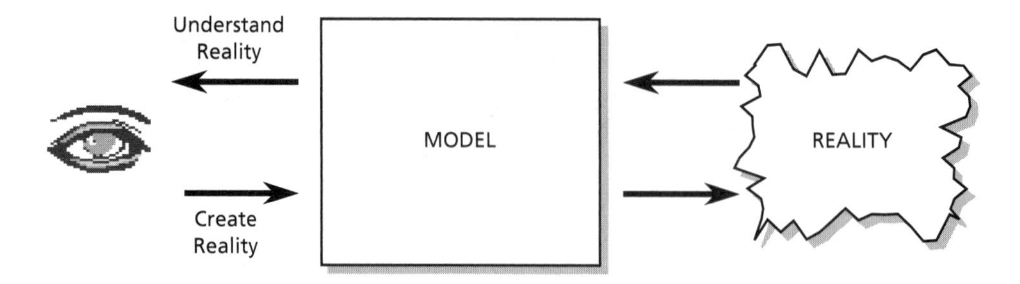

Figure 3.1 Advantages of modeling (after Unhelkar, 1999; © CRC Press)

views of the single model of the system we are about to create. Why is modeling so important? As seen in Figure 3.1, modeling has two main purposes: (i) to understand reality in all its complexity (the business problem or the user needs) and (ii) to create a new reality (to be embodied in our system) which represents the solution to some business problem.

Definition

A model is an abstraction of the existing reality and, as such, hides much of the detail. This permits the modeler to focus completely on those characteristics of immediate relevance and to ignore those aspects that are merely distracting and of no significance. A model is also an abstraction of the new reality we are trying to create – enabling experiments and trials before creating the actual work product.

Of the 30 Tasks documented in *The OPEN Process Specification* book by Graham *et al.* (1997a) (Table 3.1), only a small subset pertain to modeling. In this book, we have chosen to focus primarily on those modeling tasks together with appropriate modeling techniques (Table 3.2). In each of the following sections, we 'lump

Table 3.1 The 30 documented Tasks of OPEN grouped under contextual headings. Those in parentheses are actually subtasks but are included here for information/completeness

1. **User interactions and business issues**
   Identify context
   Identify source(s) of requirements
   Identify user requirements
   Analyze user requirements
   Model and re-engineer business process(es)
   Undertake feasibility study
   Obtain business approval
   Develop Business Object Model (BOM)
   Write manuals and prepare other documentation
   Deliver product to customer

2. Large-scale architectural issues
Undertake architectural design
(Construct frameworks)
Optimize the design

3. Project management issues
Develop software development context plans and strategies
Undertake feasibility study
Develop and implement resource allocation plans

3.1 *Quality issues*
Test
Write manuals and prepare other documentation
Evaluate quality
Maintain trace between requirements and design
Undertake in-process review
Undertake post-implementation review

4. Database issues
(Identify user database requirements)
(Select database/storage strategy)
(Identify persistent classes)
Map logical database schema
Design and implement physical database

5. Distribution issues
(Identify user requirements)
(Establish distributed systems strategy)
(Develop security plan)

6. Modeling/building the system
Analyze user requirements
Identify CIRTs
Construct the object model
Design user interface
Map roles on to classes
Optimize the design
Undertake usability design
Code
Write manuals and other documentation

7. Reuse issues
Optimize reuse ('with reuse')
Create and/or identify reusable components ('for reuse')
Manage library of reusable components

Table 3.2 The modeling Tasks and Techniques of OPEN together with reference to the sections in which they are discussed.

OPEN Tasks related to modeling	*Section in which discussed*
Identify CIRTs	3.2
Construct the object model	3.2, 3.4, 3.12
Map roles on to classes	3.11
Code	3.14
Write manuals and other documentation	3.2
*OPEN Tasks related to modeling as part of RE and BPM**	
Analyze user requirements	3.13
Model and re-engineer business process(es)	3.13
OPEN Techniques related to these modeling contexts	
Abstract class identification	3.10
Abstraction utilization	3.2
Class internal design	3.14
Class naming	3.2
Collaborations analysis	3.4
Completion of abstractions	3.6
Contract specification	3.9
Creation charts	3.14
CRC card modeling	3.5
Delegation analysis	3.4
Design templates	3.14
Generalization and inheritance identification	3.10
Granularity	3.4
Hierarchical task analysis	3.12
Implementation of services	3.14
Implementation of structure	3.14
Interaction modeling	3.4
Pattern recognition	3.4
Relationship modeling	3.7, 3.8
Responsibility identification	3.3
Role modeling	3.11
Scenario development (including use cases)	3.13
Service identification	3.6
State modeling	3.12
Stereotyping	3.2
Transformations of the object model	3.6
Textual analysis	3.2
Visibility analysis	3.4

* RE = Requirements Engineering; BPM = Business Process Modeling

together' a number of these tasks and techniques into a set of generic subject areas, e.g. object identification, responsibilities and so on. These section headings do not refer to any specific OPEN Task or Technique but merely set the context. Specific Tasks and Techniques are referred to by name within the body of each section. It is also important to note that such groupings are fuzzy. They have been determined from application of the tailoring matrices discussed in Chapter 1 and some Tasks or Techniques may appear under more than one heading. The Tasks and the Activities to which they belong are, of course, potentially executed several times in a truly iterative and incremental manner. Thus, as mentioned earlier, although this chapter describes the modeling process in a linear fashion, the reader should bear in mind that the reality is that these tasks and techniques will occur many times in such an IIP (iterative, incremental and parallel) approach typical of modern OO software developments. This IIP nature of the OPEN process is highlighted in Chapter 5.

Not only are the OPEN tasks and techniques iterative, they may also appear in different sequences in different projects. Some of them may not appear at all. This is a facet of the tailorability of the OPEN process framework which was discussed earlier, in Chapter 1. Rather, we defer to Chapters 4 and 5, the two case studies, the important issue about how you construct your own specific SEP ideally suited to the problem in hand and compatible with your organization's culture, the available skills and so on.

So in this chapter, we introduce a number of modeling areas, grouped into 13 sections plus a fourteenth on inspections and reviews. In each section we address a particular aspect of object modeling and weave into the discussion the necessary concepts, tasks and techniques together with some practical advice on how to use each individual topic area. We focus initially on the static aspects of the system (e.g. class diagrams) and then move on to the dynamic and functional aspects (e.g. statechart diagrams, use case diagrams). Of course, this is not likely to be the order in which the Tasks and Techniques are ultimately used. Use cases are often used fairly early in the lifecycle as part of Requirements Engineering, as a complement to 'object identification', as well as being used later in the lifecycle as an aid to testing, for example.

3.2 Object identification and documentation

A relevant task in OPEN is 'Identify CIRTs', where CIRT is an acronym for class, instance, role or type. Although we talk about finding 'objects'' and the 'object-oriented paradigm', in reality we normally look for concepts that are representable as either classes, types or roles. Thus we lump together these four concepts under the name CIRT.[1] Probably most commonly, when we 'find the objects' we find types

1 We will also use the word object loosely not only to mean CIRT, but also during the early activity of Requirements Engineering, a package.

or interfaces.[2] Occasionally, at a higher level, or during the early part of the lifecycle, what we might be identifying are key subject areas and/or packages, eventually resulting in 'components' rather than classes. In order to avoid confusion amongst these various terms, we recommend the use of the term CIRT.

Definition

A class is a definition that captures the concept underpinning a set of instances. These instances have the same abstraction and therefore have the same or similar features. A class consists of an interface (the specification equals the external view) and an implementation (the internal view). A type describes the external view of a class (a collective notion) of individuals. Individuals are thus instances of the corresponding collection concept. For example, an object is an instance of a class; a scenario is an instance of a use case.

So an object is an individual: an instance. In contrast, a class is a description of a collection or set which describes a shared concept. There are many objects which belong to the class. In some cases, however, it is *not* possible or advisable to create instances from a class, but only from its subclasses. Such a class is known as an *abstract class* (or sometimes a deferred class). It cannot be used to create instances for the simple reason that part of its implementation is incomplete – the complete details are usually deferred to a subclass (Figure 3.2). Further discussion on the use of abstract classes and their role in inheritance hierarchies is deferred until Section 3.10.

Recognition of classes is sometimes trivial and obvious, sometimes extremely difficult. It often depends upon the domain. For example, in an engineering domain, say modeling a water treatment plant, there are a significant number of objects that

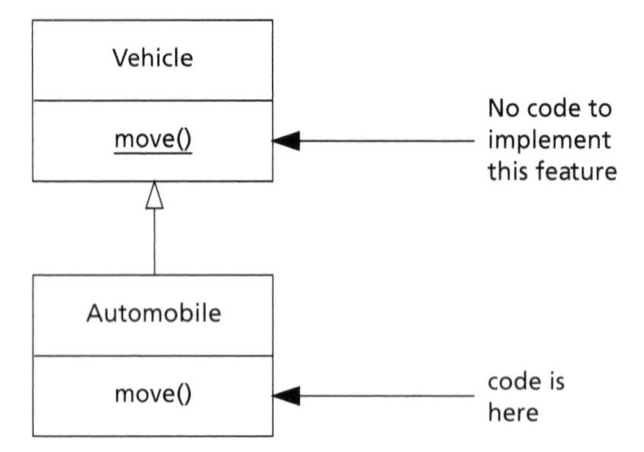

Figure 3.2 One or more methods of an abstract class are deferred (for their full implementation details) to a subclass

2 Both types and interfaces represent an external view of the 'object'. OPEN tends not to fuss about discriminating between them. The need for two terms comes from the wish to differentiate between (i) the whole of the externally visible 'face' of the object and (ii) a subset of the external view that can be related to specific roles, collaborations, contracts or abstract data types.

are obvious since they are software models of 'things' in the real, engineering world, for example filters, coagulators, pumps and channels. Note that none of these single classes can be finally implemented on their own. They need a collection of logically cohesive objects to get close to implementation. Hence, at this early stage of the OPEN lifecycle, we are more package-oriented. If, however, the focus of the development team from the outset is on 'what' is going to be developed, then the approach will become 'component-oriented', wherein the component is the final executable entity being produced by the development team.

In identifying key business entities, we should be looking out for not only real-world things but also organizational entities such as organization or department. Seek concepts that might be implicit, in addition to those that are explicit. For instance, in the negotiation of a customer buying a house, as well as the obvious classes of Customer and House perhaps there is need for a class called Purchase. Another example, quite commonly used, is a banking system wherein Customer and Account are pretty obvious explicit classes, whereas Transaction, an important class, is implicit.

We aim first to derive a list of candidate 'objects'. Perhaps the objects are intuitively obvious so that we can just look at the requirements or talk to the end user and immediately identify the key concepts, which we add to our list of potential or candidate classes. Another, slightly more formal, way of arriving at a list like this is called textual analysis (a Technique in OPEN). It is also called the 'underlining the nouns' technique by some. We can do this semi-formally by reading through the requirements document and underlining all nouns and noun phrases. For a small system like the library system, this can work. In our experience, though, it doesn't scale up all that well. We have heard of 1000-page requirements documents being analyzed mechanically in this way. More thought than just a red pen in your hand is needed! Choose whether the noun/noun phrase is of value or whether it is just part of the general diatribe of the requirements description.

Another useful OPEN technique is abstraction utilization. 'Objects' model a whole range of concepts in the problem domain. Within that problem domain, one can usually identify a whole range of scales – or levels of abstraction. Initially it is recommended that you model at the highest level of abstraction – sort of creating an overall sketch of the main 'entities' in the problem domain using the UML notation of 'packages'. Analysis and design in OO is often regarded as 'fleshing out' those originally identified key abstractions. This means adding more detail and consequently changing the abstraction level. For example, we might model a computer as a single object at a high level in a technical problem domain. Only later, and with much more detail, do we add to this original model all the details of the parts of which a computer comprises. Knowing that a PC has a motherboard is irrelevant to modeling, say, the network configuration to support a distributed information system but would need to be included prior to final coding. Generally, most people find it very hard to retain a highly abstract level of modeling for long enough. There seems to be a great tendency to rush off into detail perhaps commensurate with a great desire to produce working code. OPEN's Technique: Abstraction utilization reminds you of the advantages of selecting and focusing on a single abstraction level at any one time. Granted this will change with time, but at any stage during the development cycle the abstraction level of all the elements in the evolving object model should be the same.

To create an appropriate model (OPEN Tasks: Construct the object model; and Write manuals and other documentation) from our identified classes, we first need to choose a modeling language and then apply that to create a class model which typically will include mostly graphics but with textual annotations. Some parts of the model might indeed be totally textual. For the moment, we will not fuss about whether we are building the class model using objects, types, interfaces or classes. Earlier in this section we called these 'objects'. In keeping with UML terminology, let us now call them classes, although strictly a class contains implementation details and the classes in our class model do not. As we saw in Figure 2.9, the way of documenting a class using UML is as a rectangle with three compartments. The name is in the first compartment, attributes in the second and operations in the third. The attributes represent the structural aspects of the class. They really refer to CRUD (create, read, update and delete) services of the class rather than actual attributes which, following the OO principle of information hiding, should always be invisible from outside and used only in final implementation. Operations, on the other hand, are the externally visible parts of methods that exist within each class. Operations represent the behavioural aspect of a class. If the 'entity' identified at the business level is so 'high' or abstract that no meaningful attributes or operations are identifiable, then instead of calling them a class, we prefer to call them a package. For example, Account and Customer, in a real banking system, will not be classes but packages.[3]

Coming back to classes, though, we saw in Chapter 2 that UML permits various degrees of information and detail to be shown on the class icons (Figure 2.10). This is because, as we noted above, as you move through the development process, you tend to add more details (see OPEN Technique: Abstraction utilization). When you are modeling requirements, a simple name is probably adequate. It is not until you approach detailed design and implementation that you really need the full details that are possible: visibility markers, initial values, textual annotations on authorship (i.e. class indexing information) and so on. Furthermore, a single entity during the early stages of the lifecycle will be decomposed into more classes during later stages and, in time, two or more classes may be combined into a single class.

At whatever stage a new class is introduced, its name is most important. This statement appears to many to be overemphasizing a trivial matter. Studies have shown, however, that spending some time carefully considering an appropriate class name can avoid ambiguities, misconceptions and cross-connections later. OPEN even has a whole Technique to address this: Class naming. Names should be, if at all possible, short and informative. Of course this doesn't always work, but certainly using abbreviations can lead to severe problems. Laziness in naming is not acceptable. An example might illustrate this better. Figure 3.3 shows a model in

3 Note that a template for 'Class' documentation is provided in Chapter 5, which may also be used to document key high-level business entities or abstractions.

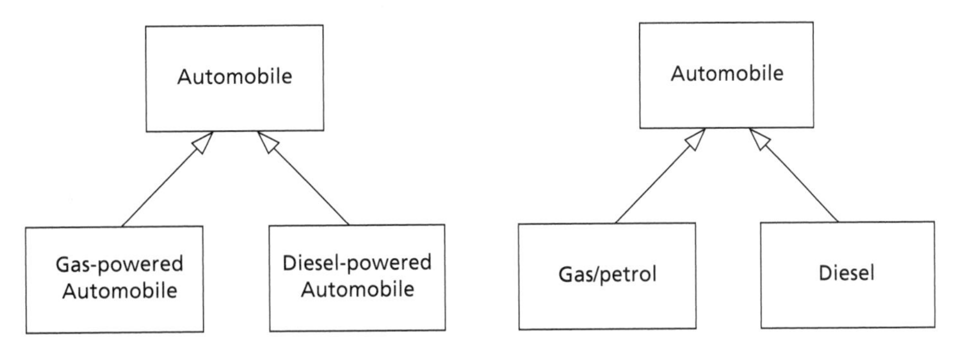

Figure 3.3 The importance of good naming

which an automobile class is subclassed into those cars powered by petrol (gasoline) and those by diesel. In reviewing this model, one would ask, 'Is the subclass a-kind-of the superclass?' A positive answer confirms that the Generalization relationship between them is appropriate. In the left-hand diagram this works out smoothly. This model seems reasonable. However, a frequently encountered 'student' answer to this question more often resembles the model on the right-hand side of this diagram. Laziness has led the student to truncate the class name of 'petrol-driven automobile' to 'petrol'. As reviewer of this model, you ask, 'Is a petrol a kind of automobile?' and the answer is clearly no. Of course, you might argue that there is a clear intention of the modeler that the class 'petrol' is really a class 'petrol-driven automobile', but if that is true then why not say so? Now take this example, multiply it by 100 and take it to a domain in which the modeler is less familiar. We hope you can see the danger of being lazy in naming classes.

Having a 'local' or departmental standard on class naming is also helpful. It is especially helpful in ensuring that classes are named in a 'general' or acceptable standard, rather than (say) prefixed by the initials of the author of the class. We have noticed, in our experience, that people are more comfortable in 'reusing' classes which are *not* named personally after their authors.

Be consistent in using singular or plural names for classes. While there is still some argument about which is logically preferable, *do* be consistent. The other thing about names is that it has been shown that they actually influence the way the designs develop. After all, names are place-markers or substitutes for real-world concepts. As we discuss above, different people often have different (shades of) understanding of any particular concept. That understanding tends to come with prejudices and assumptions that are *very* hard, nay often impossible, to see. For example, consider a web-based student course registration system that allows students to register for subjects in the 'fall' semester. If that system is used by an Australian or New Zealander student to register for a university, the seasons (or the months) will be quite opposite. A prejudice not even recognized has led to non-communication or possibly to the inability to use the software in a different region or country from the one in which it was developed, because the developer has 'frozen in' some assumptions about the concept they didn't even know they held.

A typical class diagram is shown in Figure 3.4. It shows that a car has one or more doors, a single engine and several wheels. Since the wheels can be detached and the car still remains a car, we permit a multiplicity of 0, 1, 2 or 3 as well as the anticipated 4. A Car is itself a subtype of the abstract class Vehicle. Vehicle is abstract (denoted by the word abstract in braces) since there are never any vehicle objects, only objects instantiated from one of the subtypes of Vehicle (only Car here is shown; there are likely to be others). On the left-hand side of the figure is another inheritance hierarchy which relates to People in their roles as Owners and Drivers (although we have cheated a little here and used inheritance rather than roles). Both Owner and Driver are shown as kinds of people. Indeed, if these are permanent classifications, inheritance is the best model in any case. However, there are limitations – for instance, an instance cannot be both Owner and Driver at the same time: clearly untenable in real life. Once again, the supertype is an abstract class. Finally, there is an association relationship between two classes, one from each hierarchy: Driver and Car. The Driver uses the services of the Car and only one car at any one time (hence the unity multiplicity at the Car end of the relationship). If this diagram grows too much as we develop it further, we should consider 'hiving off' the inheritance details to inheritance diagrams linked to this class diagram.

Detail and scope provide a tension and a balance that must be recognized and dealt with. A diagram with a large number of classes is good to provide overall architectural details but provides little information on the real, behavioural nature

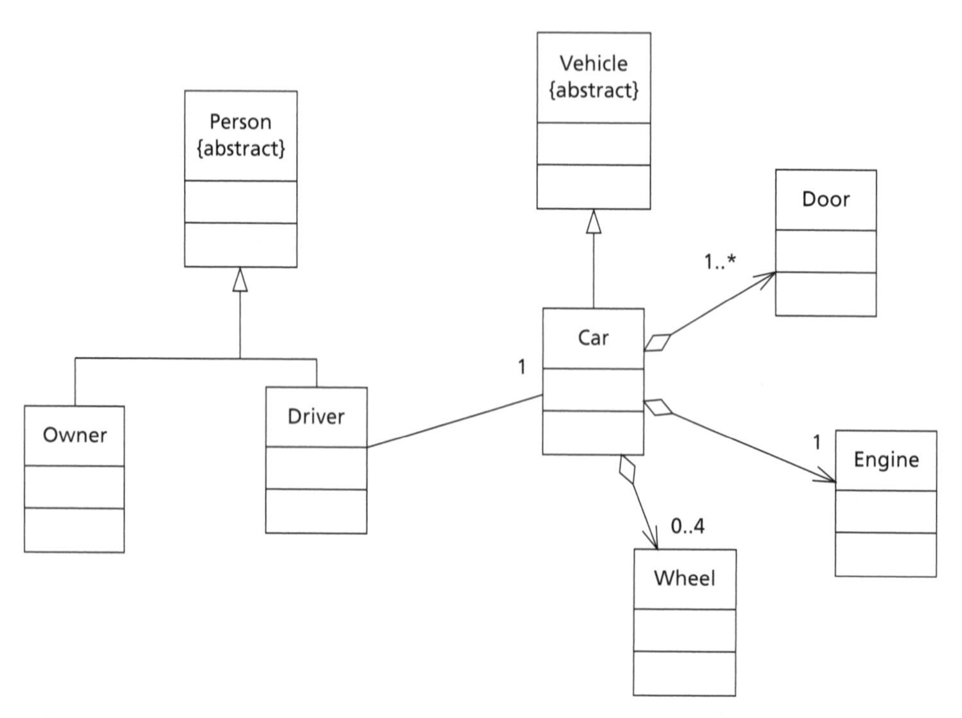

Figure 3.4 Typical class diagram using UML notation

of the classes. At the other extreme, if we use the fullest option (of Figure 2.10) to portray a class and put in *all* the attributes and operations, then it is all but impossible to see the *overall* scheme of things.

However, we should note that undertaking too much of the analysis by just using the 'class name only' style of icon can also be dangerous. Names are important but are often ambiguous. Two individuals may understand two totally different things from the same name because of their own backgrounds, prejudices, assumptions, interests, etc. For example, does OODB stand for 'Object-Oriented Data Base', 'Our Own Data Base' or 'Orange Overseas Diplomatic Bag'? Some organizations have even found that when they seek definitions of classes like Customer, Invoice or Client, each department has a different viewpoint and there may be, even in a single organization committed to doing a good object-oriented model, a dozen or so quite acceptable definitions in daily use. Hence we need additional mechanisms to annotate the class diagram.

For most purposes, UML class diagrams will suffice even if really they are intended to show types/interfaces rather than classes. If these elements are, however, required to be shown explicitly, then stereotypes can be added. OPEN has a special technique to deal with this part of the modeling process – Technique: Stereotyping. A stereotype is a way of adding a second classification to an object. While its name indicates its type, additional classification information may be superimposed. For instance, an object which belongs to the class of Automobile might also need to be shown as being an instance of a class called something like US-made things in order to differentiate it from European-made and Australian-made cars (Figure 3.5). Of course there are many other instances in the class US-made things that are *not* instances of the class Automobile. Hence, we can think of stereotypes as useful when multiple classification is required. As we noted in Chapter 2 (Figure 2.19) it is tantamount to thinking of the relationship as if it were creating subtypes (Figure 3.6).

There are two options in UML for showing stereotypes on class (and other) diagrams. The first and most normal is the addition of the stereotype name in guillemets above the class name (as in Figure 2.17). The other option is to use your

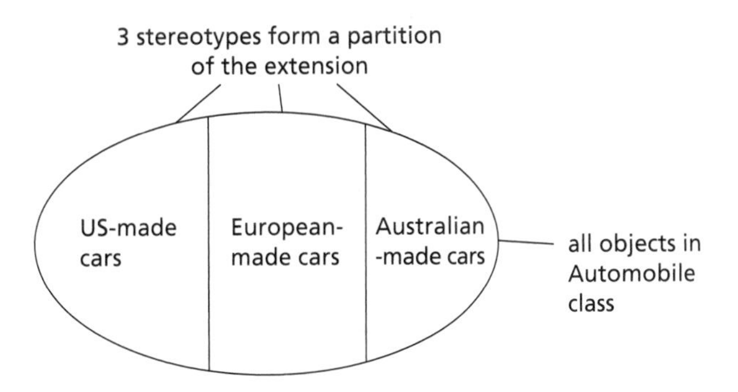

Figure 3.5 All the objects in the Automobile class are partitioned into three subsets. Each of these can be represented by a stereotype.

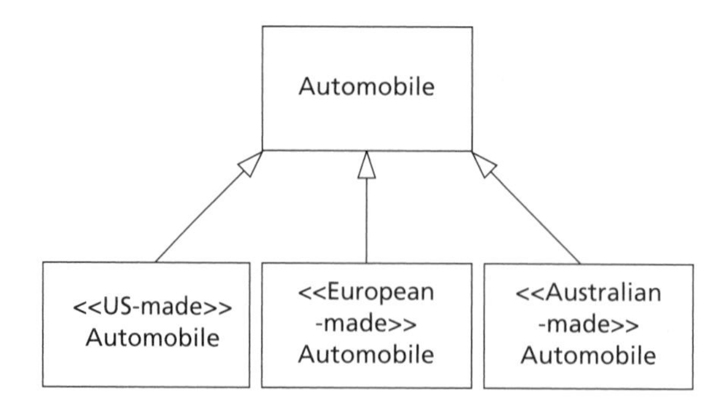

Figure 3.6 Representing the partition of Figure 3.5 using UML

own symbol. The advantage of a symbol is that it is, arguably, easier to discriminate between the stereotype and the unstereotyped classes yet, at the same time, use of a large number of non-standard or individualistic symbols can be confusing to everyone else except the drawer of the design diagram. The symbols offered by, for example, the Objectory extension of UML and the OML variant of UML strive to keep the balance between the usefulness of symbols rather than guillemets and the dangerous excesses of using a new symbol for everything. Figure 3.7 shows how these two options might look.

It is all too easy to overuse stereotypes. Remember that stereotypes do not readily translate to a type hierarchy when the design is implemented. They probably need to be translated into attributes or associations. Also remember that, since stereotypes are in effect user-defined metasubtypes, your suite of stereotypes needs to be clearly enunciated so that there are no overlaps. It is all too easy to invent stereotypes, use them liberally, and then find that you have multiple overlapping classifications that detract from the crispness and clarity that your designs should possess.

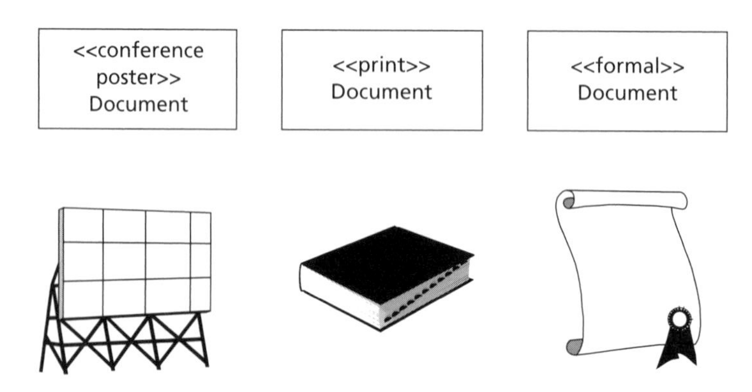

Figure 3.7 The use of guillemets for stereotypes compared with the creation and use of new icons for these stereotypes

3.3 Responsibilities

What else makes a class useful? Well, to be a real class in object-oriented thinking it needs to have responsibilities (OPEN Technique: Responsibility identification). A key business entity of a package can have only responsibilities, since packages are at too high a level of abstraction to have meaningful attributes and operations. Thus, OPEN encourages responsibilities for not only classes, but also packages.

Definition

A responsibility is any purpose, obligation or required capability of the instances of a class or package. A responsibility is typically implemented by a cohesive collection of one or more features. A responsibility can be a responsibility for doing, a responsibility for knowing or a responsibility for enforcing.

The class might have a responsibility for knowing something (like how many copies of an individual title are in the library) or a responsibility for doing something (like permitting a borrower to borrow a book or cataloguing a new book – Figure 3.8). It may even have a responsibility for enforcing some sort of business rule. In this example, we will concentrate on the first two types of responsibilities.

Since responsibilities function best in the hazier elevations of requirements gathering and analysis, it is difficult to lay down hard rules for their identification. Although often repeated, Rebecca Wirfs-Brock's analogy of a horse is a useful one to keep in mind. She recommended that one could view a horse from three perspectives, as follows:

Data viewpoint:	has body, tail, four legs
Functional viewpoint:	neighs, walks, eats
Responsibility viewpoint:	can transport people or goods between two locations or run races

Responsibilities are realized by operations and hence eventually translate into functions and methods. These in turn rely on data for the object's 'memory', i.e. in order to work correctly (Figure 3.9). Since data and functions tend to be 'general', whereas Responsibilities relate to a 'specific' problem domain, responsibility-driven

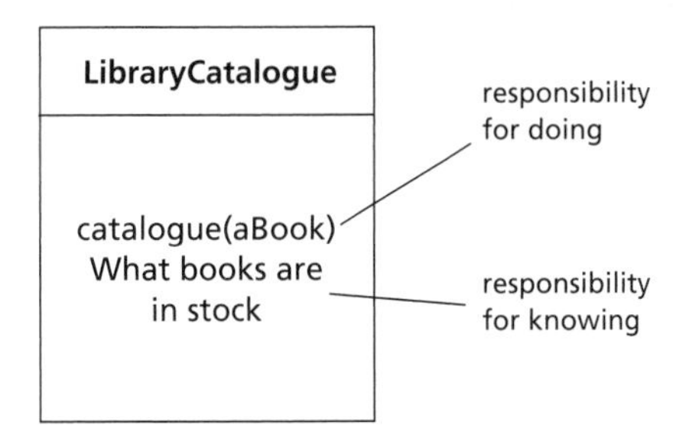

Figure 3.8 Possible responsibilities for the LibraryCatalogue class

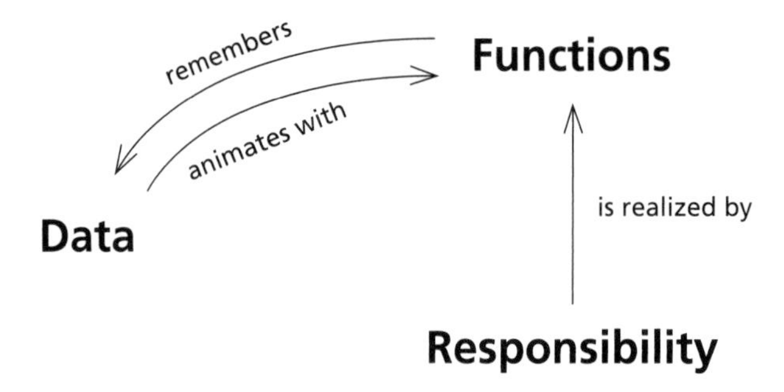

Figure 3.9 Relationship between data, functions and responsibilities

design is advisable where the system is developed in response to a specific business problem. However, a direct data-driven or function-driven approach could help in third-party or COTS developments.

Responsibilities are thus fairly abstract/high-level characteristics of classes or packages. They will later be translated into attributes and operations[4] of the class. In the case study in Chapter 4, we use a responsibility-driven approach to OPEN (the most common) and thus will spend some time looking at the responsibilities of classes. In other approaches, such as a data-driven approach, responsibilities are bypassed and the attributes and operations, rather than the higher-level responsibilities, would be identified at this stage. In a use-case driven approach (see Case study of Chapter 5), the functionality as seen by the user is the main contributor to the way the analysis and design evolve.

Responsibilities are a powerful tool particularly suited for analysis. They are at a high level of abstraction commensurate with that required in requirements analysis and early system modeling. They keep the developer's mind on modeling rather than implementation issues, the latter being facilitated by using terms like operation and method which are more closely associated with a coding domain than an analysis one. Responsibilities encapsulate the essence of a class or a package: its knowledge and its behaviour together with the rules within which it operates.

For example, one of the responsibilities for knowing of a Bank Account class might be its current balance. Seen from outside, this is a reasonable description of functionality offered to the customer. And if that is reminiscent of use cases, then it is purposely so, since a system level responsibility is very similar to a use case (although that link has not yet been explored theoretically in the literature). So a responsibility is user-focused. The flip side of that is its realization. The realization of a responsibility is by one or more operations. We can see that in order to know its balance, a Bank Account class will probably need to access information on

4 Using UML terminology. These are OPEN's services, as seen in the interface. Remember that in UML, the word attribute may mean either a query in the interface (publicly visible) or a hidden piece of 'data'.

withdrawals and deposits (part of the Bank Account class itself) and probably will need to access external objects to get information such as interest rates, possibly even duration of investment and so on. Then each of these operations will be coded using one or more methods *internally* to the class.

In UML's notation, the only direct way of describing responsibilities is by the use of textual comments – the metamodel of UML Version 1.3 supports responsibilities only by the use of a stereotyped comment (Figure 3.10). In OPEN, however, responsibilities are not just comments attached to classes but are semantically linked to features (Figure 3.11). These are not attributes of classes but, rather, provide extra information in a fairly informal way. Until the metamodel support shown in Figure 3.11 is accepted into the OMG UML standard, our use of responsibilities in OPEN has to be done by hand. Thus we create a responsibility (as in Figure 3.10) but create an additional dependency link to attributes and operations in the interface of the class. Also a semantically stronger link is probably needed between Class or Package and Responsibility – again a dependency link seems appropriate. A second, less

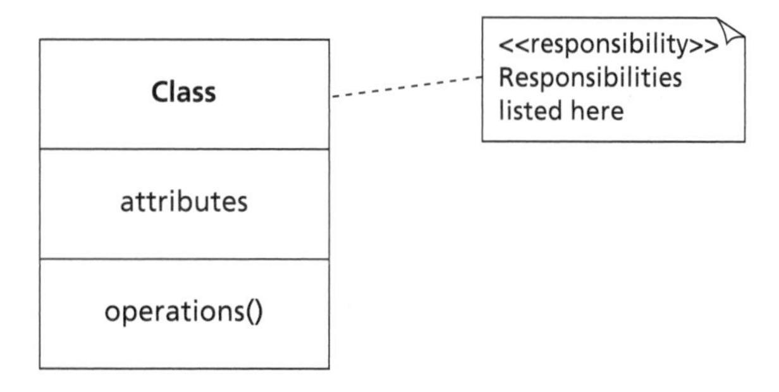

Figure 3.10 Responsibilities can be depicted using the stereotyped comment of UML.

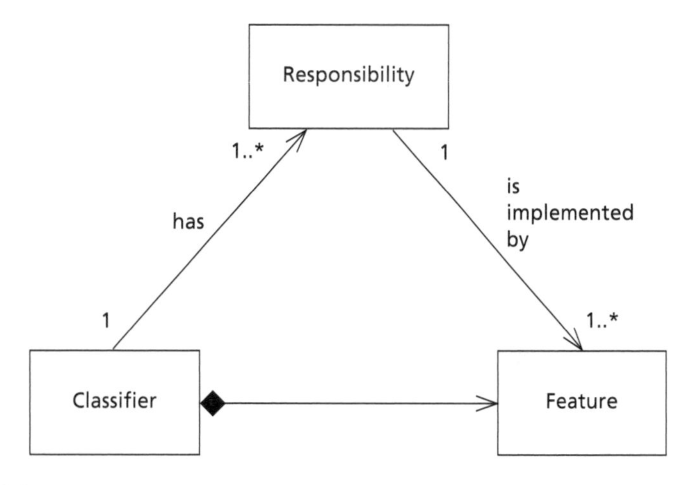

Figure 3.11 Proposed metamodel for Responsibility

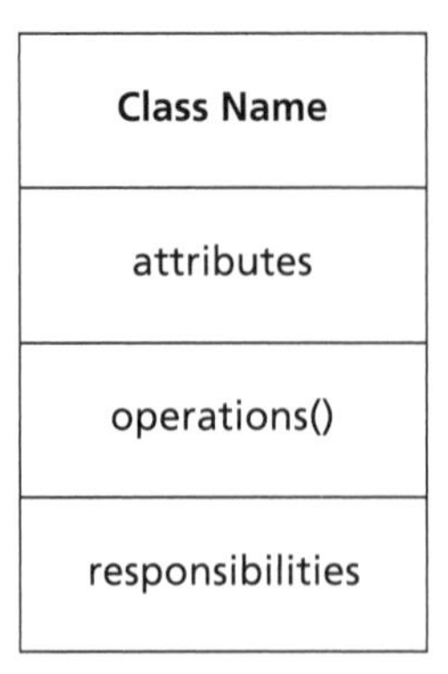

Figure 3.12 An alternative representation of responsibility can be achieved by adding a fourth compartment to the class icon

explicit way to document responsibilities, but one where the Responsibility–Feature link is invisible, is to use the option within the UML of adding a fourth box to the basic three-box icon of Figure 3.10, as shown in Figure 3.12. This, of course, cannot be done with packages.

3.4 Collaborations and patterns

While class/package identification, class naming, responsibilities and stereotypes all contribute towards the OPEN Task: Construct the Object Model, until we start to see message passing in action, we cannot complete this Task. In this section, we look at techniques relevant to collaborations and pattern identification.

Definition

A collaboration is a small-sized group of classes which interact with each other as described by the client–server model, in which the client object requests services of the server or supplier object in order to realize a specific, single purpose. A single client–server interaction is a subcontracting relationship between two classes in which the client object delegates some of its own responsibility to the server class. Collaborations often encompass several of these client–server interactions.

This means that collaborations are the next step beyond responsibilities. Whereas a responsibility is class-centric, responsibilities often imply the need to collaborate with another object in order to fulfil that responsibility. This is often known as delegation. In OPEN, we identify this special need for delegation as part of collaborations analysis by documenting it as a technique (OPEN Technique: Delegation analysis). Thus collaborations and delegations often occur as a natural consequence of the existence of a responsibility. Collaborations analysis (an OPEN Technique) evaluates how classes 'talk' to one another in order to fulfil a service request (i.e. the realization of a responsibility). They thus represent the coupling inherent in the design. A collaboration focuses on the set of interactions that need to be supported. A combination of classes and their interactions which occurs frequently is often encapsulated and documented as a pattern (see below).

Collaborations show only small sections of an analysis or design. They take a small part of a class diagram and zoom in on it in order to see how this small set of collaborating classes fulfils a specific service. This shows a particular message-passing sequence that realizes the particular service request, including the opportunity to show returned data/objects. Patterns are those collaborations that have occurred frequently enough to be deemed worth documenting officially.

Collaborations occur at different levels of granularity. This is recognized by the OPEN Technique: Granularity. A fine-granular system will necessarily utilize more classes in order to satisfy the same set of responsibilities. It will take more time to create but will result in more reusable components. Coarse-granular systems are faster and cheaper but hard to reuse outside the context for which they were originally envisaged. When the 'grains' are context-independent, they are called patterns, as we saw above. So the choice of granularity can be, in part at least, determined by the need for the organization to have reusable classes. For instance, if this is a one-off system in a one-off domain, then a coarse-granular system is probably best.[5]

Another OPEN Technique with utility here is that of visibility analysis, derived in part from the earlier fusion methodology. While the basic approach in building an OO system is to assume the default to be Visibility = FALSE (private visibility in UML), there are obviously some features of a class that require to be seen from outside and some classes in a package that need to be accessible from outside that package. A visibility analysis, either semantic or at an implementation level, will be useful in determining the minimal amount of public information that needs to be made available.

Since a collaboration occurs when one class acts as a server to a second class acting as a client, it represents coupling. However, there is no indication in a collaboration of how many different connections there are between this pair of objects, nor how many times messages are passed between them. Consequently, we also need to clarify the difference between such a collaboration and an interaction (although the definition that follows is part of OPEN and is not supported within the UML).

Definition

An interaction is a dynamic event in which a message is exchanged between two objects in a collaborative embrace. Thus for one collaboration we may have very many interactions.

Since an interaction is therefore the dynamic enactment of the (static) collaboration, there is an OPEN Technique (i.e. interaction modeling) specifically focused on

5 For futher discussion, see Chapter 5, Figure 5.17.

this more dynamic nature. This focuses more on the interaction paths and message sequencing, although both collaborations analysis and interaction modeling are really two sides of the same coin, one being focused on the more static aspects and the other from a more dynamic viewpoint.

In UML, the terms 'interaction' and 'collaboration' are used slightly differently from the definitions given above. However, since they are used primarily in the names of diagrams, this is not a problem. As we saw in Figure 2.44, the various sorts of diagrams describing these more dynamic aspects of an object model are collectively called interaction diagram. This is a generic name and is really an abstract (meta)class since we never draw an 'interaction diagram'. Instead, the collaborative/interactive nature of an object model, as described above, can be documented on either a 'collaboration diagram' or on a 'sequence diagram'. Both give much the same information but portrayed very differently, the one focusing on architecture, the second on temporal ordering. An example collaboration diagram, corresponding to the class diagram shown in Figure 3.4, is shown in Figure 3.13. Its counterpart, the sequence diagram, is in Figure 3.14. It can be seen that both represent a sequence of five message sends: startEngine, switchBatteryOn, lockDoor, pressAccelerator and, finally, turnSteeringWheel. These messages flow between the four main classes in the system of Figure 3.4 (Driver, Car, Engine and Door). Note that in a collaboration diagram, we show objects and not classes (as in Figure 3.4). Thus these two figures express a single instantiation from Figure 3.4 but one which additionally shows some of the dynamic nature of the collaboration. The difference between the collaboration diagram (Figure 3.13) and the sequence diagram (Figure 3.14) is the layout. In the former, the topology is exactly the same as that of the class diagram. The overall architecture thus remains clear and supportive of the easy collection of architectural metrics such as fan-in and fan-out. While the sequencing of the

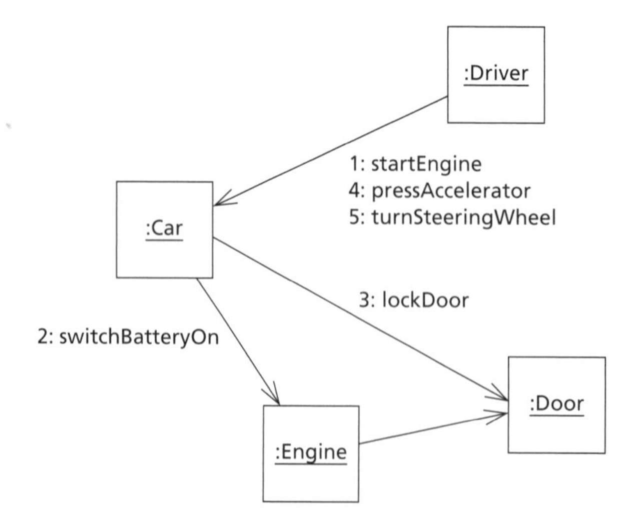

Figure 3.13 Adding dynamic message passing information to the class diagram of Figure 3.4 results in the collaboration diagram shown here

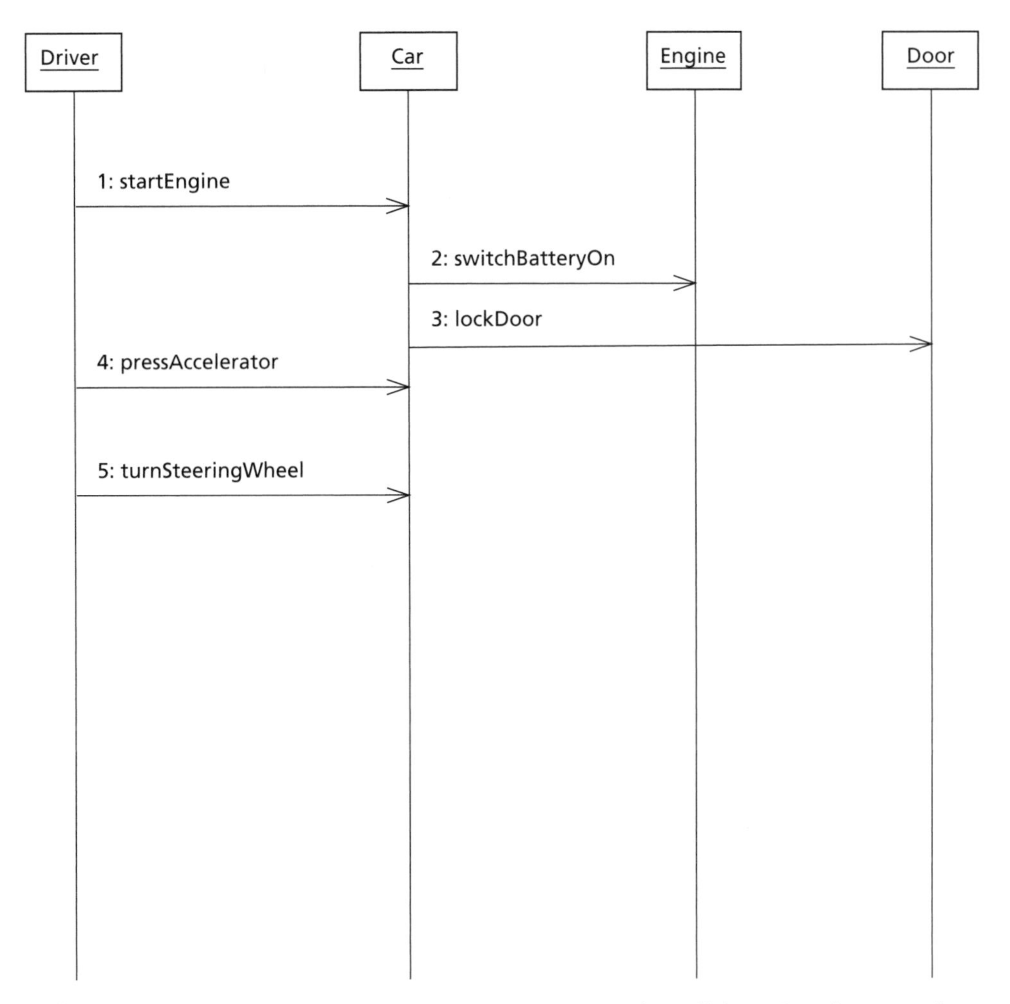

Figure 3.14 The sequence diagram counterpart to the collaboration diagram of Figure 3.13

messages is indicated by sequence numbers, these numbers have to be hunted for – they do not immediately spring to the eye. The reverse is true for the sequence diagram. In a sequence diagram, the sequencing of the messages is of paramount importance. The order of occurrence is linear down the page. The objects themselves (four here) are arranged linearly across the page and thus *all* indication of architecture of the system is lost. There are no indications of inheritance, association or aggregation relationships as there are in the collaboration diagram. However, in advanced use of sequence diagrams it is possible to show greater detail in the type of messages being sent than would be easily accomplished in the collaboration diagram. In other words, both diagrams show much the same information but their focus is very different.

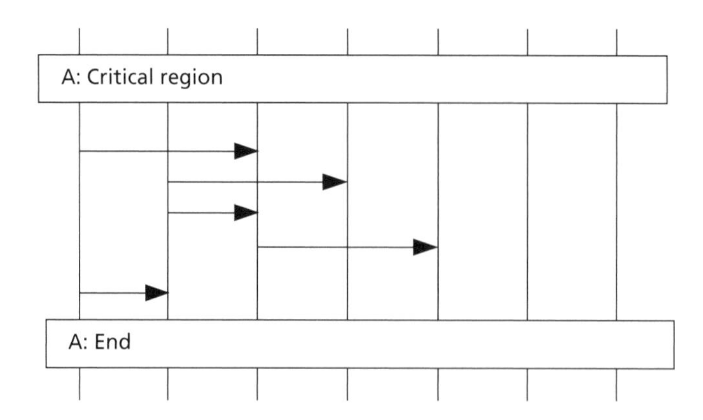

Figure 3.15 There are several possible enhancements to the sequence diagram. Here is shown one: to indicate the extent of critical regions.

OPEN's use of sequence diagrams offers some other extensions beyond standard UML. The use of logic boxes permits documentation of IF . . . THEN . . . ELSE structures and, as shown in Figure 3.15, the identification of critical regions which identify times when multiple threads are operating which must all finish (A: END) before the system continues.

Another important static aspect of a collaboration is that of a pattern, which shows *commonly occurring* collaborations.

Definition

A pattern is a (usually small) number of collaborating classes which, together, offer a solution to a commonly occurring problem in some specific context.

The OPEN Technique: Pattern recognition stresses the importance of spending time seeking parts of the design which might benefit from the application of a pattern. Since patterns are well documented in the literature, identification of opportunities for their use can save lots of time since the answer is already well known and written down. Patterns can be described, therefore, as 'designers' experience written down'.

Note that patterns can occur at varying granularities. They represent a move towards components rather than classes, since a pattern encompasses more than one class in their depiction of the specific collaboration found useful to solve the problem in question. An example of a pattern is given in Figure 3.16. This is the so-called observer pattern which 'defines a one-to-many dependency between objects so that when one object changes state, all its dependents [*sic*] are notified and updated automatically' (Gamma *et al.*, 1995).

Since there is a special symbol for a collaboration in UML (a dashed ellipse), this symbol is also appropriate for a pattern. Figure 3.17 shows the use of this collaboration/pattern symbol to revise the observer pattern of Figure 3.16.

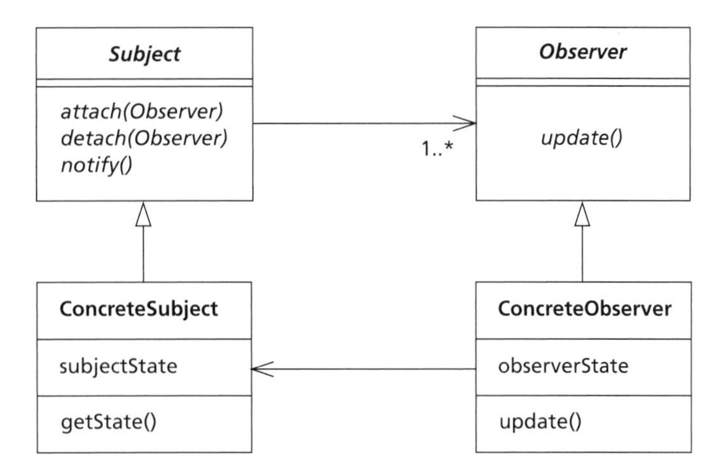

Figure 3.16 The observer pattern expressed using inheritance in UML

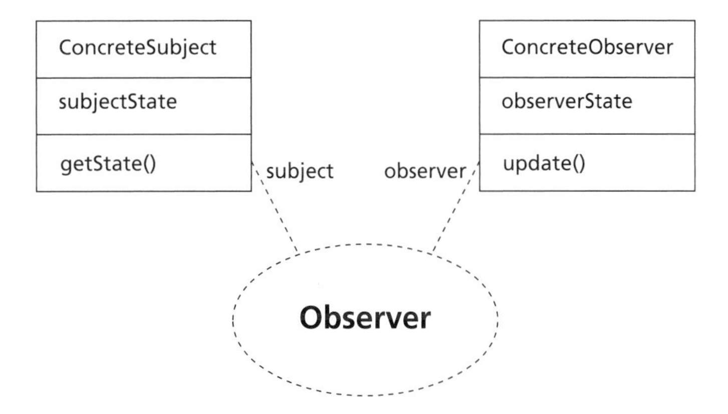

Figure 3.17 The observer pattern expressed using the pattern notation of UML

3.5 CRC card modeling

Responsibilities and collaborations and how they are allocated to and between classes can be discovered by the use of the OPEN Technique: CRC card modeling – a technique developed initially in Smalltalk development environments by Kent Beck and Ward Cunningham and popularized within the RDD methodology around 1990. It is also a Technique in OPEN. CRC itself stands for 'Class, Responsibilities and Collaborators'. CRC card modeling is a simple technique in which people act as though the objects are human (so-called anthropomorphizing). By putting themselves in the places of objects, they can ask questions such as 'What request is it sensible for me to react to?' and 'What are my responsibilities for knowing, doing and enforcing?'

In CRC card modeling, each participant is allocated the name of an object already identified (perhaps using brainstorming techniques) as likely to be in the system. (Thus this technique follows at least some class identification.) For this object, a simple index card is used to describe it. This CRC card (Figure 3.18) has three portions (class name, class responsibilities and, for each responsibility, a list of collaborating classes). In some versions of CRC cards, the reverse is also used to document inheritance hierarchies or to add free text descriptions.

A CRC modeling session is an interactive group session. Seated around a table, the members of the team each adopt the characteristics of one (or sometimes more) of the candidate objects likely to be in the portion of the system currently being analyzed. Some initial responsibilities may be identified. The dynamics are then set in motion. 'How does this system fulfil Responsibility A?' is asked. The group member representing the initial object of which this responsibility is requested has then to think whether that responsibility can be completely fulfilled internally by itself (the object being represented by the person) or whether some delegation to a collaborator is necessary. If the latter, then the collaborator needs to be identified. This may be one of the existing team members pretending to be another object in the system or, indeed, the question may reveal a concept to be modeled as an object which is not currently in the fledgling system but which, by this technique, has been identified as necessary. A new person comes into the group to anthropomorphize this new object.

Whether new or existing, the collaborating object then becomes the centre of attention. This object is, of course, being asked to exercise a responsibility in accepting the delegation from the first object. This very request may, of course, identify a responsibility not previously associated with this second object. So again, new information may be easily revealed in this way. Once the responsibility is identified, then we have effectively iterated back to the first situation: that of focusing on an object receiving a message from the anonymous external (software) world to activate a particular responsibility. That (second) object now has to ask itself whether or not it can fulfil the responsibility itself or whether it too has to delegate. And so it goes on until all the message paths have terminated.

In some of these CRC card modeling 'games', the participants symbolize the message passing implicit in the delegation by throwing a tennis ball between participants. This also helps focus the group's attention on which object is currently

Class Name	
Responsibility1	Collaborator(s) for Responsibility1
Responsibility2	Collaborator(s) for Responsibility2
etc.	etc.

Figure 3.18 Example CRC card layout

under analysis. Only the person holding the tennis ball or a person being addressed directly by this person is allowed to speak. For instance, the person modeling the bank account object may verbalize about whether they can supply knowledge about interest rates. Realizing they cannot, they may then ask the members in the group, 'Interest table object, are you able to give me interest rate information?' Obviously the person addressed has to answer. If in the positive, then the tennis ball is passed to that person and the game continues.

You, the person, need to *really believe* that you are the object in question. This is roleplay, which, incidentally, is identified as a separate OPEN Technique because it has a wide usage beyond CRC. As in acting on the stage, the best realization is the one where the person really gets into the character of the actor (on stage) or object (in CRC). Ask yourself when a request is made of you, 'Is this *really* something that I should know/be able to do/be able to enforce, i.e. is this assumed responsibility something that is the essence of my object specification or is it better allocated to someone else/some other object in the CRC group?'. Do not be afraid to decline a responsibility. A result in which responsibilities are shared around is more likely to be a better system than one in which responsibilities are concentrated into a single, god-like controller object. For this reason, the use of controller objects as stereotypes as suggested by OOSE/UP[6] is discouraged strongly. Not that they are not useful, but rather that they should be identified with care.

3.6 Services

In OPEN, the identified responsibilities are realized by services – things offered to the rest of the world; a name evocative of the OO message-passing paradigm. We can describe this object as the 'server' object and any object accessing these services as the 'client' object. In UML, the word service is not used; instead we talk of features (a synonym for services). Features can be descriptive either of behaviour (operations) or of data-like properties (attributes) – see Figure 3.19. Responsibilities have a one-to-many relationship with features and the features themselves are shown in the second and third boxes of the UML class icons (Figure 3.12).

Definition

A service (called a feature in UML) is a statement that a specific characteristic of the class may be accessed externally, i.e. by a client object. It is realized by one or more internal methods or attributes and is thus the way that the code within the class is actually used by other objects. One class thus offers several services (in its interface) to the rest of the system. When an object passes a message to another object, it invokes one of these services which in turn is implemented by a method or attribute.

Service/feature identification, an OPEN Technique, may follow relatively easily if the responsibilities have been well identified; or features may be identified

6 Object-Oriented Software Engineering (OOSE) and the Unified Process (UP) are two OO methods proposed by Ivar Jacobson and colleagues: Jacobson *et al.* (1992, 1999) respectively.

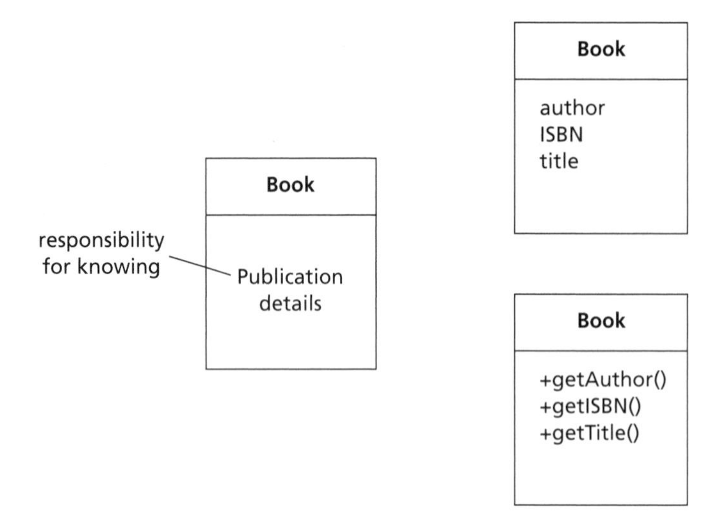

Figure 3.19 Three possible representations of the class Book

directly. In both cases, you need to remember that the invocation of an operation (by another object) effects an action, whereas the invocation of an attribute (actually a logical attribute in the interface at this stage) results in the return of an object to the client. It is the interface-implementation counterpart of a responsibility for knowing. The actual implementation of this feature may be as a data structure (attribute) or as a piece of code (a method).

Each of the public features represents a service offered by that class. As we noted above, groups of services support each, higher-level, responsibility. They also, interestingly, act as conduits between (i) the external (or specification or public) view of a class or type or interface and (ii) the internal view as expressed by private attributes and methods, i.e. the code. Thus a class is an amalgam of its interface/type[7] and its implementation (Figure 3.20).

Thus, attributes and operations are smoothly linked to attributes and methods in coding. There is an obvious advantage in that smooth linking but a disadvantage in that you might freeze in the wrong coding decisions too early. For example, if a feature of a class were to give the information on how many books a borrower currently has on loan, and this were placed on the class as an operation, then an implementation by a method would be committed. On the other hand, this sort of information perhaps would be better stored as an attribute rather than as an operation. It is safer, so the advocates of responsibility-driven design urge, to model this as a responsibility for knowing – which makes *no* statement as to what sort of feature this will be finally. Indeed, often a responsibility will eventuate as several features, i.e. several attributes and/or operations.

7 UML differentiates type and interface (although this may well change in future versions) but in a way that does not gel totally with advanced OPEN modeling. For now it is best to assume the words are used interchangeably to mean the external specification of a class.

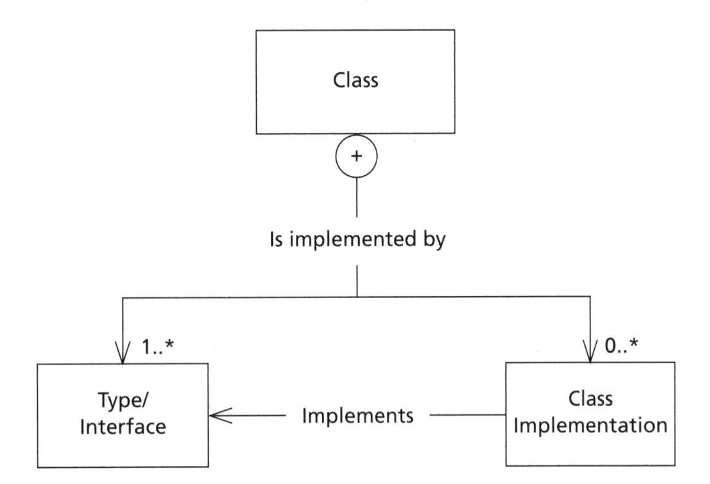

Figure 3.20 Proposed metamodel for class/type/implementation

Services are modeled (OPEN Technique: Service identification) by using the second and third boxes of the UML class icon. Services include both UML attributes and operations, the former to represent the logical 'knowledge' characteristics and the latter for the behaviour or functionality. While both types of service will be implemented by operations, since the attribute section of the UML icon really represents logical CRUD services which only indirectly access hidden attributes within the class, this differentiation into the static and dynamic sides of an object can be very useful in modeling.

Services may thus be modeled as a consequence of the identification of responsibilities or may sometimes be modeled directly from the requirements. They are documented as either attributes with the format attributeName:ReturnType or as operations, the simplest format being operationName (OptionalArguments).

There are many other annotations in UML. The most common are the indicators of visibility. In analysis, one is generally considering only externally visible features. Only in implementation, or at least detailed design, are you likely to want to show internal (hidden) features.

The interface of a class thus holds public features, i.e. public attributes and public operations – these are indicated in UML using the public visibility marker '+'. However, we should stress that it is accepted good OO practice *never* to use public attributes. On the other hand, at an early stage in analysis one could show *logical* attributes – as shorthand for accessor operations (*cf.* Figure 3.19). Later, one might want to show hidden (private) features using the '–' annotation.

The concept (of an object) is holistic. It encapsulates the essence of that concept plus the externally visible responsibilities eventually (as here) represented by a set of services. It is important that the set of services offered by each of object is as complete as possible. Hence we introduce here the OPEN Technique: Completion of abstractions. Using this technique we attempt to create a reusable object, reusable in the sense that the services offered do not relate just to your current system development but have considered the wider domain issues. Perhaps you have a Calculator class and for the present application you need to use only its functionality of addition and multiplication. But for wider application, say in your next application, you would like a more complete abstraction: one which also allows obvious functionality such as subtraction, division, logarithms, powers and so on.

Whilst it is good practice to try to get as complete an abstraction as possible, it should also be noted that this can often be very difficult in the sense that different individuals' perception of completeness can be very different. In our calculator example, if you have never used hyperbolic functions in trigonometry, you will not even be aware that some calculators offer these as functionalities. If you work in a business environment, then frequent use of percentage is called for and specific functionality may be added for this; but if you are a mathematician you probably never use this because you do the calculation from first principles. In other words, even the completeness of the abstraction can often be context (including user) dependent.

In working with services, there is another OPEN technique, taken from work by Bill Premerlani, one of the authors of OMT, which considers possible alternatives of service configurations – OPEN Technique: Transformations of the object model (although the technique has a much wider applicability than just for service identification and definition). In this it is recognized that there is not necessarily just one answer. There are often several, equally acceptable options. Services may be best offered at a supertype level or may be merged between objects at two adjacent levels in an inheritance hierarchy. Perhaps an attribute is better shown explicitly as a service call to another object rather than implicitly on the object in question.

3.7 Associations

Associations in OPEN are mappings. They are one element of the OPEN Technique: Relationship modelling. Associations represent static connections along which, later, messages will be passed when those connections are used for the purposes of acquiring service responses from the server objects to requesting client objects.

In UML, we noted in Section 2.5 that there are three options in whether or not you show arrowheads. That choice is particularly relevant to associations. Many UML users choose Option 3. With this option, a unidirectional association, as highly recommended in OPEN, would be represented in UML Version 1.3 by a line with an arrowhead to indicate the direction of navigability (Figure 2.26). In the rare cases when bidirectional navigability is required, the UML notation is a line with no arrowhead. Thus, when using UML with Option 3, as soon as you identify a relationship (here association), you also have to decide its directionality. Since OPEN stresses unidirectionality and rarely uses bidirectional relationships, the alternative option (Option 1 – see Chapter 2) is recommended. In this style, *all* arrowheads are shown. The common unidirectional association thus is indicated with a single arrowhead. No arrowhead means that directionality is undecided (also known as TBD). Bidirectional associations, shown with two arrowheads, are really an abbreviation for a pair of unidirectional mappings with added referential integrity. With 'standard' UML (i.e. Option 3), 'not to decide is to decide' – in the UML case as bidirectional. With Option 1 (as used in OML, for instance), you are allowed to prevaricate and defer decisions until later (when you hope you will have more information!).

Associations are the 'bread and butter' of the static architecture. They describe how 'objects' are connected together. They represent the underpinning structure for responsibility enactment, message passing and, ultimately, pointers and references in the code. Since we are moving towards pluggable components, based on object technology to a large degree, the notion of services offered, followed by implementation in autonomous components offering extremely well-specified services in their interfaces, is much more in line with the consistent use of *unidirectional* associations.

Associations represent visibility and also, as we saw a little earlier, a connection created when delegation is used. In UML, a distinction is made between an association relationship and a dependency relationship, perhaps uses (one of the stereotypes of dependency). In OPEN, we urge you to consider that all association-type relationships (that is, association itself, aggregation and uses) are depicting some kind of dependency between CIRTs since, as noted by Rumbaugh (1998), there is no clear distinction between the UML dependency and association. Or, perhaps more accurately, most connections are in fact both.

Associations are sometimes described as the relationships between objects that are 'left over' after all the whole–part and inheritance relationships are identified. A better heuristic would be to consider association, dependency and whole–part as a group of referential relationships all of which define differing detail and focus in the static structure. All the types of inheritance can be considered different in that they are definitional, rather than referential, relationships. In OPEN, we actually suggest you do not include definitional relationships such as inheritance on the normal class diagrams but construct a separate but highly linked and coherent inheritance diagram (not part of the UML standard) which complements the referentially focused class diagrams.

So if the class diagram is referentially focused, then we might anticipate that most, sometimes all, the referential relationships shown there might be associations. This is not a bad heuristic. Indeed, if all referential relationships were thus shown (as associations) there would be nothing lost. One would probably, however, feel the need to annotate the associations to add a little more focus/detail. This is perfectly acceptable within the use of the UML, e.g. to add a label saying 'whole–part: whole end' or something similar to a basic association arrow rather than fuss with the composition/shared aggregation confusion in the current UML notation. On the other hand, if you are going to use dependencies, uses, aggregations and other referential relationships to a large extent, introducing a 'standard' (perhaps your own standard) stereotype of icon for subtypes of association that you use frequently is a good idea and encompassed within the OMG standard for the UML.

3.8 Whole–part relationship

As noted in Chapter 2, in UML Version 1.3 the definitions of aggregation and composition are imprecise. While it is acknowledged that defining these concepts is terribly difficult, we probably need some way of describing whole–part (WP) relationships since they so commonly occur.

What WP relationships are trying to describe are configurations in which we can identify one object as playing the role of a whole and two or more playing the role of the part(s). Intuitively, the example shown in Figure 3.21, in which a yacht is made up of several component parts, shows what we are trying to depict.

Our best advice is not to spend inordinate amounts of time arguing over WP relationships – within OPEN's Technique: Relationship modeling. If there is an obvious and useful use for it, use it, otherwise use association. Indeed, until the black and white diamonds of UML are fully defined (see below), this may be the best way (Figure 3.25 below) – use an association with a label to indicate that it actually represents a whole–part relationship.

If you *do* use whole–part relationships, then there are two considerations: (i) the basic axioms that pertain to *all* whole–parts, and (ii) different 'flavours' of the WP relationship. All WP relationships need to have a set of properties. The set currently proposed is given in Table 3.3.

You may just wish to use a single symbol for all your WP relationships and stick at that. You can probably use the UML white diamond for this *but* you do need to state the meaning of it in a glossary attached to your diagrams. This is the idea behind 'prefaces' which are currently being discussed inside the OMG community.

If you wish to discriminate further you currently have a choice. You may wish to add a second flavour of WP and use the UML black diamond. But beware – there are a significant number of interpretations of this. Some believe it to focus on coincident lifetimes (Case 4 of Figure 3.22) and to mean that the whole creates the part at the

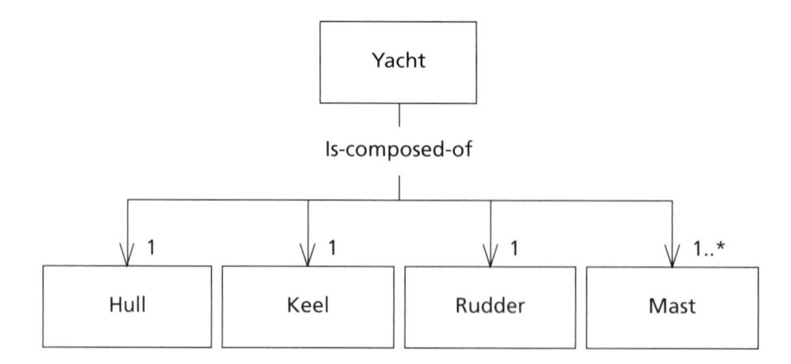

Figure 3.21 Example of relationship which is intuitively whole–part (here 'is-composed-of') – note, not a UML model

Table 3.3 Simplified definitions relevant to the primary characteristics of whole–part (WP) relationships

1. *Whole–part:* qualitatively, a whole consists of (several) parts. While the existence of the whole is contingent on at least some of its parts, the whole *does* have an independent (ontological) existence which transcends its parts – in other words, the whole can be regarded as an abstraction by which means its constituent parts are either not relevant or not visible
2. *Emergent property:* a property of the whole not evident in the parts
3. *Resultant property:* a property of the whole which can be deduced from the part(s)
4. *Irreflexivity:* a given object cannot be both whole and part at the same time
5. *Antisymmetry:* if *a* has a WP relationship to *b* and *b* has a WP relationship to *a*, then objects *a* and *b* must be the same object
   Symmetry: if an object is part of a whole, that whole cannot be a part of its own part

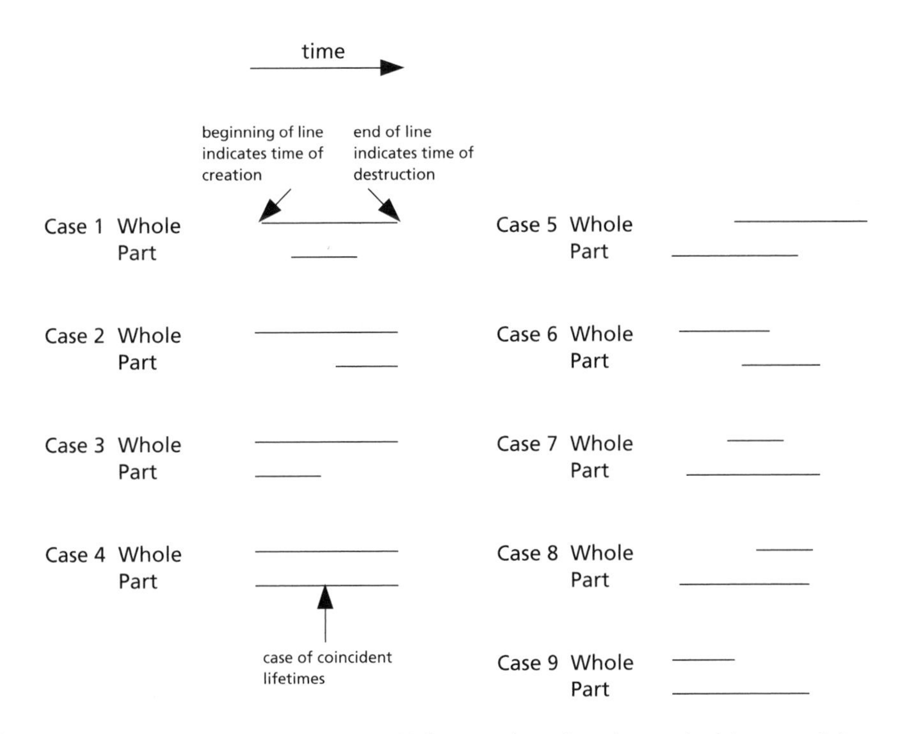

Figure 3.22 There are nine cases of lifetimes (overlapping, coincident, etc.) for wholes versus parts

time of its own creation and all parts and whole are deleted at the same time. Others think that it means the opposite of the 'shared' idea of the white diamond, i.e. that it represents not shared.

Or it may mean non-separable. If all the parts are separable it is doubtful whether we really have a true WP relationship, since one part of the definition, as seen in Table 3.3, is that the aggregate should have an emergent property. If there are no parts, then it is not possible to have an emergent (nor indeed a resultant) property. Thus, if we focus on separability, we need to recognize that in any intuitively obvious WP relationship (e.g. a car is made up of parts like an engine, a chassis, wheels, doors, etc.), there must be at least one inseparable part even if there are many separable parts. If we use black and white diamonds for separability versus non-separability, then the car example is described with a mixture of both notations (Figure 3.23). In other words, just because we think of a thing we are modeling as a whole with parts does not mean that there is only one relationship. In fact, each of the relationships is a separate association between the part class and the whole class – as seen in Figure 3.23.

Another reasonable interpretation of the UML black diamond is that it represents the idea of existential dependency found in ER modeling. If that is the case, then there is a significant overlap between the shared white diamond and the existential dependency black diamond (shown in Figure 3.24 along the three dimensions of shareability, separability and lifetime linkages).

Another good alternative is to avoid the arguments over the meaning of the current UML black diamond and instead use the OML variant of UML that is clear in its definition of 'flavours of aggregation'. In this extension to UML, there are two types of WP: aggregation, which is defined as a configurational WP relationship, and membership, which is defined as a non-configurational WP relationship. The word configurational indicates that there must be some connection, either structural or

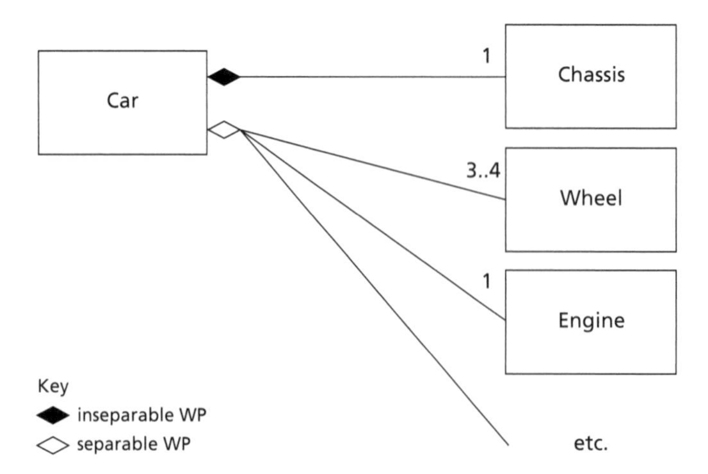

Figure 3.23 An example whole–part relationship in which some of the WPs are invariant and others are separable.

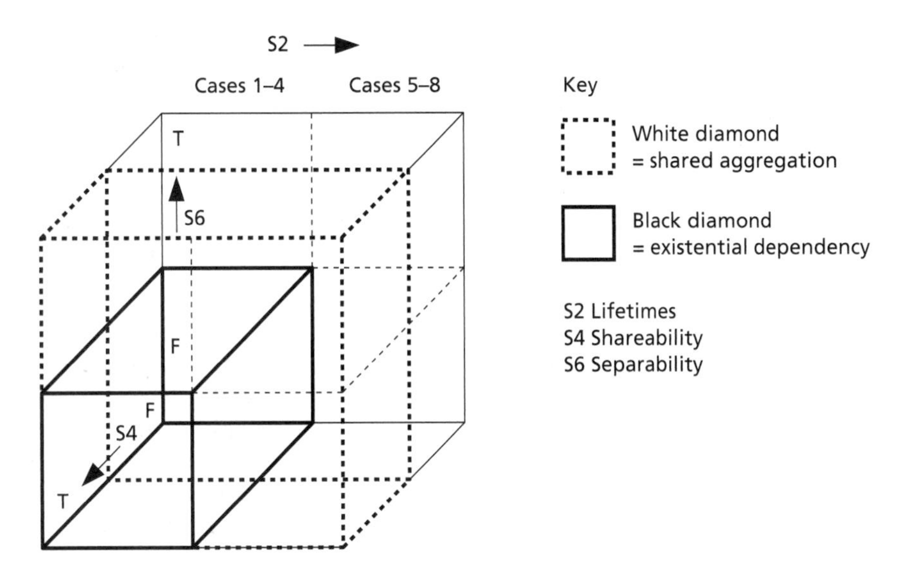

Figure 3.24 An interpretation of the current black diamond (composition) in UML is that of existential dependency whereas the current white diamond represents sharing or shareability. Drawn in three dimensions (of lifetimes, shareability and separability), it can be seen that there is a volume in which black and white diamond representations are coincident and another volume which belongs to neither definition.

functional, between at least two of the parts of a WP relationship. Thus the example we used before (shown in Figure 3.25 using UML notation) is clearly a configurational relationship, since it is critically important that the keel and rudder are attached in a particular place to the hull (i.e. underneath it!). Indicating configurational WP with a plus in a circle (Phillips screwhead to represent that the whole is (more than) the sum of the parts and the parts are attached to the whole) and membership with an epsilon, the standard mathematical set notation for 'is-a-member-of' (Figure 3.26), allows an unambiguous description of whole–part. It is

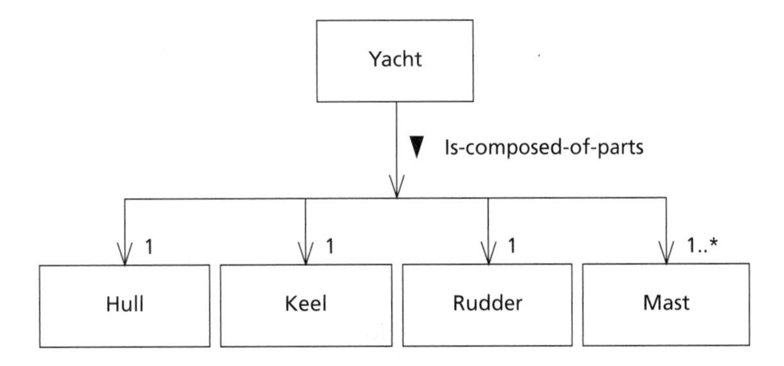

Figure 3.25 A yacht is composed of all its parts.

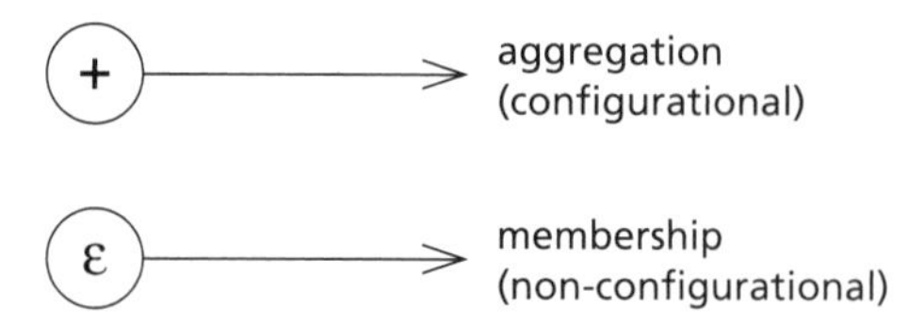

Figure 3.26 If WP relationships are partitioned based on configurationality, then the resulting two kinds of WP are aggregation and membership. This is supported directly in the UML variant known as OML.

also interesting to note that this discrimination of aggregation versus membership is found in the cognitive science and ontology literatures.

Finally, once you have decided on a simple partition between two flavours of aggregation (white and black diamond once their semantics are clear, or the configurational/non-configurational discriminator of Figure 3.26), then you can add other stereotypes to represent other characteristics of interest. For instance, you might want to show different lifetime constraints or separability/inseparability or, if you are more interested in implementation concerns, by-value/by-reference (Figure 3.27).

As a postscript, but not entirely accurately placed in this section, we should introduce the containment relationship, since it is often confused with the whole–part relationship. Although the word is sometimes used in coding texts to talk about the implementation of a true composition relationship, here we are thinking about the notion of a container in everyday life, a container like a glass or a suitcase or a car trunk (Figure 3.28). In all these examples, the basic concept is of an object into which we can put other objects for temporary storage. We put water into a glass – but then we drink it! The glass once again becomes empty. Now the first empty glass and the full glass (and the second empty glass) are all the same. At no stage did the water in the glass change the nature of the glass itself. We did not create a larger-scale composite of 'glass+water'; we are able at any time to remove the contents (the water). Certainly there was a temporary propagation of methods so

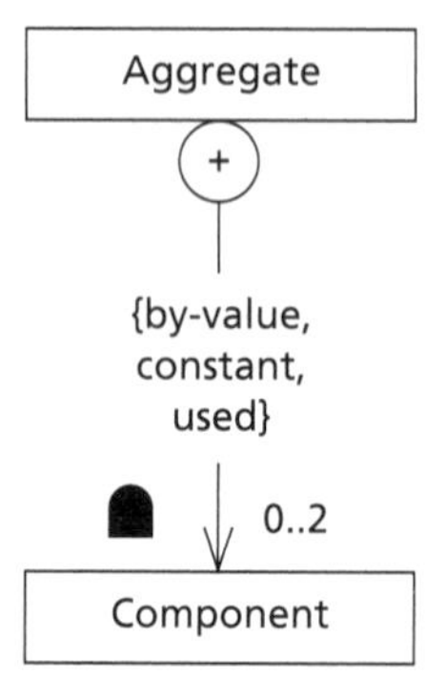

Figure 3.27 Using OML, various partitions can be drawn using a mixture of stereotypes and icons (the tombstone representing the fact that the whole and the parts 'die' together).

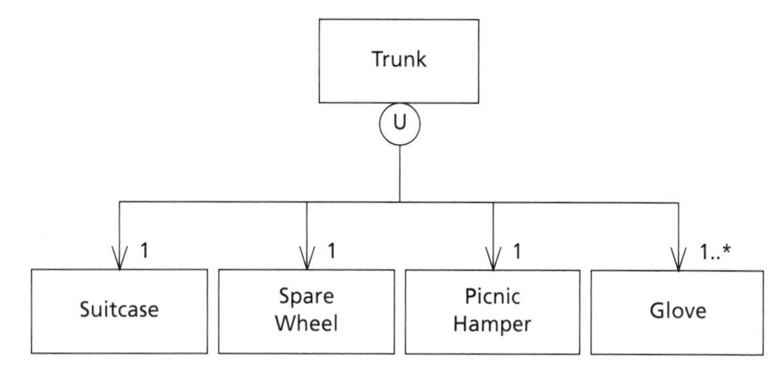

Figure 3.28 The containing relationship, as supported directly in OML.

that if we transported the glass (or the car trunk) then the contents were transported too. Similarly, adding contents into the trunk, or water into the glass, does not change the nature of those contents. In other words, *there is no semantic connection between the container and its contents.* This is very different from the basic arguments for *all* whole–part relationships. Containment, as used here in modeling, is *not* the same and should not be confused. Furthermore, these relationships translate very smoothly into code with library classes such as Stack, List, Array and so on.

3.9 Assertions and contracts

Definition

An assertion is any business rule that is a constraint on the property values of an object. Assertions may be one of three kinds: a pre-condition is any assertion that must hold before the execution of an associated operation(s); a postcondition is any assertion that must hold after the execution of the associated operation(s); and a (class) invariant is any assertion that must hold both before and after the execution of all operations.

Pre-conditions have a counterpart, the postcondition which expresses a surety that the server object will effect its service with 100% certainty. The reason it can do this is that it is well designed and, most importantly, that it is only well designed for a finite number of happenings. A bank account object might have a perfect algorithm implementing its deposit service. But it must have a pre-condition that the amount of money to be deposited is positive. So the pre-condition on the bank account's deposit service is that the incoming argument *from any other object* is strictly positive. This makes the server object autonomous – an aim of object design. It will react correctly to incoming messages from existing and future objects alike – new extensions will have no impact. It can do that *because it has restricted its inputs to a finite list of choices.* It does not have to check for incoming idiocies – using a structured language like FORTRAN, you would end up with umpteen checks at the beginning of each subroutine to catch these sorts of invalid inputs.

Pre- and postconditions are often expressed using some formal language, perhaps based on Z or VDM. In fact, UML contains one such language known as the Object Constraint Language or OCL. While originally devised to provide the capability of refining the semantics of the UML metamodel by adding well-formedness constraints, the OCL is more generally applicable. Not only can it be used to specify contractual information but it can also be used to add formal constraints to class (and other) diagrams. These constraints, for example, can be added to a class to model the invariant (Figure 3.29) or to a message in a sequence or collaboration diagram specifying just when the message can and cannot be sent. Transitions in statechart diagrams can also benefit from the addition of constraints using OCL under appropriate circumstances.

Definition

A contract spells out the obligations and benefits afforded to both the client and supplier in an interaction.

Together the pre-condition(s) and the postcondition(s) form the contract offered by the server object. Any object wishing to enter into a collaboration needs to respect and uphold their end of this stated contract. This software analogy of real-world business contracts is often referred to as 'design by contract'. Design by contract was developed in the late 1980s by Bertrand Meyer and has more recently been applied as 'analysis by contract'. If you are using Eiffel as the implementation language, then these contracts can also be seamlessly coded. Even without an Eiffel implementation, OPEN users are urged to apply the idea of contracts at all stages. Contracts spell out the (business) rules that realize the responsibilities of the CIRTs.[8] Contract specification is an important OPEN Technique.

To get to grips with contracts, consider the 2 × 2 matrix of Figure 3.30. The contract spells out the obligation of the server CIRT (to do with ensuring the response to the message request can be relied upon) and the obligation of the client CIRT (the requirements that must be met by any object wishing to use these services). There are then corresponding benefits both given and received. Until contracting is widely practised, it seems unlikely that the full power of trusted components can be achieved. Components, after all, require the user to have absolute belief that the

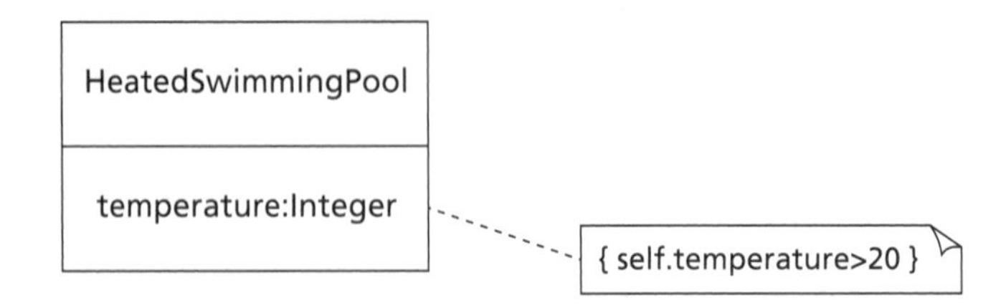

Figure 3.29 Example of the use of OCL to specify a class invariant.

8 A contract is *not* a synonym for a responsibility, as erroneously stated in the OMG UML documents. You can think of the responsibility as the statement of the rule and the contract as its realization (viz. the addition of all the fine detail) to make it work.

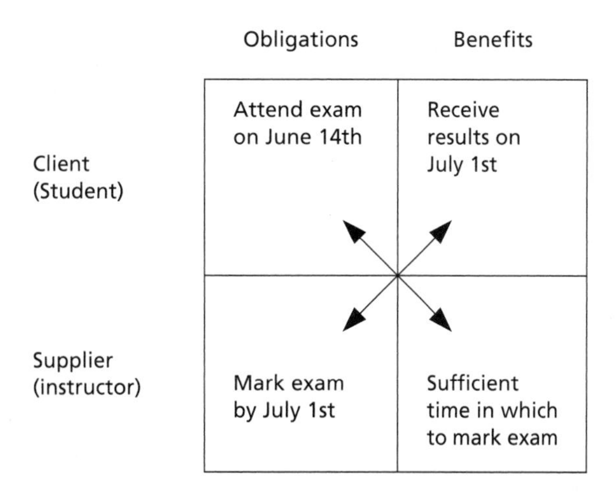

Figure 3.30 Contracting represents an interaction between a client and a supplier. The obligation placed on the client roughly corresponds to the benefit of the supplier (and vice versa). If the client breaks the obligation, there is no need for the supplier to take any action at all.

component will do *exactly* what is required and will be robust enough to handle to service requests that are inappropriate or invalid.

The matrix in Figure 3.30 is not intended to be a documentation tool – although we have seen it used in this way for small systems when it is viable. Rather, it focuses the developer's attention on the need to consider, elicit and state clearly the rules of interoperability of this particular CIRT/component. We urge *all* users of OPEN to adopt this mindset which is a significant contribution to high quality in the systems we develop.

3.10 'Inheritance'

In OPEN there is a Technique: Generalization and inheritance identification. Generalization refers to a modeling technique representing an abstraction technique in which 'parents' are identified in a knowledge tree where the 'children' are a-kind-of 'parent'. In contrast, inheritance is a computer science technique that comes in three flavours: specialization, specification and implementation inheritance. Specialization is the inheritance equivalence of generalization, so the two are generally coupled closely together, as in the phrase 'generalization/specialization'. Specification (or blackbox or interface) inheritance is really another name for subtyping. Whilst not identical to generalization/specialization, the two are often purposefully confounded. So, for the present, we will assume that the UML representation for generalization/specialization (the white-headed arrow: Figure 3.31) also means subtyping and support for polymorphism. So we can essentially replace the word specification by 'is-a-kind-of'. Indeed, this is a key phrase. Ask yourself

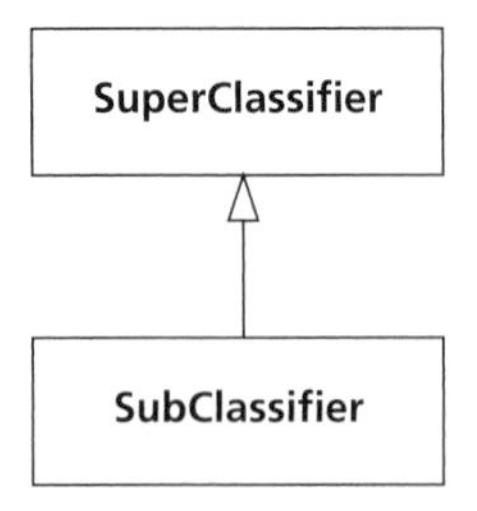

Figure 3.31 The UML generalization relationship supports subtyping and polymorphism.

when trying to decide if inheritance is useful: 'Is the subclass a-kind-of the parent or superclass?'. If it is, then we have the specialization/generalization type of inheritance and you can use the white-headed arrow in UML (Figure 2.29 in Chapter 2).

There is a third type of inheritance. While subtypes are dynamically substitutable for supertypes and therefore support polymorphism – which really is exciting in object-oriented programming – there is also subclassing which is also known as implementation inheritance. This is when an inheritance relationship is used in a language[9] to reuse code but the semantics are not necessarily considered. In other words, it is no longer possible to say that the 'lower level' object is-a-kind-of the 'higher level' one. So we cannot use polymorphism and we cannot use subtyping as the name for it. But we *can* use the word subclassing or whitebox inheritance (whitebox because we can see all the internals, since we are inheriting for code reuse, not for concept reuse – which could thus be called, in complement, blackbox inheritance).

In UML Version 1.1, generalization had two stereotypes: «subtype» and «subclass». In Version 1.3 this was changed to a single stereotype of «implementation» (Figure 3.32). Use of implementation inheritance, an agreed bad practice, does not make public the interface of the superclass in the subclass thereby violating substitutability.

In general, the UML metamodel uses the white-headed generalization arrow in a very loose way. In some contexts,[10] it is even used to represent implementation inheritance – without the stereotype label.[11] If it were to be used only to represent generalization, and to do so in a rigorous fashion, then, even allowing for the confounding of generalization and specification inheritance as above, the white arrowhead notation would be valid only between types and types or between

9 Programming languages typically have only one inheritance construct which serves to implement *all* of the OOAD inheritance types.

10 There are many examples of this usage in the UML metamodel itself.

11 Actually, it is worse than that, because the implementation inheritance stereotype («implementation») does not in fact define a (true) subset of the instances belonging to the set of generalization relationships since, as we have explained above, generalization and implementation inheritance relationships since, as we have explained above, generalization and implementation inheritance relationships are essentially two *non-overlapping* sets. Thus one *cannot* be a stereotype of the other.

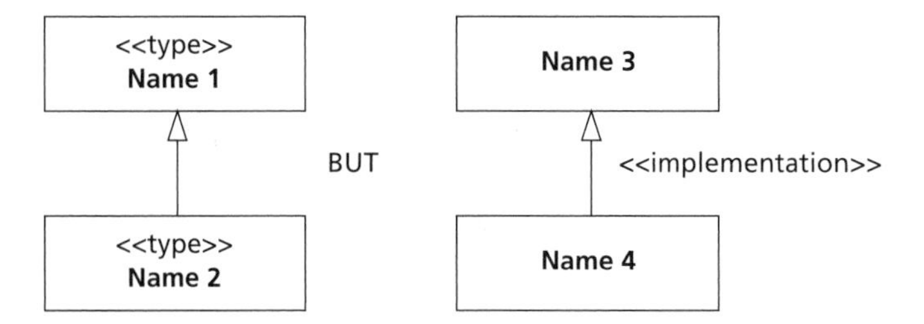

Figure 3.32 There are two stereotypes of class: type and implementation. They are shown using guillemets.

interfaces and interfaces, and *not* between classes and classes. This is because classes contain methods and other implementation details, so that a class–class inheritance is by definition an implementation inheritance relationship (Figure 3.32).

Once we start to look at classes and subclasses (or types and subtypes), the need to differentiate between concrete and abstract classes becomes evident. We thus need to use the OPEN Technique: Abstract class identification.

Definition

An abstract class is defined as one with no instances.

For example, a Vehicle class may have an operation called move(). But in the code of the Vehicle class there is no code realizing this move() operation. Rather, Vehicle has several subclasses (Figure 3.33) and it is in these classes that the code for the move() operation appears. Thus in the class Vehicle there is no information on how Vehicles move. In other words, the class Vehicle cannot be instantiated. It can have no objects belonging directly to it (it can have them belonging indirectly to it). It is an abstract class – OPEN Technique: Abstract class identification offers full support here.

The hierarchy of Figure 3.33 thus states that all Vehicles can move but that the actual way they do this depends upon to which of the several subclasses of Vehicle

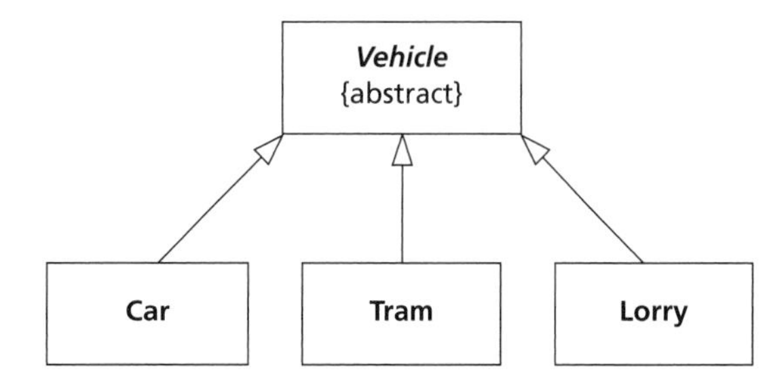

Figure 3.33 In this generalization hierarchy, instances only exist of the subtypes Car, Tram and Lorry. The supertype Vehicle is designated as an abstract class, which means it cannot be instantiated.

they belong. Such classes, which can be instantiated, are sometimes referred to as concrete classes. In UML, it is recommended that the class name of a concrete class is bold, centred and with an initial capital letter. An abstract class, in addition, has its name italicized and/or the constraint label {abstract} added below the class name.

Concrete classes usually occur at the ends of an inheritance hierarchy (i.e. the 'leaf' nodes). Abstract classes, on the other hand, frequently occur at the branch nodes of inheritance structures and never at the leaf nodes (Figure 3.34). They represent encapsulated knowledge relevant to two or more branches of the inheritance structure.

An interesting question is whether we can have a concrete class as a branch node (e.g. Class 3 in Figure 3.34). There are two schools of thought: (i) a concrete node indicates that the subtypes drawn do not form a complete partition – for example in Figure 3.33 there are vehicles we know about but choose not to identify separately; (ii) if the subtypes do *not* form a complete partition, then this should be indicated by the available constraints for a set of generalizations and shown by a keyword on the discriminator on the generalization relationship (Figure 2.29 in Chapter 2). The available standard constraints are 'complete', 'disjoint', 'incomplete' and 'overlapping'.

A useful heuristic therefore (not absolute – do not follow it slavishly) is that all nodes in the inheritance tree should be abstract classes and only leaf classes should be concrete. A consequence of this is that no concrete classes should have subclasses.

The inheritance mechanism offered by most OO programming languages encompasses all the types of inheritance. Rarely are the type and class hierarchies separated (as in the OO programming language Sather). This means that the developer, for the present, has to impose their own discipline on the use of inheritance. We urge that only subtyping is used confounded with specialization inheritance. In other words, ask the questions: 'Can I say this class is-a-kind-of another class?' and 'Can I dynamically substitute this class for its parent?'. These two questions also

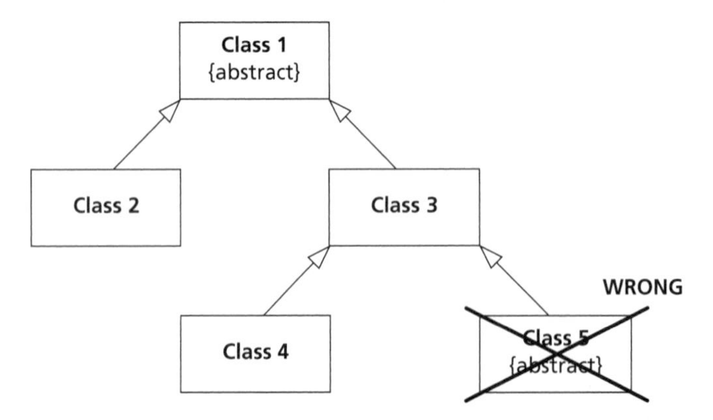

Figure 3.34 A good heuristic is to ensure all node classes are abstract classes and all leaf classes are concrete.

implicitly reflect the fact that any such identified inheritance relationship is pretty permanent. If a bird is-a-kind-of animal today then it is tomorrow also. So, use inheritance to represent permanent classification-type relationships. If something is temporary then there are two other relationships that are more likely: association (Section 3.7) or roles (Section 3.11).

Over the years, the phrase 'buy or inherit' has been used to argue the first case. The question is when to use a client server (buying a service) rather than inheritance. This originally stemmed from a feeling in the early days of commercial OO use that in order to say you were using object technology, you had to use the inheritance relationship *everywhere*. This led to its overuse, in particular, in cases where it was clearly inappropriate. This is partly because, at the coding level, both will work fine. To access methods in another object you can either declare the existence/visibility of that second object within the first (essentially an association) or you can declare it to be a subclass, in which case the methods of the superclass are immediately available in the subclass. The temptation to use a superclass in the code when an association occurs in the analysis derives from the fact that accessing a method from a superclass is faster (in machine cycles) than accessing the same method across an association link.

Our answer, in general, to the question 'Should we buy or inherit?' is buy. Our heuristic is that associations (or rather referential relationships) should be used much more than inheritance. Before you use inheritance be really sure it is the best technique. After all, using an inheritance relationship permits subclasses to 'see inside' their parent classes – thus violating encapsulation and information hiding! So, while powerful, inheritance is also potentially dangerous from a quality and reuse viewpoint, which is again relevant to components. Remember, after all, that in a distributed environment such as CORBA inheritance is all but ignored, since an object migrating across a network carries with it absolutely no information about any inheritance structure, being simply an autonomous module/component.

A different aspect of the use of inheritance arises when we consider the evolution of inheritance hierarchies. There are several heuristics here collected together as the OPEN Technique: Revision of inheritance hierarchies. One important comment here is to watch out for inheritance hierarchies that too strictly follow the notions of 'programming by difference' advocated some years ago. Not that the concept of programming by difference is incorrect, but rather that unless the difference (between superclass and subclass) is significant from a semantic viewpoint, the probable inheritance hierarchy is likely to be too deep and with few or sometimes no side branches. Such a hierarchy (as in Figure 3.35) can be immediately identified as problematical. You should check that intermediate classes (nodes in the hierarchy) really represent a useful abstraction – sometimes this may be a useful abstract class that creates a bifurcation point likely to be useful at some time in the future. You should, of course, also check that all the relationships are truly 'is-a-kind-of/subtyping' relationships.

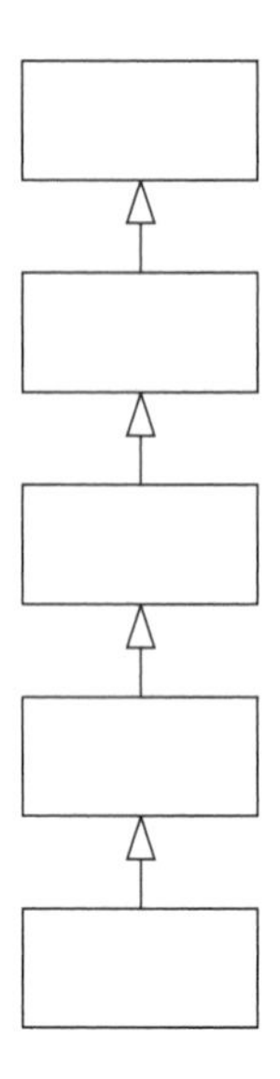

Figure 3.35 Programming by difference can often lead to deep generalization hierarchies with few or no side branches. This is usually indicative of poor design since the differences are not representative of separate concepts; rather, the hierarchy should be collapsed into a smaller number of classes such that each one represents an individual and clearly defined concept.

3.11 Roles

Roles in OPEN are inspired by the work in the Ooram method (Reenskaug *et al.*, 1996). A role is seen as a temporary and concurrent reclassification. For example, I am of type (class) Person – and am so 'permanently'. Today, I additionally can be classified as an Author object, tomorrow perhaps as a Teacher object; and so on.

The OPEN Technique of Role modeling sees roles and their use as appropriate in a number of places. Strictly, roles occur only at the instance (object) level; but they do so within and outside the scope of a collaboration diagram. Rumbaugh *et al.* (1999, p. 195) note that all participants in a collaboration diagram are in fact roles. Thus, in the context of a library simulation model (see full details in Chapter 4), the role relationships of Figure 3.36 are perfectly reasonable to be shown in either a collaboration diagram or a class diagram. This is a natural, minimal extension to the UML in that the UML permits the use, in collaboration diagrams, of both instance level and specification level (class level) versions. For example, Figure 3.37 shows the UML collaboration diagram notation for roles at the instance level and Figure 3.38 shows the same information at the specification level.[12] It is then but a small

12 The notation used here is from the official OMG UML documents. The description in Rumbaugh *et al.* (1999, p. 95) is in disagreement and, presumably, refers to an earlier version of the UML.

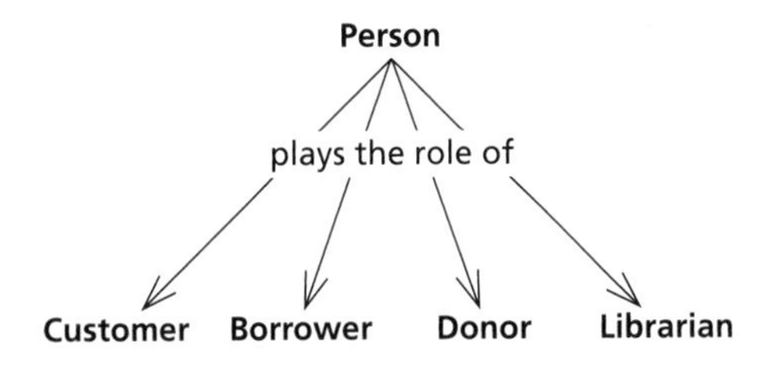

Figure 3.36 Schematic diagram (i.e. not UML) of a person playing several roles

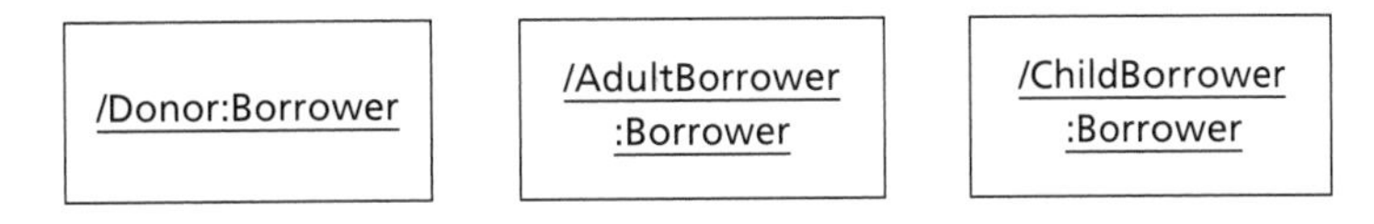

Figure 3.37 UML notation for roles as used in collaboration diagrams

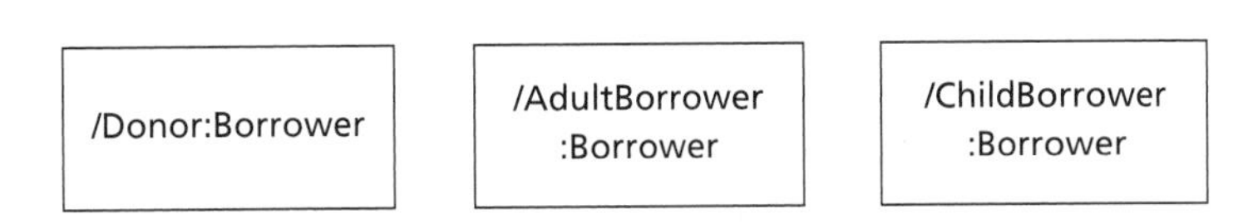

Figure 3.38 Alternative UML notation for roles at the specification level

step to permit the notation (of Figure 3.38) to be used also on class diagrams – which, after all, are the static complement of collaboration diagrams, being architecturally analogous.

In Figure 3.37, the notation is /ClassifierRoleName:ClassifierName. The solidus indicates the use of roles together with the colon preceding the BaseClassName and the whole thing is then underlined to indicate an instance. In Figure 3.38, the specification level, the notation is /Donor:Borrower without the underlining. If there is only one role being played in this collaboration, the role name can be omitted i.e. :ClassifierName. In other cases, the name of the class may be omitted, e.g. /ClassifierRoleName. If the object is named, this name precedes the solidus, e.g. donor/Donor:Borrower. (Note that this should not be confused with the notation for an object's name as objectname:ClassifierName or, for an unnamed object, :ClassifierName.)

In the context of an extended use in class diagrams, we might alternatively use a «role» stereotype[13] on the class (Figure 3.40) – as part of the extension mechanism for UML. This is a strategy highly encouraged within UML – the addition by the user of new stereotypes.

13 The OML variant of UML goes a little further and takes the OMG UML standard's option of associating an icon, rather than a stereotype label, to this figure (Figure 3.39). This permits objects of various classes to play this role which is precluded from the notation shown in Figures 3.37 and 3.38.

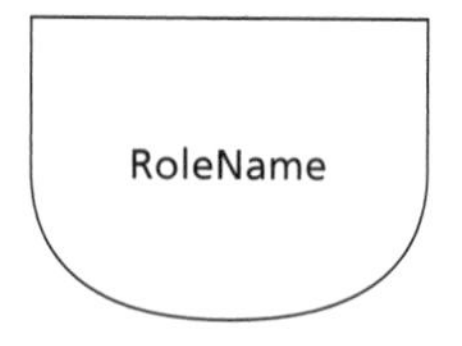

Figure 3.39 Iconification of the «role» stereotype

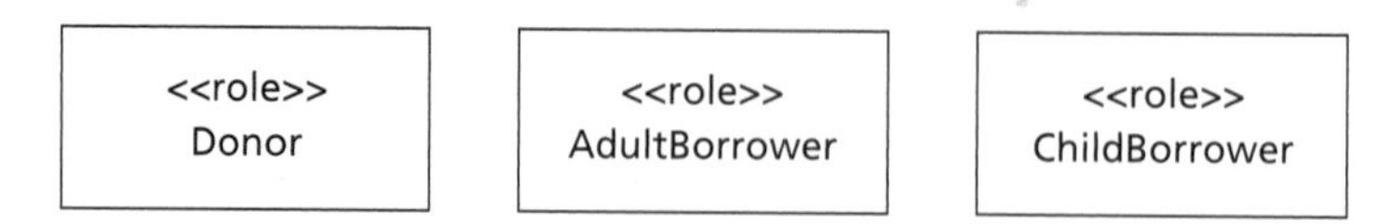

Figure 3.40 Using roles in the class diagram requires an extension to the UML. Here the extension mechanism of stereotypes is used.

Interestingly, Jacobson *et al.* (1999, p. 43) state that 'In fact, in UML a role is also a classifier of its own.' Whilst this does not seem to be borne out by the official UML documents, it augurs well for the future since it would provide exactly the sort of support needed by this OPEN Technique. For the present, the OPEN Task of 'Map roles to classes' remains.

Roles can be very useful for definitional relationships which are temporary. One might say that at this very moment I am an instance of an Author class as I type this paragraph. But this is not really true because there are many times of the day when I am not writing this book; there were periods in my life (before my first book) when I could *not* be described as an author in any way. The appellation of 'author' is temporary and, in fact, only really significant in one particular context: book publishing. It is not relevant when I attend a concert or buy my weekly groceries.

So, a temporary classification that is also context dependent might be a candidate for a role. A role in software is exactly the same as a role in the English language – on the stage. It is a temporary mask[14] added to the substantial form beneath. So in our software system we would also expect that any object identified as currently playing a role will be a superimposition of this role on top of something much more permanent beneath: a permanent type in OO terms.

Use roles for something that is temporary. Use roles for something that is a classification *in addition to* the regular classification. Consider many of the inheritance relationships in your analysis and design and apply these considerations and you may likely find that what you originally thought was an inheritance (because is-a-kind-of is as applicable to roles as to inheritance) is in fact a role.[15]

14 Hence our use of the mask icon for role in the OML variant of the UML (Figure 3.39).

15 We say this because the vast majority of examples of inheritance in OOAD and programming texts are in fact roles, not true inheritance (generalization/specialization) relationships.

3.12 States

Definition

The state of an object is represented by the current values of all its attributes, associations and aggregations.

Definition

A state changes as a result of an event which acts as a trigger for the change. The change of state effected is often called a transition.

States generally persist for a fairly lengthy period of time whereas transitions may be regarded as instantaneous. We describe interesting states and their transitions using a state transition diagram or STD (Figure 3.41). The STD is sometimes said to model the underlying 'State Machine' (OPEN Technique: State modeling). In UML, it is called a statechart diagram. States are shown as rounded rectangles joined by transitions. The transitions occur when a trigger or event occurs. Some events will occur which do not change the state. For instance, adding water to a partially filled glass will initially cause no change of state (where the states are empty; full; partially full). Only when some specific constraint is reached (the water starts to overflow) does a change of state occur.

Statechart diagrams are drawn for any classes which have interesting or convoluted states and state changes. They show the logic in terms of transitions, events and guards to those transitions. Each transition must correspond to a service offered by the same class in the class diagram. Each state in the statechart diagram must, similarly, be expressed by either a data attribute in the class or a reference to another class.

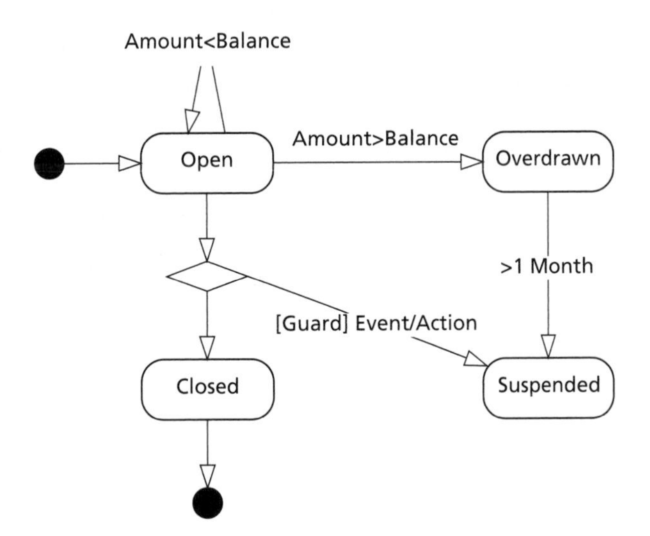

Figure 3.41 Example of a UML statechart diagram

For some domains, the statechart diagram is a more important diagram than the class diagram. This can occur, for example, in real-time control of a manufacturing plant or in an event-driven GUI interface. State models can be very precise and sometimes their formality can be offputting.

OPEN Technique: State modeling is not always used within OPEN Task: Construct the Object Model. While it is undeniable that objects have state, so many of them only have uninteresting states. *Do not* do state modeling for these. State modeling is not a penance; it is to be used only if it sheds light on the evolving model – perhaps by meaningfully tying together certain attribute values and events which may (or may not) trigger (state) changes from one value of the attribute to another.

3.13 Use cases

Use cases describe the functionality offered by a software system to a user. Use cases are often, therefore, used as part of a requirements engineering activity. They are not *the* requirements – as some seem erroneously to believe. Their use is described as part of the OPEN Technique: Scenario development, although an over-emphasis on them is seen as dangerous (Firesmith, 1999). This is especially true with respect to driving the system design with use cases.[16] Neither should use cases be used to describe non-functional requirements such as quality or performance. The following definition is taken from Cockburn (2000).

Definition

A use case is a description of the possible sequences of interactions between the system under discussion and its external actors, related to a particular goal.

The UML use case diagram (see Chapter 2 and also Figure 3.42) shows *all* the use cases in the system. Each use case then describes 'a sequence of transactions performed by a system, which yields an observable result of value for a particular actor' (Jacobson *et al.*, 1997, p. 66). Each individual sequence in the use case is a scenario and the full collection of all these scenarios defines the use case. This means that there are several courses of action, or 'paths', through each use case, for example, describing not only the straightforward path leading to success but all the optional and alternative routes that may eventuate. For example, a use case of an ATM may be 'Withdraw Money'. This might have paths linked to cases when the account is overdrawn, when the user forgets their pin number and so on. Scenarios then exist, for example, for the following: Fred Ng withdraws $100 from an account with a balance of $1000; John Smith withdraws $1000 from an account with a balance of $100.

A single scenario then describes a single thread of actions, which has no branches, decisions, etc. A use case, on the other hand, contains all scenarios and paths and therefore *does* contain many decision points, alternative routes, etc.

16 Jacobson (1999) notes that 'use-case driven development' is just the new name for 'functional-driven development'.

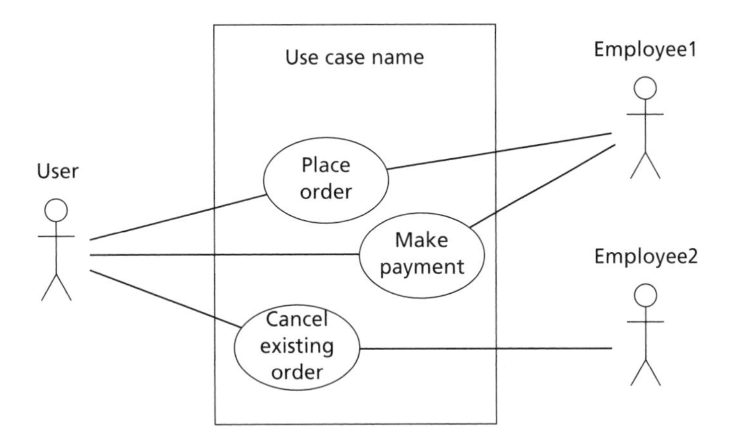

Figure 3.42 Example use case diagram

To remember the difference between a use case, a path and a scenario, two analogies have been suggested:

1. A scenario is an instance; so consider it as equivalent[17] to an object.
   A path is then equivalent to a class; and
   A use case is equivalent to a package.
2. A use case can be thought of as similar to a program; in which
   Paths are equivalent to the many branches and conditionals in the program; and
   A scenario is equivalent to a single run-time execution of the program (with specific values for all the data).

Although paths are important for testing, they are not identified separately in the UML – the term scenario is used to cover both paths and scenarios.

Each use case describes only the external view or the specification. Its realization (Figure 3.43) is in terms of cooperating objects, which are specified in a collaboration diagram. Further details are possible using a sequence diagram (Figure 2.46 in Chapter 2) and some authors also recommend the use of state transition diagrams (Figure 2.48 in Chapter 2) and/or activity diagrams[18] to document the details of a use case. Sequence diagrams would be best for showing a single

Figure 3.43 Sometimes a collaboration diagram is used to realize a use case.

17 Here we are using the word equivalent to mean 'at the same level of abstraction'.
18 A diagram type outside the core of the UML and eschewed in OPEN.

scenario (since they are both at the object rather than the class level) and an activity diagram would be most useful at the use case level since they visually describe options, choices and iterations which are contained in the use case but not in the scenario. Alternatively, the use of a collaboration diagram is recommended (Jacobson *et al.*, 1997, pp. 72, 74) as a preferred analysis option and a sequence diagram at the design level. In addition, when doing business modeling, as opposed to software modeling, a higher level of use case, called Task Script or Business Case, is extremely useful.

A use case diagram is akin to a context diagram and it is critical that the boundary of the system is clearly delineated. Everything deemed inside the system is then decomposed into a small number of key functional interactions of the 'user' (represented by the actor symbol(s)) and the software system. Each use case *must* deliver some (business) benefit to at least one actor.

The use case approach describes the system functionality. Focusing on functionality rather than data (as is more common in object modeling) can lead the use case user to deviate away from an object-oriented analysis and, instead, use a traditional functional decomposition technique. This is a real danger which you should avoid if you wish to stick closely to the OO paradigm.[19] Keep your use cases to a fairly high abstract level and keep asking if the candidate use case 'delivers a valuable service to the user'. Another way of thinking of this is whether the use case can be said to correspond to a system-level responsibility – each specifies a goal which is a request for service and a responsibility is a promise of service (Cockburn, 1997b).

While the normal use of use cases is to describe systems, the UML standard also permits them to be attached to other metaclasses. In particular, attaching a use case to a class permits specific sequences of operations to be identified which deliver a service. A simple example will suffice here. Suppose a library object needed to offer a service (operation) of borrowing a book. In implementation this would require two operations: BorrowBook and isBookBorrowed? The first is a command, the second a query. However, the sequence is important and the higher-level class responsibility requires the use case of

1. Library.BorrowBook(title)
2. Library.isBookBorrowed(title)

in order to fulfil this requirement *at the class level.*

Each ellipse in the use case diagram needs to be described. This is done in narrative form using natural language (e.g. English) (Table 3.4) using a template similar to that given in Chapter 2 (Figure 2.43). The goal is clearly stated and the use case described in a numbered sequence of steps (some authors prefer a single paragraph of free text). These describe the base (main) path of the use case, i.e. the most straightforward. Extensions are labelled and related back to the step in the main use

19 On the other hand, use cases and use case decomposition can also be very successfully used as a prelude to traditional design and implementation of a system focusing on its functional behaviour.

Table 3.4 Sample use case (after Cockburn, 1997a; © SIGS)

System under discussion:	the insurance company
Primary *Actor*:	the claimant
Goal:	get paid for car accident

1. Claimant submits claim with substantiating data
2. Insurance company verifies claimant owns a valid policy
3. Insurance company assigns agent to examine case
4. Agent verifies that all details are within policy guidelines
5. Insurance company pays claimant

Extensions

1a. Submitted data are incomplete:
  1a1. Insurance company requests missing information
  1a2. Claimant supplies missing information
2a. Claimant does not own a valid policy:
  2a1. Insurance company declines claim, notifies claimant, records all this, terminates proceedings
3a. No agents are available at this time:
  3a1. (What does the insurance company do here?)
4a. Accident violates basic policy guidelines:
  4a1. Insurance company declines claim, notifies claimant, records all this, terminates proceedings
4b. Accident violates some minor policy guidelines:
  4b1. Insurance company begins negotiation with claimant as to degree of payment to be made.

Variations

1. Claimant is
   a. a person
   b. another insurance company
   c. the government

5. Payment is
   a. by cheque
   b. by interbank transfer
   c. by automatic prepayment of next instalment
   d. by creation and payment of another policy

Table 3.5 Sample scenario corresponding to the use case of Table 3.4 (after Cockburn, 1997a; © SIGS)

System under discussion:	the insurance company
Primary Actor:	the claimant
Goal:	get paid for car accident

Scenario

1. Claimant submits claim with substantiating data
2. Insurance company verifies claimant owns a valid policy
3. Insurance company assigns agent to examine case
4. Agent verifies that all details are within policy guidelines
5. Insurance company pays claimant

case to which they apply. The 'one sentence' descriptions for both the Main Success Path and Extension sections are recommended (Cockburn, 1997b) to be of the form

<time or sequence factor> . . . <actor> . . . <action> . . . <constraint>

giving, as an example,

At any time after the clerk gets the quote, he may cancel the sale.

Since each use case contains several possible paths, it is sometimes necessary/useful to pull out individual paths or individual scenarios. An individual scenario, corresponding to the full use case of Table 3.4, is shown in Table 3.5. Since an individual scenario is a single, specific sequence, the template used is a little different, eliminating all extensions/variations and stressing the unique preconditions and unique postcondition (conditions and outcome respectively in Table 3.5).

Another useful way of writing down the use case is in the form of a dialogue between the actor and the software (Table 3.6) where it must be remembered to treat the software system consistently as a black box.

A 'recipe' for writing use cases (from Cockburn, 2000) may be given by the following 12 steps:

Step 1: Find the boundaries of the system (Context diagram, In/out list).

Step 2: Brainstorm and list the primary actors (Actor list).

Step 3: Brainstorm and list the primary actors' goals against the system (Actor–Goal list).

Step 4: Write the outermost strategic-level use cases covering all of the above.

Step 5: Reconsider and revise the strategic use case. Add, subtract and merge goals.

Step 6: Pick a goal/use case to expand. Optionally, write a system-in-use story to become acquainted with the story of the use case.

Table 3.6 Two-column or dialogue style of writing a use case (here presented as a scenario corresponding to that of Table 3.5)

Claimant	Insurance company/agent
1. Claimant submits claim with substantiating data	
	2. Insurance company verifies claimant owns a valid policy
	3. Insurance company assigns agent to examine case
	4. Agent verifies that all details are within policy guidelines
	5. Insurance company pays claimant
6. Claimant exits system	

Step 7: Fill in the stakeholders and interests, the pre-conditions, the success end conditions and the failure protection. Double-check the goals and interests against those conditions.

Step 8: Write the main success scenario for the use case. Double-check it against the stakeholders' interests.

Step 9: Brainstorm and list the possible failure conditions.

Step 10: Write how the actors and system should recover from each failure.

Step 11: Break out any sub-use case that needs its own space.

Step 12: Start from the top and readjust the use cases. Add, subtract, merge. Double check for completeness, readability and failure conditions.

We now have a formalized description of (the functional part of) the requirements. Thus use cases can be thought of as adding such formality to a more 'accidental' form of requirements specification. The problems remain of (i) how to add detail to the use cases and (ii) how to link them into or create from them object diagrams (semantic nets).

Adding detail can occur when the 'realization' of the use case is considered, for example by using sequence diagrams (e.g. Figure 3.44) which show a number of objects and the messages sent between them. However, sequence diagrams are essentially whitebox diagrams.[20] In other words, they expose internal details and thus have a focus very different from the external, blackbox viewpoint of a use case. It also begs the question as to where the objects (at the top of the diagram) came from. These have to be found in parallel with use case development using OPEN Techniques appropriate to the OPEN Task of 'Identify CIRTs'.[21] While it is suggested

20 Although a blackbox variety can be supported (Firesmith *et al.*, 1997, p. 195)

21 CIRT: Class or Instance or Role or Type – the Classifier types recommended for use in OPEN. Ofter CIRTs are in fact packages, particularly in coarse-granular analysis diagrams.

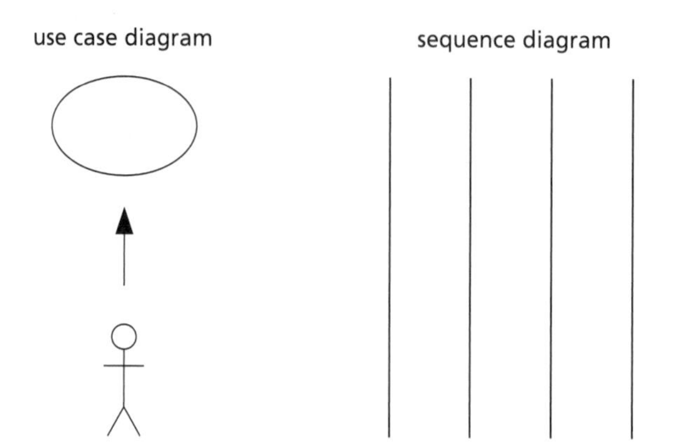

Figure 3.44 An instance of Figure 3.43 in which the sequence diagram is the realization of the use case

that this is done by an analyst who 'searches through the descriptions of the requirements and use cases, looking for the elements that can become the types in the analysis model' (Jacobson *et al.*, 1997, p. 69), a more considered approach is urged here. Certainly textual analysis can be one of the contributing techniques (also known as 'underlining the nouns'). In fact, when using OPEN, we strongly suggest that CIRT identification and use case modeling proceed in parallel. Use traditional 'object-finding' techniques to identify CIRTs (e.g. CRC card modeling, textual analysis) and only then merge together the functionality as expressed in use cases with the already-identified CIRTs. The advantage of this is that you already have some confidence that the CIRTs are the right ones. Identifying CIRTs mechanically from each use case in turn (as advocated, for instance, in RUP) tends to identify only fragments of CIRTs. Building up CIRTs layer by layer as each RUP iteration occurs gives no guarantee that the final CIRTs have semantic integrity. Rather, spend the time earlier on serious CIRT identification. That way, assigning functionality (from the use case) to objects becomes more natural and straightforward.

In fact, use cases can also be used to provide a second check on object behaviour. The system model must satisfy the use cases. To do this, express the steps in the use case in the SVDPI[22] format advocated in OPEN Technique: Hierarchical Task Analysis. Grammatical objects in these SVDPI sentences becomes CIRTs, verbs become actions on them, and grammatical subjects are usually collaborators or clients of that CIRT. Use cases are thus highly valuable for testing.

Several authors, including Jaaksi (1997) and Lilly (1999) upon whose work this discussion is based, offer advice on how best to use use cases.

1. *The system boundary must be well-defined and consistent.*
   The box around the use case represents the 'system' – but is it the computer system? Or a computer subsystem? Or an application? Or the whole business

22 SVDPI = Sentence Verb Direct-object Preposition Indirect-object.

enterprise? It should focus on one and only one of these. A common problem is mixed scope – some use cases pertaining to the overall business level and others to the application level. For example, in Figure 3.45, the business level and computer system scopes are mixed together. Separation into two use case diagrams is essential: one for the computer system scope (Figure 3.46) and one for the business enterprise scope (Figure 3.47).

2. *The use cases shall be written from the actor's (not the system's) point of view.* Beginning with the use case name which describes what the system does rather than the goals of the actor, leads to an incorrect focus on the system functionality *per se*. Good names might be Order tickets and View schedule rather than Process ticket order and Display schedule (for the use case of Figures 3.34 and 3.35). An incorrect focus on the systems leads you to start to decompose the use case in a functional way such that it ends up looking like a data flow diagram.

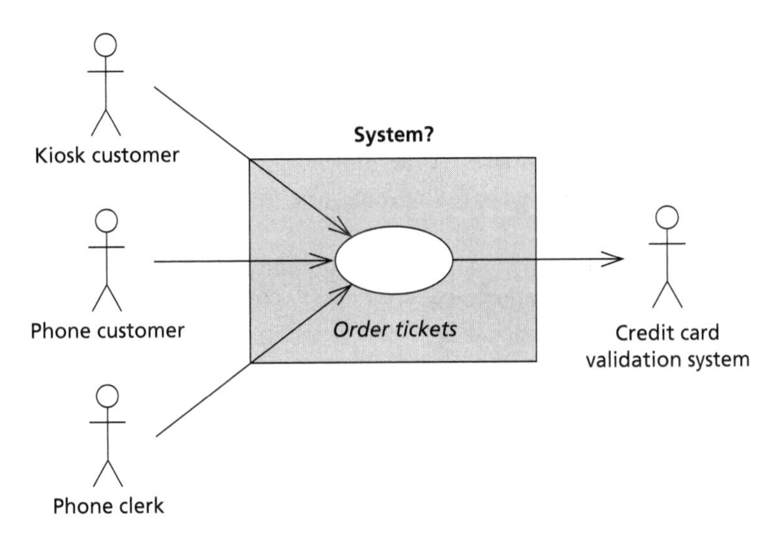

Figure 3.45 Use cases showing confused scope (after Lilly, 1999; © IEEE)

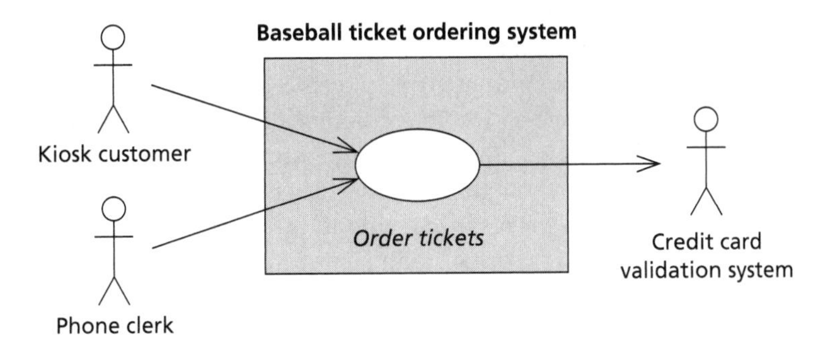

Figure 3.46 Use case focusing on the computer system (after Lilly, 1999; © IEEE)

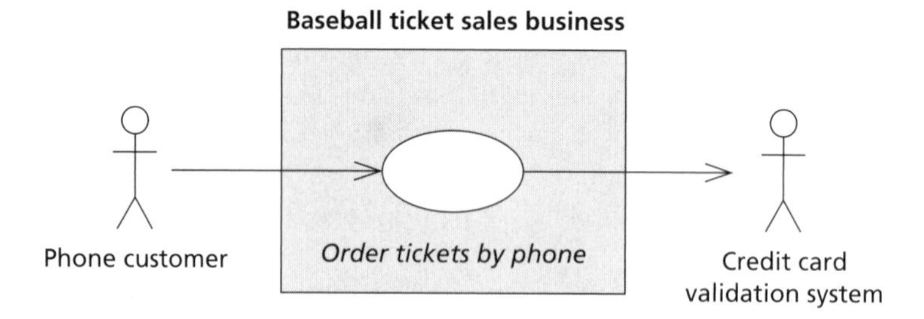

Figure 3.47 Use case focusing instead (*cf.* Figure 3.46) on the business (after Lilly, 1999; © IEEE)

This is particularly a danger when using the «include» and «extend» relationships, since this uses use cases which do not adhere to the rule that a use case must interact with an actor across the system boundary, being entirely inside the system boundary and interacting only with other use cases (a point also noted by Korson, 1998).

3. *Actor names should be consistent.*
   An easy mistake is to allocate several actors with different names when in fact they all relate to the same role. This arises from the use of synonyms in different parts of the requirements, originating probably from different sources. Constructing a glossary of terms early in the process can be highly beneficial in creating an agreed, common vocabulary across the whole project.

4. *The most important functional requirements must be specified in use cases.*
   For each functional requirement there should be a corresponding use case. Sometimes an overly enthusiastic attempt to make the use case 'object-oriented' results in fat use cases that try to do everything, e.g. 'maintain system' or 'manage the business'. It may merge together responsibilities of several actors, i.e. different actors have different levels of security access, so combining them as a single, more general actor is not a good idea.

   The granularity of a use case is often a question raised in the use of use cases. Remember that the use case should represent *the delivery of result(s) of value to the user/customer.* Use cases that describe internal processing should be removed and any trivial use cases should be merged together or into larger, existing use cases. One clue here is that a single actor in the use case diagram may be associated with a large number of use cases. This suggests the possibility of an overly granular use case model. This can often arise if a single use case is created for each individual option in the GUI (Figure 3.48). If you correctly conclude that there are in fact a large number of use cases in the model, all at the correct granularity, then use UML packaging techniques (Figure 3.49).

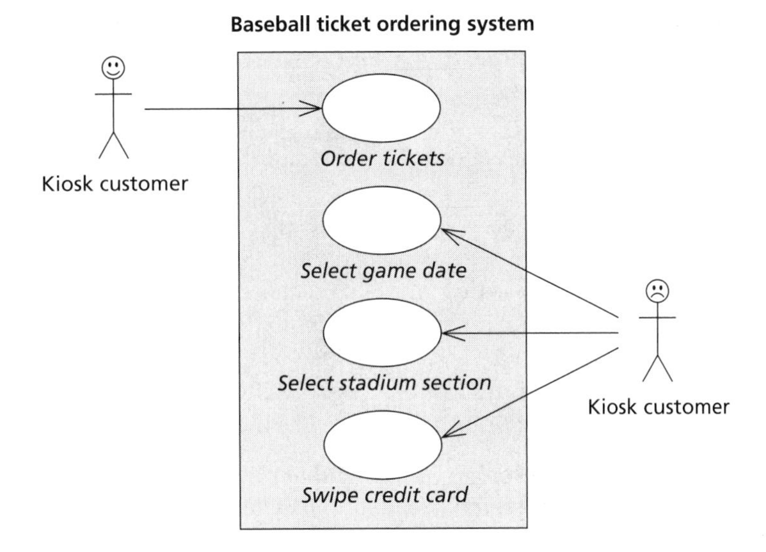

Figure 3.48 Real use cases versus incidental actions (after Lilly, 1999; © IEEE)

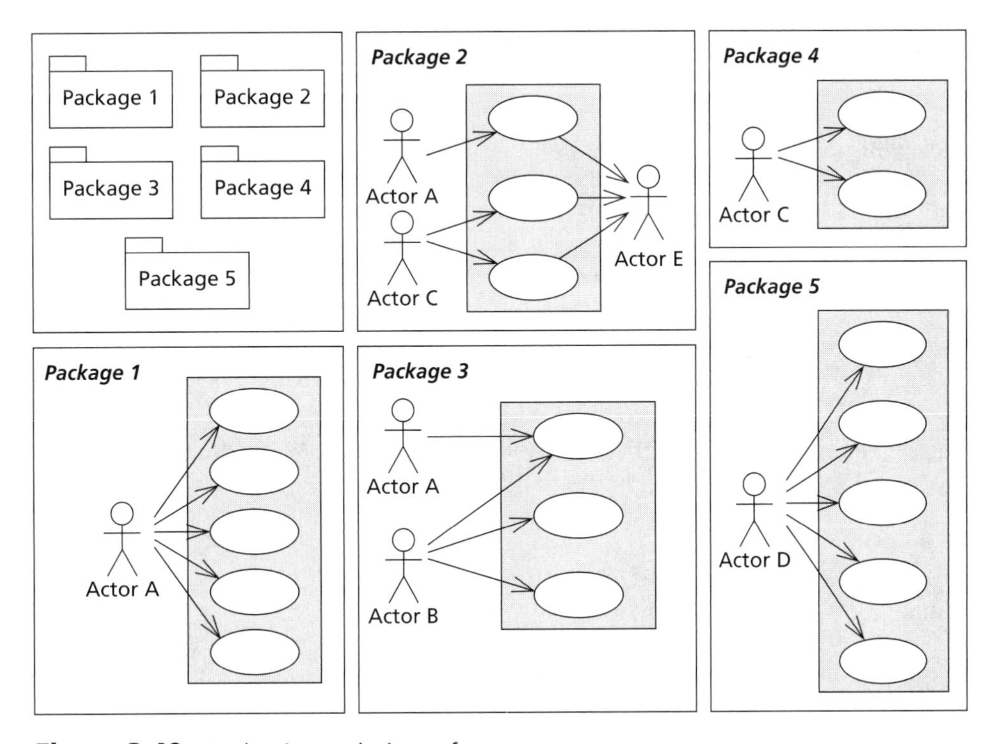

Figure 3.49 Packaging techniques for use cases (after Lilly, 1999; © IEEE)

5. *A use case describes something that the designer can be proud of and the customer is willing to pay for.*
   Use cases should not be so broad as to provide no value; neither should they be so narrow as to be too detailed. The guideline states that the developer should be proud of the development and the user pleased to pay for it.

6. *A use case depicts a typical way of using the system – but nothing more. It has a beginning, a main body and an ending.*
   Each use case describes one recommended way of using the system and should be complete in itself. It should start with a trigger supplied by an actor and end with delivery of the prescribed business benefit.

   A description of the use case should therefore contain a succinct and short description of its goal. Some bad examples are

   The user changes the desired temperature of the room.
   (This is not a requirement, but rather an observation.)

   The user shall change the desired temperature of the room.
   (This constrains the user. It is not a requirement on the digital thermometer.)

   whereas a good example in the same domain would be

   The digital thermometer software shall permit the user to change the desired temperature of the room.
   (Written as a requirement 'shall' – on the digital thermometer.)

7. *A use case is a play.*
   Like a play in which any person can take on a specific role, the use case should be general enough that any external (person or software) should be able to take on a particular role just by 'reading the manuscript'.

8. *A use case is like an essay written by an elementary school pupil.*
   Use cases should use simple sentence construction. The story is a sequence of first do this, then do that, with no analysis or attempt at literature. Confusion often arises in the reader's mind when the story-telling nature of a use case is ignored. Perhaps writing the use case as a dialogue between user and system will be helpful here.

9. *A use case should not be too long and ideally should fit on one page, with a maximum of three pages.*
   Overly long use cases are hard to understand and suggest that the granularity may be too fine. Lengthy use cases should be considered for breaking down into two or more use cases.

10. *A use case should be loud and clear.*
    Use cases should be able to make the reader form a firm opinion on the usefulness and validity of the use case.

11. *Customers and software designers can sign the use case.*
Use use cases as contracts between user and developer and get sign-off from both. This means that the customer must understand the use case. Optimally, users should be involved in the development of the use case documents. But when they are not, they often do not understand the documents without some explanation. When delivering a use case document to an end user not involved in their preparation, it is therefore wise to include a short explanation/glossary which explains and defines the terms in a use case model – as a preface or appendix. You may even think about a short training session to explain the concepts involved. Using «include» and «extend» may exacerbate this problem, since they are really a modeling convenience and not at all intuitive.

Other situations causing this problem are when (again) the use case does not tell a story; or when the use case organization does not match the way the customer looks at the problem; or when the use case is written in computerese rather than the language and terminology of the end user/customer. There are also customers who, for whatever reason, just 'hate use cases' – in which case, alternative modes of presentation should be sought, even if use cases are used internally by the requirements engineering team. Thus the use case must be verifiable by the user and implementable by the developer.

12. *A use case can be used in system development and system testing.*
Use cases need to be explicit enough that they can be used later in the project, e.g. for testing.

13. *The actor-to-use case relationships should not resemble a cobweb.*
The number of relationships in the use case diagram (actor to actor, actor to use case, and use case to other use case) is excessive. This suggests incorrect delineation of the actors – they are too general. As in the identification of inheritance in class models, the observation of several actors all using the same use case (Figure 3.50) suggests that the use of an inheritance structure for the actors might be useful (Figure 3.51) – but remember the basic rule that inheritance (actually generalization/specialization) should only represent a relationship which truly describes the 'is-a-kind-of' connection between classifiers (here actor classifiers).

There is also a serious danger that the use cases are never finished. When changing interface requirements lead to changes in the use cases, it suggests that they are too tightly coupled together. Consider here the discussions of 'essential use cases' (Constantine, 1997) which abstract away from specific technology to a more generic description. Use events in the business domain to trigger use cases rather than screen navigation details. Similarly, avoid including any design details in the use cases.

Baseball ticket order system

Kiosk customer

Phone clerk

View schedule

Order tickets

View daily sales report

Figure 3.50 Actors with overlapping roles (after Lilly, 1999; © IEEE)

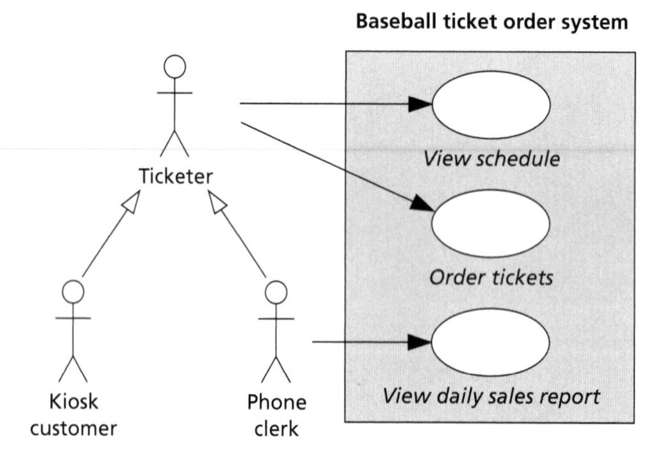

Figure 3.51 Use case model showing generalization of actors (after Lilly, 1999; © IEEE)

Implementation

As a prelude to implementation (Task: Code), we need to consider programming language-dependent design decisions (OPEN Technique: Class internal design). Within the seamless transition across the lifecycle, there comes a time when the facilities offered in the implementation language will begin to affect the fine detail needed to finalize the design. Up to then, the design has concentrated on offering solutions at the interface level to the problems identified in 'analysis' – but still from the interface viewpoint. In class internal design, we work out the best design for the implementation. Since many of the OOPLs are in fact procedural in nature at the method level, we can roughly equate the class internal design Technique of OPEN with traditional structured design techniques at the subroutine scale.

On the one hand, methods should be sufficiently short (2–5 lines of code) that the need for a design technique at all is minimal. On the other hand, should the algorithmic and control flow complexity warrant a pre-code design, then a range of options are available – all basically traditional techniques such as ER modeling, dataflow diagramming, HIPO and so on. Other, more recent techniques such as sequence diagrams also focus on internal design. In OPEN these are known as whitebox sequence diagrams and complement the external-view-only blackbox sequence diagrams. In such a whitebox sequence diagram, each horizontal line segment corresponds to a message pass and the subsequent activation of a method of the object which is the target of the message. For example, in Figure 3.52, the fact that a message *choose* is sent from the graphic object to the menu object means that the menu class *Must* have a choose operation. In this case, the class internal design for the method implementing the choose operation has an IF THEN ELSE structure to it.

There are two relevant, more detailed OPEN Techniques for coding that we need to discuss here: Implementation of Services and Implementation of Structure. Both rely on the existence of detailed class internal designs as a pre-requisite. Together they assist in making coding level decisions regarding state and behaviour (attributes and operations) – thus fulfilling OPEN Task: Code.

Implementation of services is usually done by methods (member functions in C++). The visible (public in UML) methods should be a minimal set – to maximize

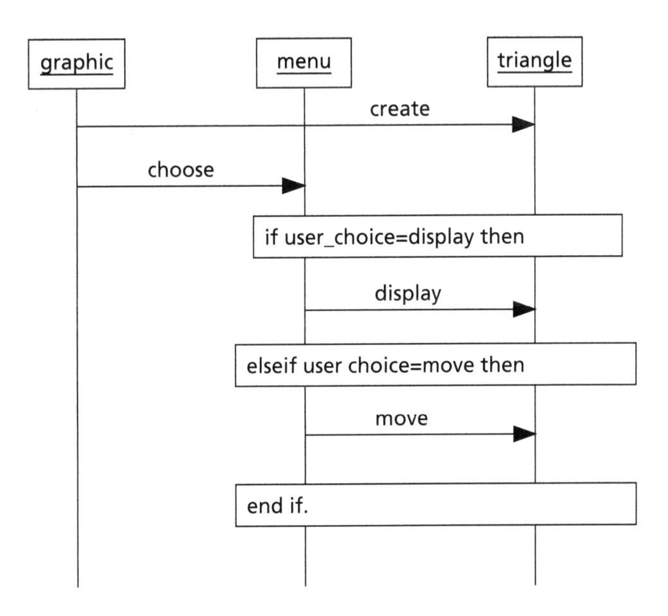

Figure 3.52 Example whitebox sequence diagram showing support for selection (IF . . . THEN . . . ELSE) using extensions provided in the OML variant of the UML (after Henderson-Sellers *et al.*, 1998; © AWL)

on encapsulation and information hiding. Some of these may use the same private methods.

Classes need to have full CRUD (create, read, update and delete) facilities even though these are not shown explicitly in the detailed design. Create requires a constructor method and, depending upon the OOPL, the class may also need a destructor method to be coded manually. Access methods need to be coded for all data items – these are *get* and *set* methods (the R and U of CRUD respectively).

Two other OPEN Techniques are sometimes used at roughly this stage in the process. The first is to document creation – for instance, as shown in Figure 3.52, a message sent from the graphic object to the triangle object clearly requires the Triangle class to have a create routine accessible from objects of the Graphic class. One way of documenting interactions that pertain to the creation of objects is the OPEN Technique: Creation Charts. These are diagrams with two columns, the first listing classes by name and the second listing which other classes the first class is responsible for creating instances thereof. Other techniques adopted into OPEN include that of Design templates from the work of Martin Fowler and Jim Odell. These are similar to idioms in that they offer pre-packaged options for implementation.

3.15 Inspections and reviews

3.15.1 V&V

Under the heading of Verification and Validation (V&V) are a number of OPEN Techniques. We will discuss briefly just four here: inspections, walkthrough, unit testing, and package and subsystem testing. (Reviews may also be used – see Section 3.15.2.)

Definition

Reviews, inspections and walkthroughs all focus on examination of workflow products for errors. Their focus and purpose are, however, different. Reviews are used to evaluate the progress of the project, inspections identify defects in the work products, and walkthroughs have an educative focus in which alternatives may be examined.

Inspections can in fact be applied to code and to designs. They offer a static evaluation of these work products and do not attempt to assess performance or runtime failure. As the name implies, the development team members 'inspect' these various work products. Most documented inspection techniques owe their heritage to the work of Michael Fagan in the mid-1970s. Typically, six distinct stages are needed:

1. Inspection planning
2. Inspection overview
3. Inspection preparation
4. Inspection meeting

5. Rework
6. Follow-up.

The core of the technique is the inspection meeting at which a moderator conducts the meeting review in which defects are identified and recorded (in a small number of classes). The agreed list of defects is then allocated to a developer for fixing. These are checked either directly by the moderator or in a follow-up meeting.

Walkthroughs are semi-formal examinations of a work product by a small team of peers. The walkthrough is led by the author of the design or code. He or she explains the objectives and then the detail of the work product. Readability is considered, as is an examination of alternatives – a think-tank atmosphere prevails. The aim is not to identify defects (this is the role of an inspection) although, if these are found, they are of course noted.

Testing is a formal approach built on many sophisticated mathematical theories to ensure that test plans are adequate and as broad as possible. In OPEN, testing occurs throughout the lifecycle. It can be regarded as part of the post-conditions of each Activity object. Since it is applied in conjunction with each Activity, it is clear that the word 'testing' has different meanings depending on when in the lifecycle it is being used. This also has an effect on the scale of work product under test. So we can consider testing at the unit, subsystem/package and system level; we can look at alpha testing versus beta testing versus user acceptance testing; and the level of comprehensiveness to which the test plan is developed depends strongly upon the required quality of the system. Testing of a system to be used in real-time control of a nuclear plant, for instance, requires more extensive testing than for a system which does payroll updates and batch processing of salary payments.

In unit testing, individual classes are tested. Data need to be fully encapsulated; each method must work, in the sense of satisfying all pre- and post-conditions. Newly added classes, particularly within an inheritance hierarchy, need to be carefully evaluated. It is said that, just because the superclass is well tested, there is still the need to test these same services when accessed via a newly constructed subclass. You should note that when testing, whether at unit or another level, it is *imperative* that there are expected results for the experimental results to be compared with. In other words, you need to know what the correct answer should be in order to evaluate whether the class is behaving correctly or not.

Unit testing is usually undertaken by the developers themselves. They start with classes with zero fan-out followed by testing of those classes which use services of the zero-fan-out classes. And so on.

When groups of classes collaborate, they are often grouped into a package or subsystem. That very grouping, while valuable in abstracting away detail to aid understanding, can often create more possibilities of failure. Any sort of integration testing is usually a concern – although with objects, integration test failures are less common than with traditional subroutine-structured systems. Since we are now dealing with larger 'objects', other ways of delineating the test strategy are needed. Often scenarios (use case instances) offer that integrating mechanism. We can think of driving a scenario through a package as a good measure of its integrity.

As before, testing needs to be approached rigorously There are generally three stages:

1. Package test plan
2. Review
3. Test plan execution.

3.15.2 Reviews

Some potentially useful OPEN techniques for *undertaking user reviews* are:

1. Responsibility identification
2. Class naming
3. Inspections
4. Walkthroughs
5. Complexity measurement
6. Coupling measurement.

We have already seen how Technique: Responsibility identification is useful in analysis and design. Here, as part of our review, responsibilities (and often use cases) can be used as a yardstick against which to make our evaluations. Similarly, the utility and succinctness of appropriate class names can be very important in quality reviews of designs. The actual review techniques can be grouped as either inspections or walkthroughs.

Inspections focus on direct evaluation of work products such as the design or the source code. In trying to identify defects, a typical software inspection process has six distinct stages: inspection planning, inspection overview, inspection preparation, inspection meeting, rework, and follow-up. In contrast, while an inspection focuses on the identification of work-product defects, a walkthrough relates to the elucidation and examination of alternatives. It is a semi-formal examination of a work product by a small team of peers led by the work product author. Since the focus of walkthroughs is alternatives, any defects identified during the process are often ignored.

In any evaluation technique, quantifying the outcome is useful. In that context, OPEN provides several metrics techniques. Two useful ones here are complexity measurement and coupling measurement. Their importance for quality evaluation is now discussed.

3.15.3 Quality

The two OPEN Techniques relevant to *quality evaluation*, which we have not yet discussed at all, are the two metrics ones: complexity measurement and coupling measurement.

Complexity metrics, the topic of a whole book (Henderson-Sellers, 1996), encompasses the many aspects of complexity understood to be the difficulty of understanding a work product. The harder a work product is to understand, the more complex it is and the harder it is to debug, maintain and attain a high quality. While there is no one single metric (and never will be), there are a number of useful complexity metrics that can be collected and analyzed. These include measures of central tendency (averages, modes, medians) and measures of the distribution (histogram shapes, skewness parameters, standard deviations of continuous distributions, and so on). Metrics should also be kept on the shape of all inheritance hierachies. Heuristics tell us that deep hierarchies with little branching are bad and, conversely, shallow broad leafy hierarchies may be less than optimal.

Coupling measures how tightly components (CIRTs) are connected. A high degree of coupling means that individual classes cannot really be regarded as autonomous and are certainly not (re)usable as small transferable components. However, it is also clear that a near-zero coupling metric value is equally suspicious. A class that is not coupled to anything else in the system is either useless (because it is never accessed) or the only class in the system (since its 'godlike' nature means it never needs to delegate any service request to any other object in the system).

Summary of Key Points

- OPEN has a large number of tasks and techniques covering the full lifecycle.
- OPEN's modeling tasks and techniques are a subset which aid in the understanding of the requirements as well as in creating a model prior to implementation (coding).
- OPEN's modeling tasks and techniques are used to support people in producing products (UML diagrams, code etc.).
- In utilizing OPEN's tasks and techniques to create models, we have used the UML (Unified Modeling Language) to draw a set of appropriate diagrams .

Discussion Topics

- Let us say that there are three OPEN Techniques available for identifying CIRTs. How do you choose between them?
- What are the critical differences between roles and generalization/specialization?
- What is the scope of local standardization for elements of OPEN and the UML notation?
- What are the pros and cons of use cases?

Bibliographic Notes

The activities and tasks of OPEN are described in the book by Graham *et al.* (1997a) and the techniques in a later book (Henderson-Sellers *et al.,* 1998). There are also shorter articles in the more academic literature as well as *JOOP* (*Journal of Object-Oriented Programming*) columns which describe particular techniques, such as Relationship Modeling, in gruesome detail.

Case Study 1

Library Management

Abstract

In this first case study, we use a simple library information system to illustrate the basic principles of using a tailored OPEN process. The prime focus is the Build Activity in which we illustrate how to use the various OPEN modeling techniques documenting the work products using the UML notation.

4.1 Scope of case study

The first case study is a relatively simple one of small scope. In it, we will introduce simple process ideas and undertake the *modeling* element using classes together with association and inheritance relationships between them. Other, more advanced, topics will be discussed in Chapter 5 (e.g. use cases, architecture, aggregation relationships). In this first introduction to the application of OPEN, we will also minimize consideration of the project management and business elements which are discussed in other books in the OPEN series.

For this example only, we initiate the project with the assumption that we have been given all the requirements – so we do not have an activity for Requirements Engineering. The requirements[1] read as follows:

> Develop an interactive library management system to manipulate information regarding the normal transactions of a library. Customers borrow and return books. Books are added to the library collection and some may be lost or stolen. New customers may wish to use the facilities of the library. At any time the information system must be able to be interrogated regarding who has borrowed which books. The basic transactions possible are thus

1 Originally supplied by R. Rist, University of Technology, Sydney.

A: add a book to the library catalogue – watch out for multiple copies of the same book.

D: delete a book from the library catalogue (lost or stolen).

B: borrow a book.

R: return a book.

S: display the list of books or customers.

X: exit from the system.

and these should form the basic six options offered to the administrator in the menu of the information system.

The following 'business rules' should be noted:

A child (less than 12 years old) can borrow up to 3 books at a time.
An adult can borrow up to 5 books at a time.
Customers who have donated more than $1000 to the library (known as 'donors') can borrow as many books as they wish.
For every book that a customer loses, their borrowing allowance is decreased by one. (This does not apply to donors.)

Although you can assume perfect typing skills on the part of the administrator (i.e. you do not need to validate data for typing errors), you should ensure requests are meaningful – for example, checking that when a book is returned it does exist in the catalogue, that the borrower is a valid user of the library and that this particular title had indeed previously been borrowed by this customer.

In this first, introductory case study we will focus on modeling. However, we first need to establish the OPEN SEP (Software Engineering Process) that is most appropriate. Creating this SEP is done with an OPEN Task: Tailoring the lifecycle process. To do this, we start with the full OPEN process framework described in earlier chapters. Since we are not going to be concerned too much with project management, and particularly project planning Activities and Tasks, we can focus on a very much trimmed down set of Activities with their main focus as the Build Activity (Figure 4.1). We supplement the Build Activity, as can be seen in this diagram, with some project planning and, of course (although these will be minimal in this particular case study example), project initiation and final evaluation. For this first example, we have also not added too many iteration paths; in fact, just the one, back from evaluation to planning, as well as the standard ones inside the Build Activity as indicated. Since this is our first project in OO, many of the concerns of larger OO projects, including reuse, domain analysis, detailed fits between technology and business, and inclusion legacy systems, can be deemed outside our scope. Similarly, the added 'complications' of a fully IIP (iterative, increment and parallel) process can be avoided. Iteration and incremental delivery are seen partly in the interactions indicated in Figure 4.1 between the evolutionary development subactivity (labelled Modeling, Implementation and Testing) and the user review subactivity.

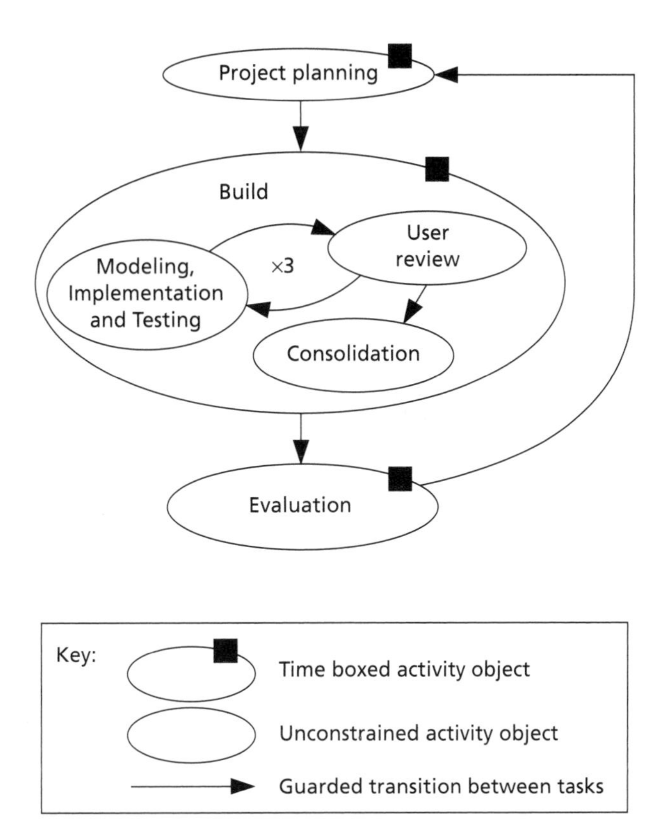

Figure 4.1 Contract-driven lifecycle instantiation (of the OPEN process framework) suitable for the library case study

We must now ask, given these chosen Activities, what are the best tasks? In Figure 4.2 we see these six chosen activities/subactivities listed across the top and appropriate Tasks linked in down the side. When we are designing a matrix to link Tasks and Activities (or Tasks and Techniques) for an organization, we will add fuzziness into the matrix by using all five levels of possibility supported by OPEN. However, if we are tailoring OPEN for a single project or, as in this instance, as a small teaching example, we can be more categoric in our choice of linkages. In other words, we will make the entries in the Activity/Task matrix and the Task/Technique matrix binary: either the combination is used (effectively mandatory for present purposes) or it is not. Thus in Figure 4.2, we elect to use four subtasks for Activity 1 (Project planning), four tasks for Modeling and Implementation; and so on.

Finally, Figure 4.3 links the selected Tasks,[2] as shown in Figure 4.2, to a selection of appropriate and useful Techniques. These are chosen to fit in with the skills of individuals, the organizational culture, the available tools and so on. As you

2 All except 'Write manuals and other documentation' since (i) it is all pervasive and (ii) we will not be discussing this formally in this book.

	Activity					
Task	1	2	3	4	5	6
Code		x				
Construct the object model		x				x
Develop and implement resource allocation plan						
develop iteration plan	x					
develop timebox plan	x					
set up metrics collection programme	x					
specify quality goals	x					
Evaluate quality			x	x		x
Identify CIRTs		x				
Map roles on to classes		x (OOP)				
Test		x	x	x	x	
Write manuals and other documentation			x	x	x	x

Key:
1. Project planning
2. Modeling, implementation and testing
3. V&V
4. User review
5. Consolidation
6. Evaluation

Figure 4.2 Tailored Activity–Task matrix for the library case study

develop your own skills, and depending upon the domain in which you work, you might finally settle on an organizational OPEN culture in which you always use collaborations analysis and collaboration diagrams but never sequence diagrams – or vice versa. You may decide to focus on responsibility identification as your major technique for object identification; or you may use textual analysis based on use cases. You may decide to spend a lot of time using CRC cards or decide that this technique is not for you because of particular skills sets, domain constraints or the availability or preference of other brainstorming techniques. But, for the moment, that is in the future and here we will take a more prosaic approach in order to introduce you more slowly to the ins and outs of the OPEN process and, in particular, its Build Activity.

In the next sections we go through each of the *modeling-focused* Activities. Within each of these sections we then discuss the Tasks and Techniques you might find useful. These are the ones listed in Figures 4.2 and 4.3 respectively.

4.2 Project planning

Let us start by planning the project which is essentially focused on OOA/D/P, i.e. 'Modeling, Implementation and Testing' (Figure 4.1). The tasks relevant to this activity are listed in Figure 4.2: develop and implement resource allocation plan, with its subtasks of developing the iteration plan and the timebox plan, setting up the metrics collection programme and specifying the quality goals.

In this case, because the problem is so small, we can plan on a single major iteration – although we expect several *ad hoc* iterations amongst team members and

Technique	Tasks 1	2	3	4	5	6	7
Abstract class identification		x					
Abstraction utilization		x			x		
Class internal design	x	x					
Class naming		x		x			
Collaborations analysis		x					
Complexity measurement				x			
Contract specification	x	x			x		
Coupling measurement				x			
CRC card modeling		x			x		
Generalization and inheritance identification		x					x
Implementation of services	x						
Implementation of structure	x					x	
Inspections				x			x
Interaction modeling		x					
Package and subsystem testing							x
Prototyping	x	x					
Relationship modeling	x	x					
Responsibility identification	x			x	x		x
Role modeling		x				x	
Service identification		x					
State modeling		x					
Textual analysis					x		
Timeboxing			x				
Unit testing							x
Walkthroughs				x			x

Key:
1. Code
2. Construct the object model
3. Develop and implement resource allocation plan
4. Evaluate quality
5. Identify CIRTs
6. Map roles on to classes
7. Test

Figure 4.3 Tailored Task–Technique matrix for the library case study

probably back to the user as well. We might also imagine that this project has a small team (two or three) people involved in it. Thus their roles will be several and potentially overlapping. In Chapter 5, on the other hand, we have tried to show two or three iterations for the relevant activities.

So we aim to have a single deliverable, but involve users as team members if possible – certainly in the user review subactivity. Internally, let us plan for the delivery of a first cut object model within a week and a final and agreed model, perhaps with some preliminary code, within three weeks. If we simply state these temporal objectives and we are delayed, the product delivery date may slip. If it is more important that the deadline should be met even if the deliverables are less than 100% complete, then we might impose a timebox of three weeks. A timebox simply states that at the end of the stated period, the product (version/build/release, whatever word you prefer) ships – come what may, the deadline is always met. Since we are building in an iterative and incremental manner, probably using a component-based approach, if there is slippage, it will be in the percentage of the modules configured and delivered. We might hit the deadline but with only 85% of the functionality. But the client at least has a working system which can be put into action for user evaluation and feedback. However, if you are using a timeboxing approach the customer needs to be aware of this, since it affects their planning too. Unfortunately, many customers have become so accustomed, over the years, to delays in software delivery that they come to expect it – and therefore plan with an anticipated delay in mind. Delivery *on time* in a timeboxed environment may cause them surprise and discomfort if you do not agree this with them first.

The deliverables will be a set of class diagrams with any worthwhile state transition diagrams that we discover. There are also envisaged to be several collaboration diagrams (identification of this as a deliverable would normally be part of the early analysis activities) together with code and full user manuals, test reports, and so on.

Deliverables and effort expended should also conform to the level of quality required. For instance, if the software you are building is life-critical, such as aircraft control, tomography scanning, etc., you will require a higher quality standard to be met. This will need more careful testing, for instance perhaps a careful look at response times and code efficiency. On the other hand, if you are developing a word processor, CASE tool or theatre booking system, concerns about sub-millisecond response or guaranteed downtimes of less than 1 second per year are not likely to be relevant.

If this is a one-off or a pilot project you might think it valueless to set up a metrics collection programme. But in either case, this project will provide you with valuable experience. You need to document it, monitor it and measure it so that when you look back at what you learned in 6 or 12 months' time, you have some reminders as to what went right – and perhaps more importantly what went wrong. Humans tend to learn by their mistakes. Yet software developers never publicly admit their mistakes[3] which means that, unlike other branches of science and engineering, there is no collective culture in which you can learn from the mistakes of others – know which paths *not* to follow, which techniques do *not* work well. Set up a metrics programme, even if only a small one, to collect data at least for yourself and your organization. This will help to create a learning organization and one in which you can, at some time in the future, start to think about process improvement, 'climbing the CMM ladder', attaining ISO9000 accreditation and so on. Without measurements, you can never achieve these advantages of higher productivity, higher product quality, effective and efficient work practices, and so on.

Process comment

One of the interesting questions that 'project planners' have always asked is 'is the activity of project planning a part of the project plan?'. The answer is not a plain 'yes' or 'no'. In OPEN, we recommend that the activity of project planning be made the first,

3 Sometimes because of commercial confidentiality and non-disclosure agreements (NDAs).

albeit short, activity within the project plan. This can help in putting the work associated with planning the project in perspective. This also indicates that the project planning activity, in larger and more complex projects, can be made to 'iterate'. This iteration of the project planning activity will need more care and subtlety, as this really implies iterations in two dimensions, one of the actual project and the other of the planning activity.

4.3 Build

Most of the activities that typically precede the Build Activity can be loosely referred to as higher-level or management/project management issues. The Build Activity, on the other hand, epitomizes the technology side of software development. So much so, that in many so-called OO methodologies, the only elements you find in them are Build tasks and techniques.

During Build, we go deep inside the lower-level or design aspect of the model, and very close to coding. The advantage in using the OO approach is that the semantic gap, as shown in Figure 4.4, is much less than in a traditional software development approach. Therefore, when we start using some of the modeling techniques as described in OPEN, we are producing the business models (made up of key business entities such as Flight, Passenger and Seat in Figure 4.4) on the one hand and corresponding software realizations (classes Flight, Passenger and Seat, in Figure 4.4) of these on the other. In other words, the language of objects is not that far removed from the language of the user and the manager. You might say that object-oriented technology is a 'client-focused' approach to building software applications.

Project management is needed to identify releases and builds. These are times when partial systems are handed over to management or to the users for evaluation and/or release (to beta testers or finally to the users). Commercial software often uses builds internally to the development team and releases to the external client. These

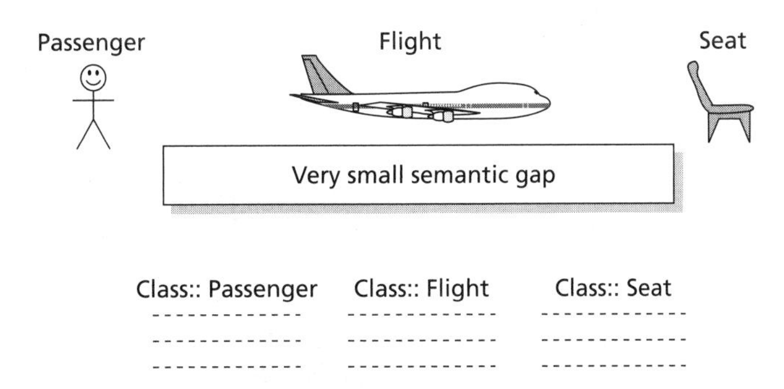

Figure 4.4 The advantages of modeling and implementing using 'objects' is that there is a very small semantic gap between reality and the software implementation (after Unhelkar, 1999; © CRC Press)

might be identified by way of their new version number. Each iteration of the build (and this is a highly iterative activity) must involve not only the technical ideas behind object-oriented analysis, design and programming, but also validation and verification (V&V), user reviews and, finally, a consolidation, before there is any thought of release to the client. In the next sections we explore each of these sub-activities in more detail, focusing particularly on the modeling aspects and the use of the UML notation.

Process comment

While it was still possible to iterate to some degree in traditional development, that iterative nature of software development was not supported by traditional/procedural languages. OO programming languages, on the other hand, are very conducive to iterative and incremental development, as described in the Build Activity. However, it is still vital to note that the full advantage of iterative and incremental development is not *recognized when 'component integration' is desired. This is so because despite the use of OO languages on the front-end, the back-end legacy software continues to remain rooted in the traditional technologies. For example, a persistent component that is stored in a couple of relational tables will be very difficult to be developed iteratively, as the corresponding relational tables may not lend themselves to this iterative development.*

4.4 Modeling and implementation: OOA/D/P

In this case study, we focus on modeling techniques and how to document the results from application of these techniques (described in detail in Chapter 3) in diagrams using the UML as a notation.

We start with reading through the requirements derived earlier in the process. These are given in Section 4.1. We see that we are dealing with a domain of which we have some intuitive knowledge: a library from which we can borrow books. The system we are to design caters for not only borrowing and returning books but also adding new books to the collection and for deleting those from the library catalogue which are lost or stolen.

Since this is a physical domain containing physical objects, a simple read through of the requirements document starts us thinking about books, borrowers, librarians, libraries and, perhaps, book allowances. These are all potential 'objects' in our system. We have identified, on our read-through of the requirements, *concepts* such as book and borrower which we can add to our (new) list of candidate classes (Table 4.1).

We call Table 4.1 a 'candidate' class list since at this stage we are not sure if all of these will turn into real classes. For example, book allowance, whilst a noun phrase, may turn out to be better modeled as a property or logical attribute of some other object. But for the moment, we keep them all as possibilities (Figure 4.5). Do not worry if the list is too long. It is often easier to cross things off than add them later. We will eliminate items from this list if we find they have no responsibilities. We

Table 4.1 First draft at candidate class list

• book	• menu
• customer	• donation
• borrower	• request
• adult borrower	• title
• child borrower	• typing skills
• donor	• valid user
• library	• library card
• book allowance	• account
• librarian	• information
• book catalogue	• transaction
• book collection	• library collection
• administrator	• information system
• staff	• business rules

will also look for possible synonyms. For instance, in Table 4.1, is the administrator class the same as the librarian class? Is customer just another name for borrower? Is a borrower or an administrator inside or outside the system? If outside, it will be represented by an actor, not a class. We cannot decide as yet until we have more information as the OOAD progresses.

An interesting and difficult question to answer (at least right now) is what is the best way to model the candidate classes of borrower, adult borrower, child borrower and donor. Whilst an inheritance structure might seem all too obvious, take care! Freezing in an inheritance right now, while tempting, might lead to a less than optimal design later. Let's bear in mind that an adult borrower seems to be a subclass of borrower – but let's not rush to draw it that way.[4]

We are focusing in this initial cut at classes at a consistent abstraction level: that of real things in the system. We have not considered fine details like whether a book has an ISBN number and how to differentiate different physical copies of the same title. Neither have we considered how the library class might be part of a much larger national or international library system with inter-library loans facilities and so on.

4 A strong recommendation here, especially if you are using a CASE tool, is to let the designer 'toy around' with the key business entities *without* formalizing their relationships. Furthermore, the relationships should also be designed in an iterative fashion, making provisions for changes to the relationships. Finally, note that classes/CIRTs should not be qualified (i.e. their attributes and operations specified) in the first iteration at all.

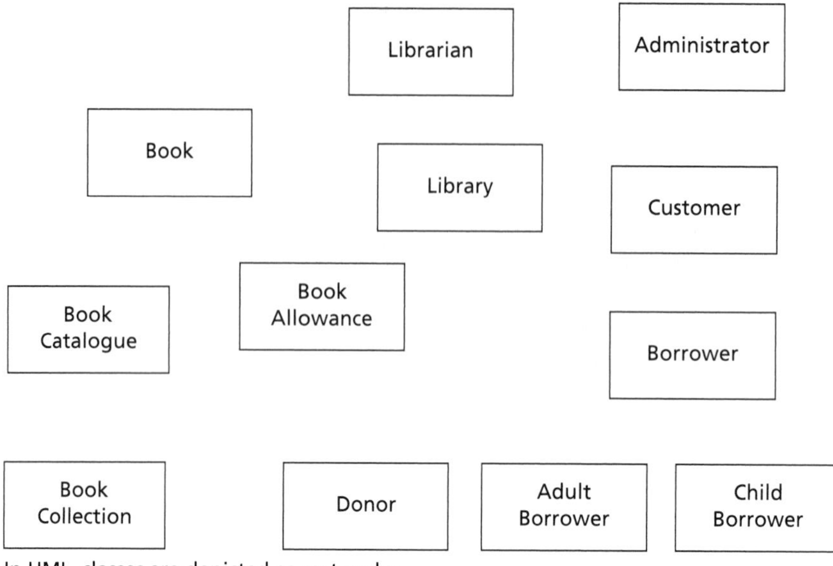

Figure 4.5 First set of candidate objects for the library case study

We now have, in Figure 4.5, a number of potential classes. But are these really all classes or are some unnecessary? Let's look at what makes a useful class. A class represents a concept, like book. We all have a shared understanding of what a book is so it qualifies as a concept. Representing it in an object-oriented system as a class also says that the concept called 'book' has a (potentially large) number of instantiations: individual objects that are members of the set of items described by the book class. (Later we may differentiate between type and class as well as between class and object, but for the moment let's just use the term class, since that is the basic notational icon we have used so far, e.g. in Figure 4.5.)

A good rule-of-thumb would then be that if a class had no identifiable responsibilities, its existence as a class should be severely doubted. This might occur not just because the class is spurious but because the responsibilities of the real-world entity being modeled are outside the context of the system being built. That is why a context model can sometimes be useful. For example, we know (from our real-world experiences) that a borrower (which is probably a person) has all sorts of features like a name, address, the ability to walk, talk, etc. But if none of these is relevant to the library system, borrowing a book, etc., then, as far as we are concerned in modeling the library system, the class (here borrower) would have no responsibilities *relevant to the domain* and would therefore be redundant.

So what might appropriate responsibilities be for some of the candidate classes in Figure 4.5? Well, a librarian might have the responsibility of checking out a book – but so might an administrator! A borrower might have the responsibility of knowing what books he or she has borrowed. But that might not work because if they forget . . .! So perhaps the responsibility of knowing what books the borrower has is the responsibility of something else in the system, perhaps a new class called BorrowerRecord. So, in this case, looking at responsibilities turns out to be yet another method of identifying missing (still candidate) classes. Another question: what are the responsibilities of BookAllowance? This seems to be something with a fixed value depending upon the age of the borrower and whether or not they are a donor. It sounds like (potentially) a single integer. So this candidate class seems less likely to survive the 'class cull' than some of the others.

What are the responsibilities of Borrower?
Know how many books in possession

What are the responsibilities of Customer?
Know how many books in possession

Both Borrower and Customer seem to have identical responsibilities. Unless we can identify some differences in their responsibilities, then we may have to conclude that they are synonyms (at least in this domain) and merge the two classes. One good way to start to answer these questions is to use yet another OPEN Technique: CRC card modeling.

Responsibilities belong to individual classes, being made visible as the features or services (queries and commands) offered by that class. However, for each class to be valuable to the system, it must enter into a collaboration.

For example, a BankAccount class may have a responsibility for knowing its current balance. In order to provide this information, however, it may choose to delegate part of the calculation of 'currentBalance' to another object called InterestTable.

Collaborations are often indicated when one class begins to acquire a large number of responsibilities. Collaborations also represent coupling and, so, at the same time, minimization of coupling is a goal to be aimed at. A good responsibility-driven design distributes its responsibilities equally over all classes in the system. Minimizing coupling then attempts to simplify the collaboration call patterns.

Initially, only the object name is likely to be known; although if you are modeling in a domain you know well, this itself may suggest to you some likely responsibilities. Tracking how one particular service is fulfilled may identify other responsibilities. So, the person playing the role of the bank account object in a CRC card modeling session (see Chapter 3 for details) may identify that a reasonable responsibility is one for 'knowing the current balance'. Further investigation then suggests that it is not possible for the BankAccount object to fulfil this responsibility alone and that a collaborating object is needed. There may, of course, already be a person playing the InterestTable object, in which case a discussion can ensue about how the responsibilities are variously apportioned between these two classes. In many other cases, the need for an InterestTable is likely to be the discovery of a new and previously unidentified object. Thus, in this context, CRC card modeling is an additional technique for 'finding the objects'. Perhaps a better phrase would be 'refining the list of candidate objects and classes'.

Another use of CRC card modeling sessions might be to trace through a much longer series of connected service requests, perhaps as identified by a use case or task script (see Chapter 5). When a service request requires many interactions, the role play group may choose to pass a token around the group, say a ball thrown between two interacting objects (people representing objects, of course), to symbolize the passing of a message between the two objects thus represented. Indeed, many people find this dynamic aspect of CRC card modeling extremely valuable in envisaging what it means to have a message passing system and, then, for this particular system, how the classes are likely to interact. For example, a ball repetitively ball thrown back and forth between two objects, ignoring all others, is likely to be indicative of one class incorrectly split into two.

In our library example, each of the team members would write out a card for one (or possibly two) of the candidate objects listed in Table 4.1. Perhaps the person playing the role of the Borrower declares that a Borrower 'can borrow books' so that the service *borrow* represents a responsibility of each borrower object. Such a service would have to take as argument an object of type Book. But just a minute. When a borrower borrows a book, that is an old-fashioned description of an actor initiating an action. It is functionally oriented, not object-oriented. In OPEN (and other OO methods), the best way to translate a statement like 'a borrower borrows a book' is to parse it. While the verb does indeed become a service (probably eventually a method), the object to which this service is attached is an object identified by the grammatical direct object of the sentence, in this case 'book'. The grammatical subject of the sentence is then the client of the object which we have just identified: Figure 4.6. Now the normal rule for client–server interactions in object-oriented design and programming is that the server object has no knowledge of the client object. This is clearly seen in a diagram like Figure 4.6 because of the unidirectional visibility indicated by the arrowhead. But in being borrowed, a book needs to be told about 'by whom'. In other words, when the message borrow is received, there needs to be an argument borrower:Borrower (Figure 4.7). But then is borrower still the

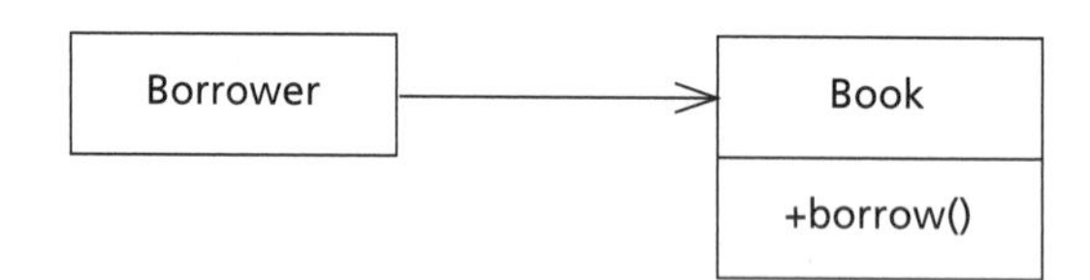

Figure 4.6 Classes Borrower and Book identified by textual analysis of the requirements document

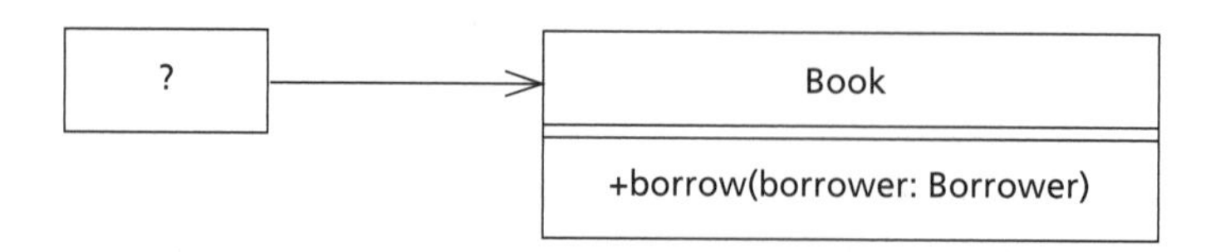

Figure 4.7 Revision of Figure 4.6 leads to indecision as to what the client class should be.

client object if it is the argument object? Somehow the link between a book object and a specific borrower object must be made. Perhaps there is something missing.

It may take some time and discussion before the abstract notion of a Loan object emerges. A Loan consists then of a Borrower and a Book (and probably also information about a time period and so on). A loan is created each time this Borrower–Book link is made (i.e. in real life a borrower borrows a book). Who creates this loan object? Probably a Lender abstraction – although this now means we have two new objects (and two new CRC cards with people role-playing them). Try out different possibilities; try out different objects; try to identify concepts, like Loan, *not* in the requirements specification or in the initial list of objects. Experiment. Often objects consolidate because their need becomes apparent from study of *more than one* particular service invocation.

Operations can all too easily be misidentified with respect to the object to which they apply (Figure 4.8). Ask yourself the question 'Can I do this operation if I were this class?' Does the Account class in Figure 4.8 know how to deposit money? Most likely, the answer is yes. Depositing is an intrinsic part of being a (bank) account. This correlates also to a second way of identifying correct location of operations. If class A (here Teller) requires class B (Account) to be in some specific state before it can execute an operation, then there needs to be some way to change that state. In other words, there needs to be some service in the interface of B which is provided for changing the state. So deposit and withdraw are part of account, because I may need to make several deposits to put the Account into a state of 'withdrawals possible' since the bank's rule is that I cannot withdraw money from my bank account unless the balance exceeds some prespecified threshold.

CRC card modeling started us thinking about how objects collaborate. And when these objects, which we have just been anthropomorphizing, collaborate, so typically do the classes of which they are instances. This means that we have started to identify relationships between classes (OPEN Technique: Relationship modeling).

There are many relationships that can exist between classes in an OO system. In

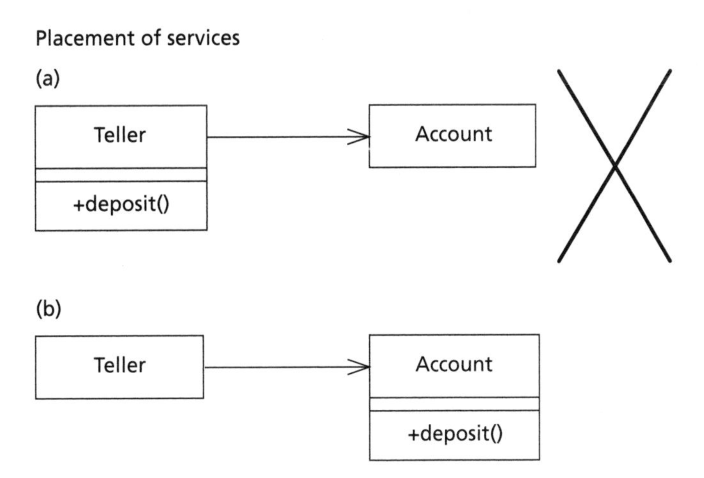

Figure 4.8 Service placement needs careful consideration.

The OPEN Toolbox of Techniques[5] the main categories are association, aggregation, membership, containment, dependency, usage, subclassing, subtyping and powertypes. Here we discuss only associations or mappings and their dynamic counterpart of usage as well as subtyping.

Associations are identifiable as being structural and not transient relationships between pairs of objects. UML also permits ternary associations but the OPEN process suggests that these can generally be decomposed into binary associations without loss of information. While identification of association relationships can occur through many methods, here we identify them when we realize that certain pairs of objects need to inter-communicate. Generally this will be when one object requires the service (or the activation of a feature) of a second object. So in the CRC card modeling exercise, any pair of objects between which a message was passed indicates the need to add a structural relationship – an association – between the two classes corresponding to the objects in the CRC role-play game.

In this (library) example, the CRC exercise identified the equivalence of Administrator and Librarian, Borrower and Customer. It also identified many of the collaborations that are required. Figure 4.9(a) shows how Figure 4.4 has evolved when these associations are added to the diagram. In Figure 4.9(b), the CRC-discovered Loan class is then added and the realization that the librarian is in fact an actor *outside* the system (i.e. a user *of* the software system) is also incorporated into this next version of the class diagram.

Adding relationships between two objects means that one object is offering a service to another object. When the software is run, those services will be requested by message sends. However, there need to be rules governing when such a message send is appropriate and when it is not. For instance, the idea of a customer borrowing a book does not make any sense if the book is not in the library catalogue or if another borrower already has it out on loan. There is a *pre-condition* on the service. Before the 'borrow' service can be invoked, there is a need for the book to be in a state of 'available-for-loan' i.e. it must be in the library and ready to be borrowed. The pre-condition is the business rule that must be met before anything happens. It is part of a contract between the supplier object and the client object. It is usually regarded as part of an individual service of the *server* object.

As well as association and their contracts, we might look for other types of relationships between objects. For example, we might be tempted to look for subtypes as well. Let us resist. Inheritance breaks encapsulation so we need to be *very* sure it is the best relationship to use. We will return to discussion of inheritance later in this case study example.

There is an important, yet seemingly innocuous, OPEN Technique called class naming. Let us utilize that now (and probably repetitively again later). Class naming is an important and influential activity. It can actually influence the way the design develops. And it all sounds so trivial – but it is not! The first guideline is not to be lazy. Do not use short, acronymic names that only you understand. One very important reason for using object technology at all is so that you can communicate with

5 See Bibliography for details.

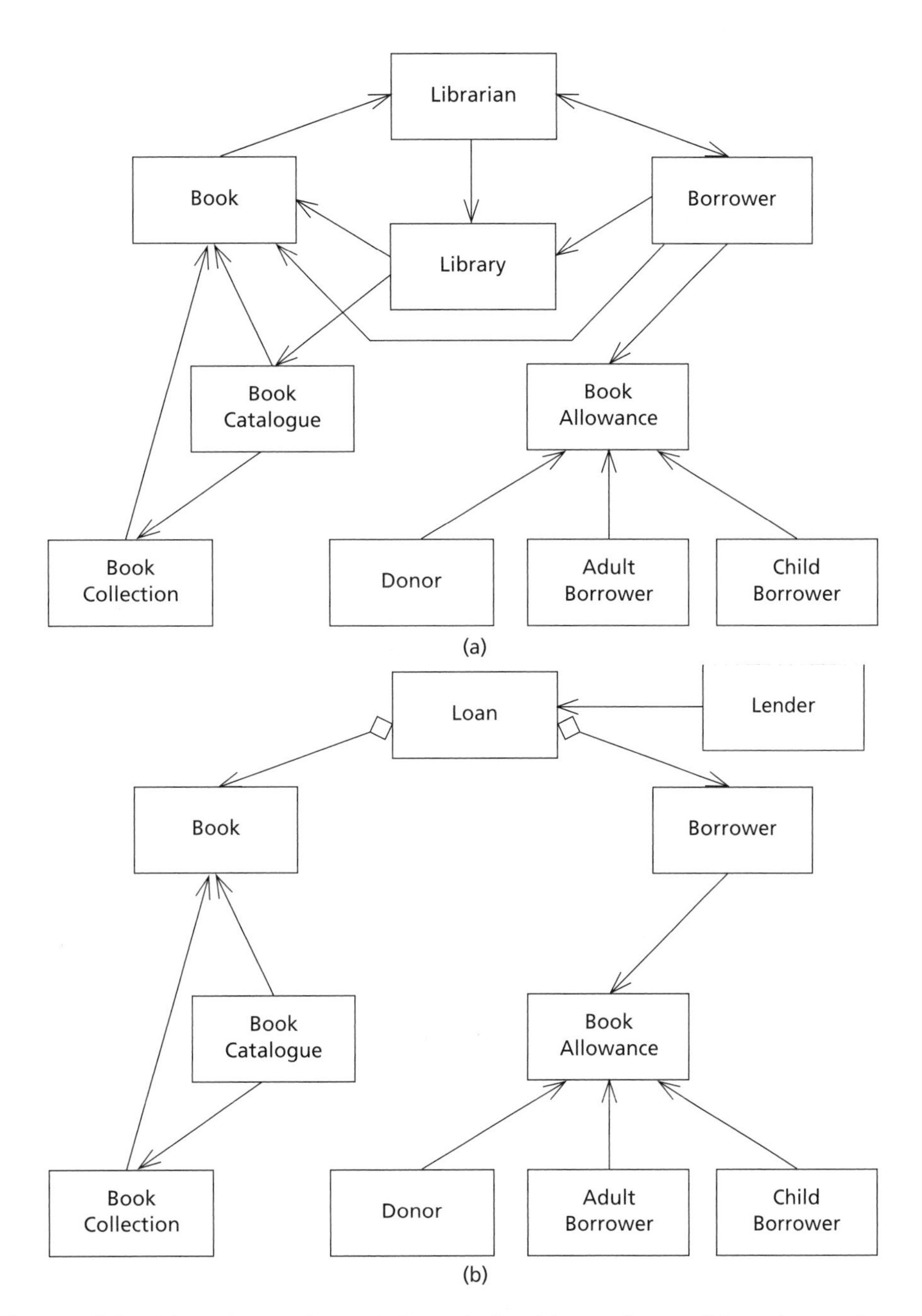

Figure 4.9 (a) Addition of association relationships to the candidate classes of Figure 4.5; (b) revision following introduction of new Loan class

the users and managers. Good class names assist. But even calling a class 'librarian' may not be enough. Is this a software model of the librarian person; or is it really a model of the reservation system? Let us be clear in this, our initial, analysis and design diagram. Decide on a standard way of naming in terms of how to indicate compound names. Is it to be AdultBorrower (the UML standard) or Adult_Borrower or Adult_borrower or ADULT_BORROWER or . . .? If you are bound to a specific programming language you might use the standard forms for that language, e.g. by use of an underscore preceding the name to indicate a system variable if you are using C++. But beware that such pseudo-acronymic approaches might not be understandable by the users and managers. Sometimes two 'standards' pull in opposite directions!

In using UML, there are suggested standards. Here we use some of these, since we do not have any information on the implementation language. UML tells us, wherever possible to

- centre the class name and use bold typeface
- use bold and italic typeface for abstract class names (again centred)
- for stereotype names, use a plain font in guillemets above the class name, again centred
- begin the classname with an upper case letter
- use left justified, plain font for attributes and operations.
- use initial lower case letter for attribute and operation names
- use, in addition to the above, italic font for attributes and operations that are abstract.

Features represent services *offered* and never services demanded. When a service is offered, it is offered equally to all other objects.[6] So, in our example, Teller may send a message to an account object to request a deposit. So could another account object (which might then facilitate the notion of inter-account transfers at a later date). This approach is also a boon to reuse, since the objects we design in this manner are holistic and self-contained. They are autonomous components offering services to the world. It is up to the world (or objects in that world) to take advantage of these offers and send messages. To do this they need to establish a relationship, initially an association which is then turned into a usage relationship later. Note, however, that in OPEN we purposefully confound usage and association as being two sides of the same coin: the dynamic and the static aspects of referential relationships.

Service or feature identification and relationship modeling (particularly for associations) go hand in hand and, although they really are separate techniques, they often occur concurrently. Relationships are the paths between objects but, without services, they are meaningless. Similarly, identification of services of an individual class tends to lead one to think of which other classes are likely to want those services. Sometimes we design services without considering which other classes will access these services. This occurs when we are focusing exclusively on reuse and aiming to design a class that has services that we think future classes might want,

6 This isn't precisely true, since we can use OPEN Technique: Viewpoints to add security and make certain features visible only to a select band of other classes.

despite the fact that current classes in the system under present development might have no use for them at all.

OK. We now have a number of classes with identified features and some associations connecting them (Figure 4.9). But AdultBorrowers, ChildBorrowers and Donors are still unconnected and semantically you are probably by now keen to explore some generalization hierarchy. Generalization and inheritance in general are often identified with OO as being the really exciting concept brought into programming. Yes, but . . . . It certainly helped to sell OO in the early days (late 1980s) but is increasingly being downplayed. The members of the OPEN Consortium have been leaders in suggesting that inheritance is often *not* the best relationship for solving problems. Sometimes it is, sometimes it is not. Do not just assume that, because an AdultBorrower seems to be a special kind of Borrower, an inheritance relationship is going to be best.

But we can see you are not convinced, so let us succumb to your excitement and add some inheritance relationships between AdultBorrower and Borrower, ChildBorrower and Borrower, and Donor and Borrower.

Returning to the library example, can we answer yes to all these questions?

- Is an Adult Borrower a kind of Borrower?
- Is a Child Borrower a kind of Borrower?
- Is a Donor a kind of Borrower?

Well, yes we can. So it seems reasonable to draw the inheritance structure as in Figure 4.10. The white arrowhead can be taken to mean 'is-a-kind-of' and to permit dynamic substitutability by use of subtyping and polymorphism. If I send a request to a borrow object and it is rerouted to a donor or a childBorrower object, then I can expect everything to work fine.

Some further work can be done by realizing that the 'business rules' for these three types of borrower fall into two groups: child borrowers and adult borrowers are identical except for their borrowing limit; whereas donors make a payment and have an unlimited borrowing capacity – this also means that if a donor loses a book, no action needs to be taken to adjust the borrowing limit. Thus an improved hierarchy might be as shown in Figure 4.11. In fact, we might go even further (Figure

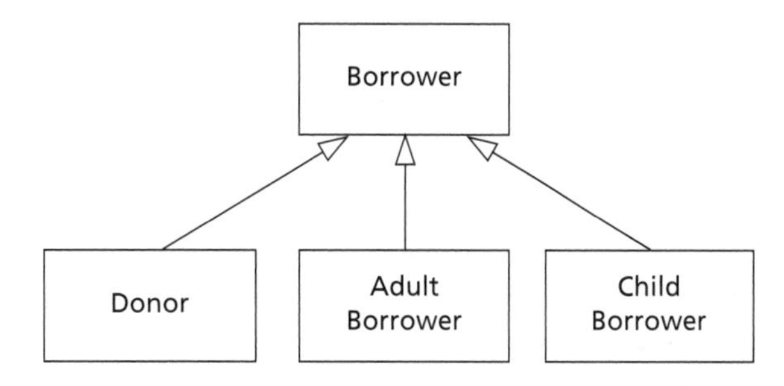

Figure 4.10 Identification of potential generalization hierarchy

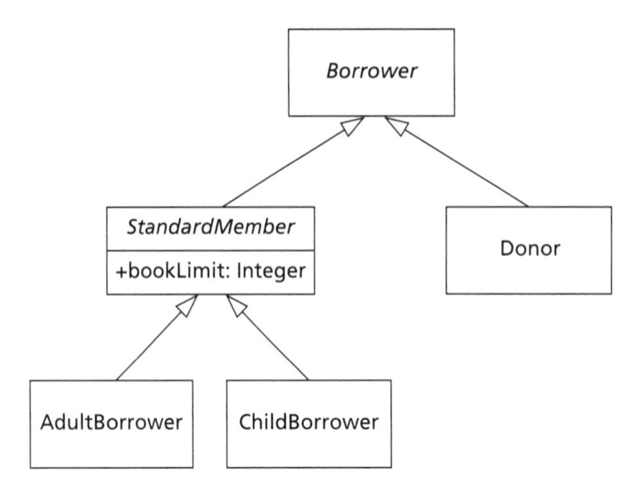

Figure 4.11 Revised hierarchy (*cf*. Figure 4.10) for Borrower and its subclasses

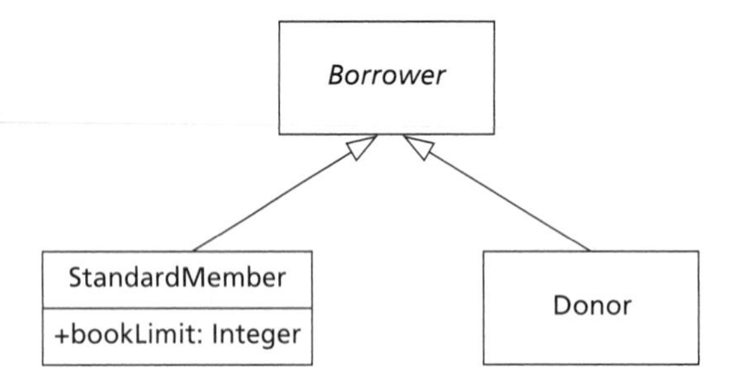

Figure 4.12 Elimination of AdultBorrower and ChildBorrower – replaced by more sophisticated business rules in the StandardMember class

4.12) by simply associating a business rule with bookLimit. This would be used upon creation as follows:

```
If standard_member.age .lt. 12
    bookLimit = 3
else
    bookLimit = 5
endif
```

Another service might update this upon a child's 12th birthday.

Another small improvement (with reusability in mind) might be to add an abstract supertype of Book called LibraryItem. This would permit the library in the future to lend videos, CDs, etc., which would then be readily representable as subtypes of this LibraryItem class.

So what is the problem? Well, there are two issues to look at regarding generalization/specialization inheritance. Firstly, are the subtypes permanent? Specialization inheritance is closely akin to knowledge representation and it is essentially static. If the subtype is a kind of the supertype then it is always a kind of the supertype. Is this correct here? Yes, but there is another problem (see below). Secondly, do the subtypes partition the supertype so that it is correct to say that an instance of the subtype is also an instance of the supertype? If so, then conversely, if I send a message to an instance of the supertype without clear knowledge of which of the partitions is currently being referred to, I will still get a successful response because the supertype can be replaced at runtime (dynamically) by the subtype. This is polymorphism – one of the major elements in the object paradigm. In terms of relationships this is often known as either generalization, knowledge representation, is-a-kind-of or subtyping.[7]

Now we consider that other problem we mentioned above with regard to static inheritance hierarchies. We have here the general idea that a Borrower may be either a child or an adult. While you might argue these partitions are static at the class level, they are clearly not static at the dynamic level. An individual instance of ChildBorrower does not remain an instance of that class. He or she grows up and changes into the AdultBorrower class. So how is that supported? Before we answer that question, consider also the question about whether Borrower (which may be adult or child) is even the appropriate concept to be modeling. How about considering that the main concept should be Adult and Child playing a role of Borrower? That is nearer to real life and is an important alternative to the static model of Figure 4.10. We will discuss the OPEN Technique of Role modeling below. But before we do that, let us continue in the (perhaps mistaken) belief that the inheritance structure of Figure 4.10 is optimum. Before we finish, we need to employ the OPEN Technique of Abstract class identification.

At this stage, we may undertake another round of two OPEN Techniques, described and used earlier: collaborations analysis and interaction modeling. In addition, we might begin to use OPEN Technique: Role modeling.

Earlier, we raised in your mind doubts about the validity of describing the relationship shown in Figure 4.10 by generalization. Let us return to this vexed question of role modeling in more detail – vexed because our desire to redraw Figure 4.10 as in Figure 4.13 is not fully in accord with the use of role models in UML. In UML, while ClassifierRoles and AssociationRoles *are* available in the metamodel, their use is only permissible on UML collaboration diagrams – and we want to use them on class diagrams.

For example, in the library system, we may model the states of a book as

TO BE CATALOGUED
AVAILABLE
BORROWED
LOST OR STOLEN

7 These are only approximate synonyms – the differences are not important at present. If you want more information consult *The OPEN Toolbox of Techniques* book.

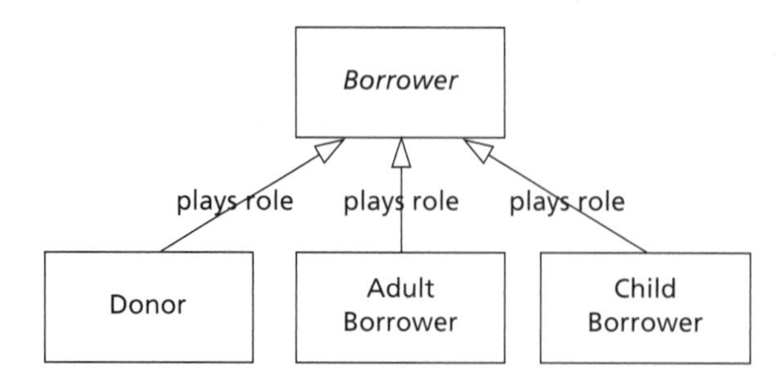

Figure 4.13 Realization that the generalization hierarchy of Figure 4.10 is inappropriate since all the relationships are better described by the 'plays role of' relationship (note: not UML notation)

What events occur to change the state of a book object? A borrower borrowing a book will change the book's state from AVAILABLE to BORROWED; an administrator may catalogue the book and thus change its state from TO BE CATALOGUED to AVAILABLE. These state changes need to be linked to services offered by the book object. For example, when a loan object is created, the message that is sent by the loan object to the book object changes its state to borrowed (Figure 4.14). Note that since the borrow method has a pre-condition of 'state-available', it would be a wise design that preceded the 'borrow' message by a 'check-if-available' message (a query on the state). Thus we have identified a new service that must be offered by each book object – 'is-available' (Figure 4.15). This will probably need to be added to both the class diagram (as in Figure 4.15) as well as to the state transition diagram (Figure 4.16).

Having neared the end of one iteration towards a reasonable cut at the class model, it might be an appropriate time to consider how to make the necessary

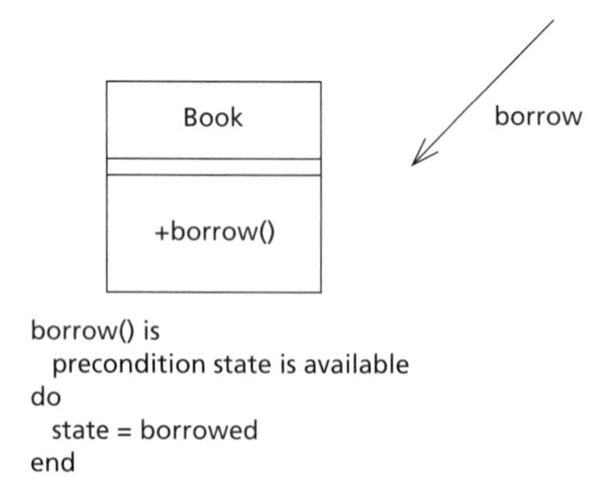

Figure 4.14 Incoming messages (here borrow) need to meet the pre-condition on the service being requested. Request for action (a command) will change the state (in contrast to a query which does ***not*** cause a state change).

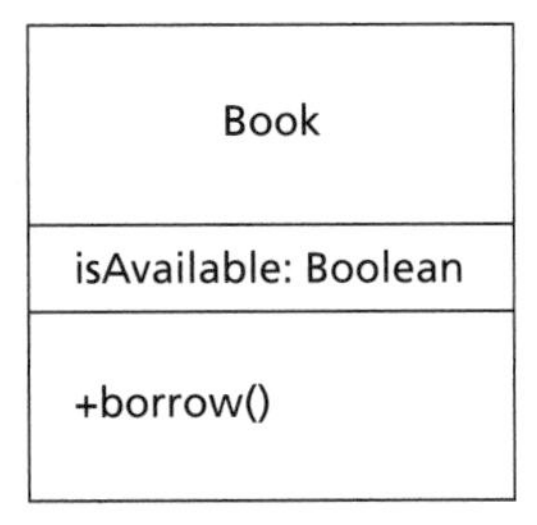

Figure 4.15 Adding dynamics (as in Figure 4.14) has led us to identify a missing feature.

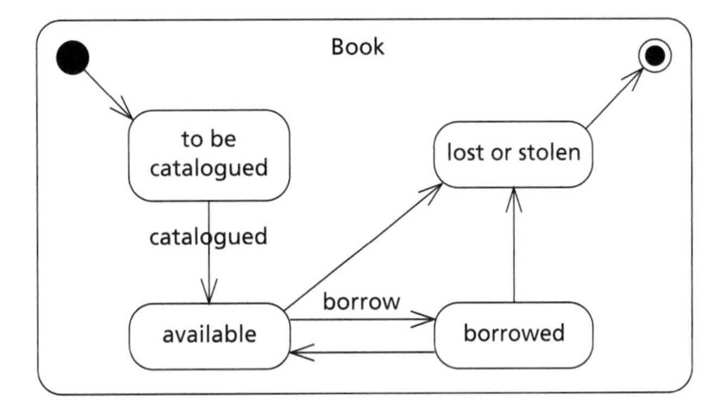

Figure 4.16 State model for the book object

objects persistent. If you are using an objectbase (object-oriented database) product, then the mapping is straightforward since the database will use the same model as you have been doing during the application development. Using a relational database is a little more difficult.[8] Annotating persistence can be readily done in UML using a stereotype (Figure 4.17).

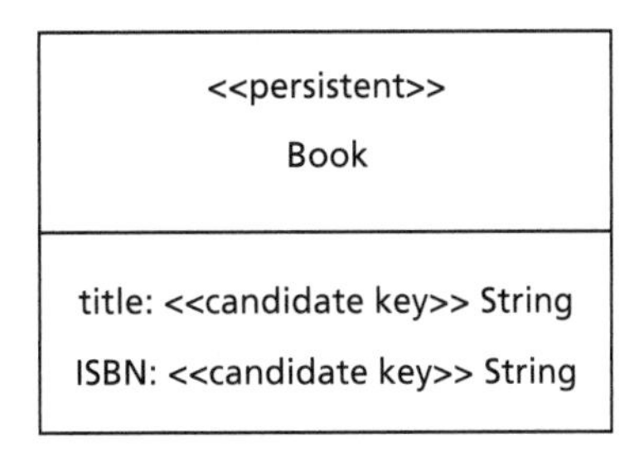

Figure 4.17 Using a stereotype in UML to indicate persistence (based on Ambler, 1999)

8 See discussion in *The OPEN Toolbox of Techniques.*

At some stage in the iterative process, we also need to consider the design of the GUI interface. We will not spend a lot of time on this because that is not intended to be the focus of this book. There are other excellent books on this topic.[9] However, we *do* note that the requirements were couched in terms of an implicit user interface: one with options selected by the user. These could be represented by the inheritance model shown in Figure 4.18.

Prototyping is an OPEN Technique that might be considered at around this time as we refine our model. Prototyping is the rapid creation of a mockup of the system to test out a portion, or an idea – perhaps how one particular user screen may look, perhaps whether a specific role model fragment makes sense and/or is not hopelessly inefficient. Naturally, prototyping involves translating the evolving design into code. So let's look now at some of the issues relating to class internal design and implementation.

Before coding, decisions have to be taken at a very low level. Should you use by-value or by-reference semantics (if that choice is available in your chosen language)? How will you code the various relationships – the OPEN Technique of Design templates may be useful here (for details see the full *The OPEN Toolbox of Techniques*)? Are logical attributes (queries) to be coded as physical attributes or associations? Do you need to build in destructors and a garbage collection policy (e.g. in C++)? What visibility (public, protected, private) will each method have? How are 'selection' control structures to be coded? What use is to be made of existing libraries (of coded classes)? Is there any opportunity to use patterns and, increasingly, of existing third-party components? A myriad of questions, only a few of which will pertain to any one project.

Since OPEN fully encourages a 'programming by contract' metaphor, the code needs to include explicitly pre- and post-conditions on all its public methods. In addition, exception handling should be treated seriously and with care.

If the system is a distributed one, it is best to design and code it first as if it is a

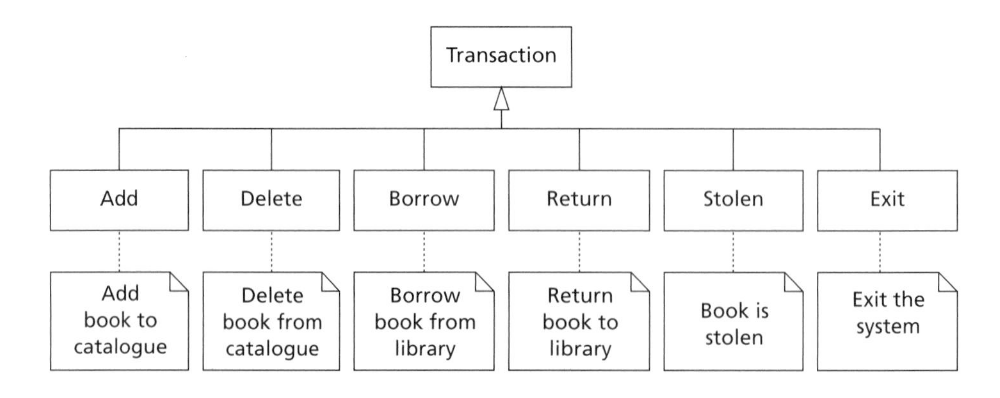

Figure 4.18 User interface design shown using UML (based on Ambler, 1999)

9 We recommend the book by Constantine and Lockwood (1999).

non-distributed system and satisfy the distributed requirements later, once the design is stabilized and thoroughly tested.

Implementation of structure in OPEN requires coding decisions to be taken between implementation of (logical) attributes as either data or associations to other objects. Patterns (such as Mediator) or design templates – as described in two other OPEN Techniques – may also offer some support here. In addition, an aim of ensuring loose coupling is to be encouraged.

As an example, in Figure 4.19 we show the Java code for the classes of Figure 4.9(b). Each class is a separate module, headed by 'public class'. The internals here are simply references to other classes with which it may wish to communicate. Since there are, as yet, no features specified on the classes in Figure 4.9(b), none appear in Figure 4.19.

Figure 4.19 Java code showing some of the details of classes from the design shown in Figure 4.9(b)

```
public class Librarian
{
 private Book Librarian_Book;
 private Borrower Librarian_Borrower;
 private Library Librarian_Library;
}

public class Book
{
 private Librarian Book_Librarian;
 private Library Book_Library;
 private BookCatalogue Book_BookCatalogue;
 private BookCollection Book_BookCollection;
 private Borrower Book_Borrower;
}

public class Library
{
 private Book Library_Book;
 private Borrower Library_Borrower;
 private Librarian Library_Librarian;
 private BookCatalogue Library_BookCatalogue;
}

public class Borrower
{
 private Librarian Borrower_Librarian;
 private BookAllowance Borrower_BookAllowance;
 private Library Borrower_Library;
```

```
 private Book Borrower_Book;
}

public class BookCatalogue
{
 private Book BookCatalogue_Book;
 private BookCollection BookCatalogue_BookCollection;
 private Library BookCatalogue_Library;
}

public class BookCollection
{
 private BookCatalogue BookCollection_BookCatalogue;
 private Book BookCollection_Book;
}

public class BookAllowance
{
 private Borrower BookAllowance_Borrower;
 private Donor BookAllowance_Donor;
 private AdultBorrower BookAllowance_AdultBorrower;
 private ChildBorrower BookAllowance_ChildBorrower;
}

public class Donor
{
 private BookAllowance Donor_BookAllowance;
}

public class AdultBorrower
{
 private BookAllowance AdultBorrower_BookAllowance;
}

public class ChildBorrower
{
 private BookAllowance ChildBorrower_BookAllowance;
}
```

4.5 V&V

Once we have some code, we can start to worry about checking its validity. Loosely grouped under the heading of Verification and Validation (V&V) are a number of such OPEN Techniques. In the context of our small case study example, we will use one or more of the four recommended in Chapter 3 (Section 3.15.1): inspections, walkthroughs, unit testing, package and subsystem testing.

Walkthroughs are semi-formal examinations of a work product by a small team of peers. The walkthrough is led by the author of the design or code. He or she explains the objectives and then the detail of the work product. Readability is considered, as is an examination of alternatives – a think-tank atmosphere prevails. The aim is not to identify defects (this is the role of an inspection) although if these are found, they are of course noted.

4.6 User review

We have already seen responsibility identification from the point of view of the developers. But since responsibilities also exist in the real world, the user can often identify missing responsibilities directly as they participate in the user review. Similarly, inspections and walkthroughs now involve the user rather than just the development team and are likely to shed new light on many issues – although, of course, a good OO team will have had significant input from at least one user all the way through the development cycle!

Class naming now has a different focus. Developers' names may not (but we hope they do) have meaning in the user's domain. If the development has gone well, then the OPEN Technique: Class naming may be insubstantial here. If not, then it is crucial that the user understands the names in order to make a useful assessment of the design and ultimately the product to be delivered and used by themselves and their colleagues.

Even with a small system such as the library simulation, it is wise to start to collect some metrics. Let us focus here on design metrics: measures of the way in which the architecture can be said to represent a good (or a bad) design. While there are many ways of assessing complexity, some measures of size as well as coupling may be useful. Size should be assessed at the method level as well as the class level. Thresholds should be considered at least to provide 'rules of thumb'. So, for instance, any methods longer than a few lines of code (maximum 15) should be regarded with high suspicion (good methods are 2–4 lines of uncommented code). Coupling can be measured in several ways: the easiest is in terms of fan-out. An example is shown in Figure 4.20 in which fan-out values are shown explicitly. Ideally, coupling should be pretty evenly distributed across the system. In Figure 4.20 we find that fan-out values do not exceed 2. There is no 'god class' with a large fan-out value supported by lots of classes with a zero fan-out value. On the other hand, there are a couple of classes with zero fan-out which we might double-check on to make sure they are viable as independent classes rather than as attributes of some other class. In this case, we can justify their inclusion.

Metrics are a critical part of a quality programme. Not only do they give insights into current designs (as illustrated above) but they also provide an increasing baseline of knowledge across many projects for future use in cost estimation, quality assurance, and so on.

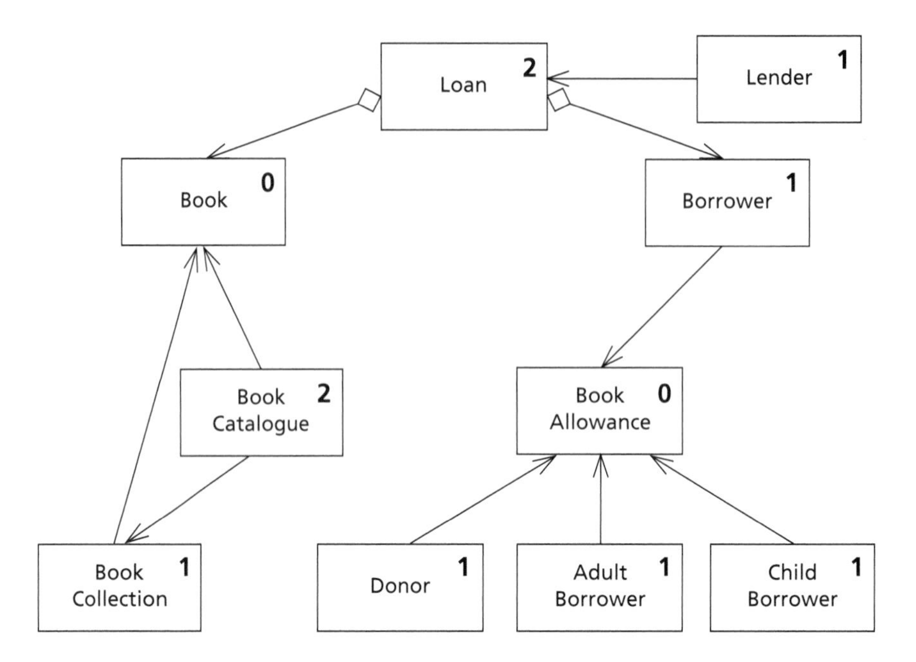

Figure 4.20 Fan-in and fan-out values for the design shown earlier in Figure 4.9(b)

4.7 Consolidation

Consolidation is an activity in which no new techniques are introduced. It takes place after the OOA/D/P and V&V iterations have been completed and typically after user review. It is most useful to consolidate timeboxes when these have been used as well as consolidating the choice of classes and their potential reusability, and the quality of user and technical documentation. It is a final check on *everything*.

4.8 Evaluation

This is an important Activity, particularly for large-scale commercial systems. It is a formal review and evaluation, prior to implementation (deployment) at the user's site. Again it involves the users or their representatives as well as the project sponsors and developers. It is a decision point on whether the software is deployable or should be reworked or abandoned.

Inspection techniques (see Chapter 3) are useful here, as are metrics. Reuse potential should be considered and any remaining defects identified. The objectives of the evaluation include the following.

1. Authorization for continuation of the product (YES/NO)
2. Authorization of delivery to user (YES/NO)

3. Reusability identification
4. Acting as focal point for metrics
5. Comparison against plan
6. Finalizing deployment plan (or rework plan if not yet ready for deployment)
7. Evaluation of impact of any remaining defects and a plan to rectify them as soon as feasible.

The activity should ideally be undertaken within one working day, and in no circumstance be allowed to extend to more than 10.

Summary of Key Points

- Using a responsibility-driven approach applied to a simple problem of a library information system has permitted us to explore that part of OPEN pertinent to the analysis and design level of modeling.
- To do this, we made the (gross) assumption that we were starting with a known and immutable requirements specification.
- This then permitted us to focus clearly and concisely on just those OPEN elements relevant to modeling.

Case Study 2

Small Business Loans System – a use case study for the Web

Abstract

OPEN, as a process environment, is extremely helpful in large-scale software development. This chapter accentuates the use of the OPEN process in a relatively larger system developed for business loans given out by a bank. This chapter is replete with process and modeling comments which highlight the practical issues related to the development. Since almost all 'new' development has to integrate with some 'existing' system, relevant integration issues have been pointed out in this chapter. Thus, although the focus of this book is 'modeling' and the process related to modeling, this is a more extensive chapter that takes us through many important activities and tasks of OPEN that also deal with issues other than lower-level design. As one of the available approaches, we have based this discussion on the use case approach to requirements modeling.

5.1 Scope of the case study

This second case study is relatively larger and more complex than the one in the previous chapter and also deals with process-related issues for web-based development. This case study includes significant aspects of the OPEN configurable lifecycle – and highlights the way in which development for a relatively large web-based application can take place. In this chapter, we show you how to:

(a) tailor the OPEN lifecycle to create a specific SEP or Software Engineering Process for large system development, and

(b) apply the process in detail in the specification and development of a sophisticated system that handles the small business loans for a bank.

While we give more 'process' advice here than in the earlier case study, the discussion is still focused on how the modeling issues fit in with the overall process.

Almost all software development in the new millennium is likely to have an element of web-based architecture. This new development is also going to face the problem of integration with the existing 'legacy' applications. As a result of these requirements, 'distribution' will be an invariable part of the architecture of the system. In this chapter, we discuss process and modeling issues that are related to these issues of web architecture, interfacing with an existing legacy architecture and distribution.

Furthermore, in contrast to Chapter 4 in which we used the 'responsibility-driven design' (RDD) style of modeling, in this chapter we adopt the 'use-case-driven' approach and highlight *its* advantages and limitations in modeling software systems. In this context, it is worth mentioning that all our discussions related to a use case apply only to this current discussion in which the decision to use a use-case-driven approach is a *pre-condition.* There are a number of software development situations wherein a use-case-driven approach *may not be* appropriate – a classic example being back-end systems development or integration, wherein there are *no actors.* These issues are also highlighted in this chapter.

We discuss, in this chapter, the technological and methodological aspects of development which, as you will recall (Figure 1.4), form two of the three major dimensions of a process. However, any large and complex project, such as the one we are discussing in this case study, will also involve sociological and project management issues that are important and that should be handled right from the outset to ensure the success of the project. These issues have a greater impact on the business processes than on the software development processes, as shown in Figure 5.1. Although their detailed discussion is outside the scope of this 'modeling' book, they are mentioned wherever relevant, albeit briefly. Detailed discussion of such

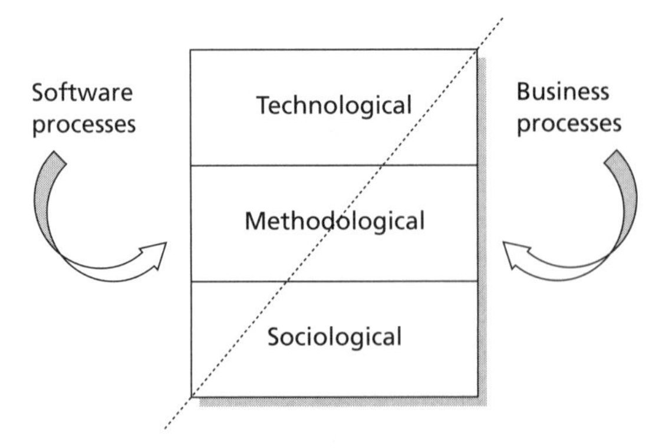

Figure 5.1 Mapping of business and software processes with the OPEN process environment (after Unhelkar, 1999; © CRC Press)

sociological and project management issues, particularly the extent to which they influence the software processes as well as the business processes, are discussed in other books in the OPEN series.

5.2 The OPEN process in practice

We have shown in Figure 1.15 in Chapter 1 how the various artefacts of the OPEN process are brought together in order to create a specific Software Engineering Process (SEP) that is relevant to a particular domain (such as banking or finance) or to a particular organization (i.e. specific to a company). That discussion on the creation of a SEP can be applied to any project – mostly before the start of the project – to ensure that the SEP followed during the project is *optimum*.[1] Based on the discussion in Section 1.2, we create, in this chapter, a SEP that is specific for our web-based development example.

Creation of a SEP for our development depends on a number of factors, including:

(a) The main artefacts of the OPEN process, namely the Activities, Tasks and Deliverables/Work Products
(b) The iterative and incremental lifecycle represented by the fountain or 'contract-driven' model of software development
(c) A set of rules and guidelines, together with the experience of a process engineer to bring together the lifecycle and the artefacts of the process into an *executable* SEP.

Detailed description of the repository of all Activities, Tasks, Techniques and Deliverables/Work Products has been provided in the reference manuals of OPEN (see Bibliography). Here, we discuss the way in which these artefacts will be combined to create a specific SEP for web-based development of a Business Loans System (called BLS for short).

OPEN's SEP is made up of a 'contract-driven' set of Activities. Some of these Activities are performed *iteratively,* meaning that the same activity may be repeated in two or three iterations (see Chapter 1) during the actual development. Some of these Activities of OPEN either are at a higher level of abstraction (such as project initiation) or, during their initial iteration, remain at the higher level. As against these 'higher-level' activities or their iterations, there are other activities that are more concrete in nature. These are performed approaching and during the implementation of the system (which would happen during the later iterations of the same Activity). These two types of activities and/or their iterations can be 'loosely' called *higher-level* and *lower-level* activities, as shown in Figure 5.2. The focus of the higher-level activities is more strategic and at a higher level of abstraction – typically performed during the earlier stages of the lifecycle. The lower-level activities, which

1 Not too heavy with all Activities, Tasks and Techniques included, and not too light with only a few sketchy Deliverables.

Requirements Engineering
Architecture:
Needs *abstract* thinking
Experience and domain knowledge helpful
Easily *changeable*, not implementable
Need to think *FOR* reuse
Design; Coding:
Concrete lower-level implementation thinking
Programming language, database knowledge essential
Not easy to change
Need to think *WITH* reuse

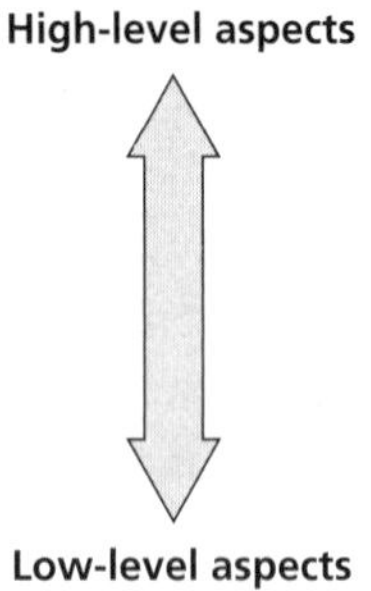

Figure 5.2 High- and low-level activities in the OPEN process

tend to be tactical or operational in nature, are usually performed during the later stages of the lifecycle when the core or final iteration of the Activity is being performed.

We will consider activities that belong to both 'levels' in creating and using a SEP for the Business Loan System development. A point to note from the *process* viewpoint is that the creation of an SEP is itself a higher-level activity performed early in the project. In order to demonstrate this SEP creation and its subsequent application in the development of an object-oriented model for Business Loans, we will delve briefly into the problem statement.

5.3 The problem statement

Let us spend a few minutes understanding the problem statement. The problem dealt with in this case study is that of a bank, hypothetically called COMMERCIAL Bank. It has an existing client base that comprises personal customers, small businesses and large corporations. The bank has successfully carried out its operations within a developed country within the Asia-Pacific region (let's say Australia, for the sake of this case study).

The corporate strategic planners of the bank have identified numerous areas in the banking sector in which COMMERCIAL bank needs to lift its game – especially in the new millennium. One of these areas is that of loans taken out by 'small businesses'. Small business loans are differentiated from personal loans and large commercial loans by the amount and duration of the loan. The small business loans area is 'hotting up' primarily because the business strategists and planners have identified a large area of potential market that, in the new millennium, will be trying to set up its own businesses and will be attempting to ride on the wave of ebullience sweeping throughout the world. However, in order to succeed in the small business sector of the market, COMMERCIAL bank needs a *technologically 'savvy'* software system that will support the business in a large geographical region focused on the countryside, where a single branch of the bank supports a large number of small businesses in and around the town. The bank's planners also believe that it will be essential to create a web-enabled application, since this is the only viable way to reach its potential customers who are geographically distributed over a wide region. A web-enabled application is also a major way to take on the competition from the foreign banks coming to the Asia-Pacific region, riding on the Internet wave.

Small business loans are typically taken out by borrowers who are running small-time businesses such as restaurants, take-away food outlets and flower shops, or who are tradesmen. Small business loans may also be taken out by 'mums and dads' investors to participate in public floats of large companies, or to borrow money to invest in the property market. More often than not, the small business owners are also personal account holders in the bank. If the borrowers are not already customers of the bank (i.e. having existing accounts with the bank), the business requirements state that all information that is stored for any other customer should be stored for them as well. If the person is already a customer, then that information can be strategically used by the bank to 'cross-sell' the new loans product to potential borrowers. Otherwise, the new 'customer-related' details of a person provide the bank with a personal profile that can be used in the decision-making process for granting loans. Thus, the scope of the loans is relatively small in terms of the amount of money ($50,000 to $500,000) that would need to be tracked over a relatively long time frame (2 to 5 years and occasionally even 10 years[2]).

The purpose of the BLS (code name for Bank Loan System) is to provide system support for the entire process of small business loans. Starting with the process of identifying potential borrowers, BLS should provide support in managing the information related to the borrowers, identifying and valuing their assets (which they plan to use as security against the loan) and accepting and processing the loan application. Once the loan has been approved, and the amount disbursed, the BLS should also provide mechanisms to monitor the loan throughout its life. It is envisaged that the Internet will provide an important mechanism in helping the borrowers monitor their loans on a day-by-day basis as well as reducing the load on the bank staff.

With this background information on the BLS, we now start applying the OPEN process in the analysis, design and development of the application. It has to be stressed again that the industry standard UML provides the notations for documenting the various object-oriented models appearing in the deliverables or work products of OPEN. For an industrial-strength development, however, we need more than a set of modeling notations – we also need the *process* that helps us understand, plan and execute the development. While the UML provides the notations and models for 'what' gets documented (documenting the technological requirements of the project), the methodological aspect of the OPEN process describes the 'how' of the deliverables. This relationship between OPEN and UML is shown in Figure 5.3. Further note that Figure 5.3 shows an *instantiation* of the OPEN process environment as comparable with other known processes in the industry such as

2 As against the large corporate players who would go for large sums of money (>$1m) over a relatively short period of months or even days.

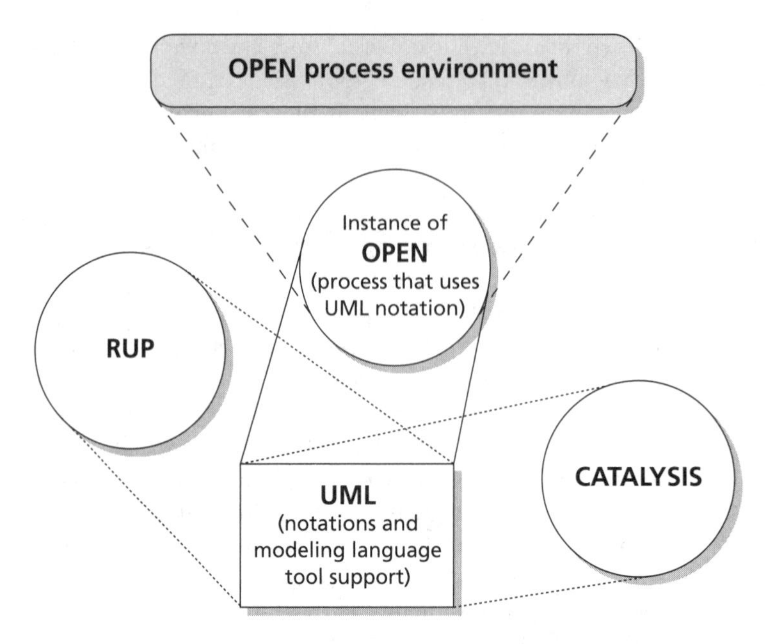

Figure 5.3 Relating the Unified Modeling Language to OPEN and other processes

Rational's Unified Process (RUP™) and Catalysis™. Thus, the significant aspect of comparing these processes with OPEN is that it is an *instantiation* of OPEN that should be compared. OPEN itself is a 'process environment' from which various processes can be 'instantiated' depending on the needs of the user. The relationship between an instantiation of OPEN and the OPEN process environment is also shown in Figure 5.3. When we use the words 'OPEN process' in this chapter, we mean one instance of the OPEN process environment, as used here.

Thus, in practice, we use UML, together with the OPEN process, in order to (a) understand and describe the problem itself, (b) describe the solution, and (c) produce the solution. Diagrams from the UML, such as use case diagrams, use easily understood notations to describe the business reality by documenting a model of the same. Thus, UML together with OPEN can be used to describe the problem through *higher-level* modeling even before it comes within the domain of software development. Once the business reality is properly understood, models of the solution can be created once again using the UML, e.g. class diagrams and component diagrams. Thus we use models to understand the problem as well as create a new solution, as was discussed earlier in Figure 3.1.

Finally, once the project has been initiated (and sometimes, even, during the initiation of the project), the controlling and *tracking* aspect of the entire development comes into play. This is the time when we start applying the process in greater detail for the actual development of the software, as against simply documenting the requirements. The BLS is a relatively new development with very few areas of the system needing integration with existing systems. Therefore, the need to create detailed models for *existing* processes is not that pressing. Instead, we start applying some of the architectural aspects of the OPEN process in dividing and understanding the problem statement itself – which is described next.

Process comment

Note that although we have started describing the problem statement in terms of its higher-level subsystems or 'packages', in practice the 'flow of events' could be slightly different. For example, we may spend some time up front deciding on the activities and tasks we want to perform and the deliverables we want to produce. This 'tailoring of the OPEN lifecycle' is an important higher-level activity in itself, and may be performed either in parallel with the architectural work described next, or before any work on the project begins.

Also note that, although we are starting the process as if it is a totally new development, some integration would be required even in this case study. As described later in detail, this is the integration of the new application with the existing customer-base of the bank.

5.4 The subsystems of BLS

One of the groups of tasks within the OPEN process includes 'large-scale architectural issues'. These tasks deal with 'development of layered designs' as well as 'partitioning the application into subsystems'. Usually, these tasks are undertaken after the initial iteration of the Requirements Engineering activity is complete. This is so because the initial iteration of the higher-level requirements-capturing activity can provide a good understanding of the way in which the application architecture should be layered and partitioned. This approach can be called the 'bottom-up' approach to architectural work as shown in Figure 5.4. However, if the modeling team has sufficient domain expertise and a good understanding of the problem, then some of the architectural group of tasks can be undertaken up front, as is done in this case study. This approach to the architectural work may be called a 'top-down' approach, as shown again in Figure 5.4.

Process comment

Note that while 'top-down' and 'bottom-up' represent the two approaches to architectural work, the actual process of creating the architecture may not be an 'either or' situation. This means that, in practice, the application and system architecture tend to follow both approaches, and may be called 'middle-out'. Thus, the thoughts on 'top-down' and 'bottom-up' only provide a lead-up to the architectural work; once inside the tasks related to architecture, it may not matter how the actual process appears to the 'outside world'.

A re-read of the BLS problem statement will indicate three to four clear *groupings* or *areas* within the problem. Identification of these groups is the beginning of a *top-down* approach to the application architecture. For the sake of our discussion here,

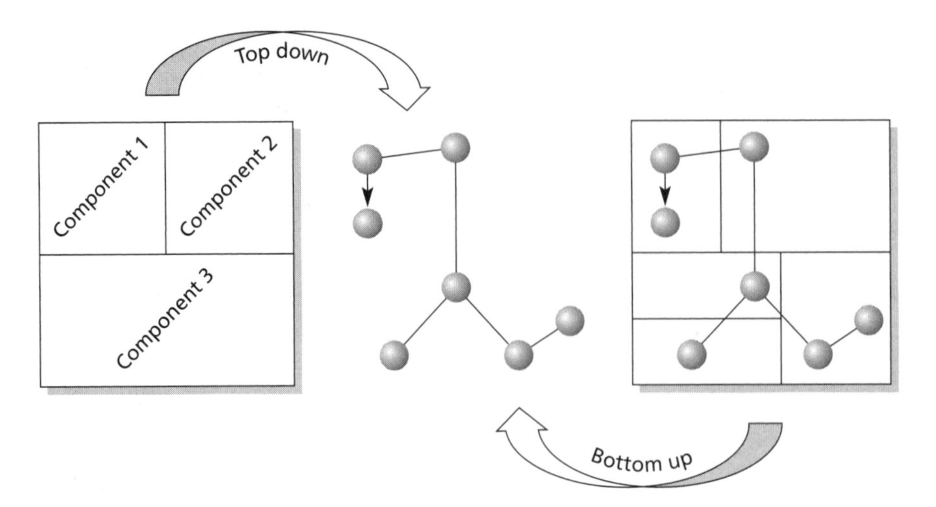

Figure 5.4 Top-down versus bottom-up architectural approaches (after Unhelkar, 1999; © CRC Press)

these *groups* of requirements that emerge from the description of the problem may be described as follows:

- All details related to the customer – this area primarily deals with all details of existing customers of the bank. Details of new borrowers, who are made up of either existing or new customers, are also maintained in this 'module'. Thus, from the outset, it becomes apparent that this module will have to deal with 'integration' issues – the existing system that deals with maintenance of current customers, and the area of the new system that will be storing additional details related to the borrower and new customers making up the borrower.
- All information related to the assets, which will be provided as security against the loan. Since the Bank Loan System is primarily focusing on the new development of the small business loans, and since the bank must be having some mechanism related to storing asset details, it may be said that even this area of the problem will have to deal with integration issues – integrating the existing mechanism to store and maintain details of customers' assets, and the new mechanisms needed in order to 'mark' the value of the asset to its current market value. A major new functionality that has to be added here is the calculation of the total 'collateral' that the assets offer.
- All details related to the making of the application, registering and approving the loan, as well as tracking the loan. All these are new areas in the development of the Bank Loan System.
- Finally, there would be a controlling group of requirements that would include the overall management of the system itself, printing and dispatching reports

with control totals, and so on. These group of activities would deal with providing the bank itself with information related to how its product is shaping up in the market and whether the bank has made or lost money. Since the focus of the current book is 'modeling', we will not delve into the details of this controlling group of requirements. However, a practical system will have to consider these additional requirements that may not deal with the functional aspect of providing and tracking loans.

The groupings or areas of the requirements will start shaping up as subsystems or packages. The major subsystems or packages of the BLS, identified at this early stage, are readily shown in a package diagram in Figure 5.5. This diagram shows that the Bank Loan System (BLS) *depends* on three distinct subsystems (or packages) which are outlined above. Further description of each of these subsystems (as a part of the overall requirements capturing exercise) is now provided.

Modelling comment

From a pure modeling viewpoint, this dependency between the BLS and its corresponding subsystems (viz. CISS, LASS and SASS) is semantic. If this dependency is viewed at a more concrete or 'syntactical' level, then it would translate to a class or classes from BLS depending on – or sending messages to – the interface classes from one of the three subsystems. In the process that we are following, this is only an early attempt to identify subsystems. We have not yet reached the later iterations, wherein the dependencies shown in Figure 5.5 become more concrete.

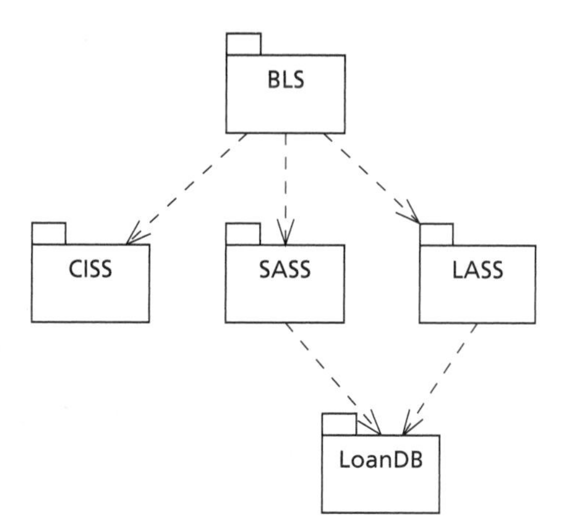

Figure 5.5 BLS (Bank Loan System) package diagram showing how the BLS package is dependent upon three other packages: CISS (Customer Information Subsystem), SASS (Security Asset Subsystem) and LASS (Loan Approvals Subsystem). In turn, these last two are dependent upon a fourth package called LoanDB (Loan DataBase).

5.4.1 Customer Information Subsystem (CISS)

The CISS provides all the customer-related information to the BLS. This includes (but is not restricted to) the name, address, phone/fax/email details, personal interests of the customer and so on. Each of these entities can have many variations. For example, address can be residential and mailing, local and overseas and so on. The business experts have clarified that when customers of the bank take out loans, they become 'borrowers'. The bank rules currently state that in order to become a borrower, a group of two or more customers will have to form a 'borrowing entity'. This also happens to be a legal requirement, wherein loans for business purposes can be given out to a 'business entity' that is made up of at least two individual customers (these rules do not apply to personal borrowers). Thus, a borrower is a group of two or more customers of the bank who have formed a legal entity to borrow funds for business purposes. They are called a 'borrowing entity' or, simply, 'borrower'. These borrowers may be pre-existing business partners (e.g. father and son(s); husband and wife; brothers and sisters, friends, and so on), or may have been created anew. Furthermore, the CISS is also meant to provide information to the BLS on the '*value*' of the customer to the bank. This will depend on factors like the number of years or months the customer has been with COMMERCIAL bank, their balance amount and so on.

Modeling comment

As already mentioned in the discussion on 'groupings' or 'areas' of the problem statement, note how, on re-reading the problem statement, it becomes evident that some areas of the CISS already exist in the bank's software. For example, there are existing customer-related details already recorded in the bank's database. These are the areas of CISS that will be modified as a result of the new loan system requirements. Other areas of the system are 'new' requirements. These are related to the 'customer' becoming a 'borrower', which require a new place to store borrower-related data. In a large and complex system, there will always be a need to modify existing software and integrate with the existing software, in addition to writing new software. If models for the existing system do not exist, only minimal effort should be spent in modeling the existing system. And during such modeling of an 'existing' system, note that it is quite acceptable to represent the existing (or legacy) modules as packages or components in the new diagrams. This is an important modeling aspect of integrating newer developments with the existing systems.

5.4.2 Security Asset Subsystem (SASS)

This SASS subsystem deals with all information related to the 'Securities and Assets' that will be offered by the customers as collateral for the loan. Each customer can have many assets. Also, one asset can be owned by many customers. This has to be translated into a relationship of 'assets to borrowers'. The SASS should be able to accept various types of assets such as personal homes, commercial properties, stocks and shares, and specialized assets (such as taxi licences), as well as being able to value them. Valuation of these assets will be based on a number of factors, such as the book value of the asset, the duration it has been with the customer, whether there are other loans existing on this asset, and so on.

Modeling comment

Modeling the asset component should be straightforward, and so also the relationship between asset and customer. What is special here is the need for SASS to go 'outside' its domain and retrieve some information related to the market value of the asset being offered as security for the loan, otherwise called collateral. Most medium to large software projects have a need to access external data needing collaborations with external systems. This requires some 'interface-related' work. Furthermore, this need to retrieve external data would also call for some 'distributed architecture' work. The market value of, say, a residential property being offered as collateral may be available from a server that is physically kept in another building or even another city. The system architects will have to ensure that the classes of SASS are able to understand and use the right 'transfer' protocols, in order to access the information they need, if that information is kept on separate machines.

5.4.3 Loan Approvals Subsystem (LASS)

The LASS has two primary functions:

(a) Accepting and approving the loans by balancing the Assets of the customer with the loan amount and term applied for. This will be done by considering the valuation of the asset provided by the SASS and ensuring that the valuation is sufficient to cover the loan amount. If the customer is going to use the returns from the small business in order to service the loan, then it will be essential to determine the potential revenue from the small business. This may be done by comparing the trading results of this business with other similar businesses. The initial loan application process may take place on the phone, but the final loan application will have to be settled in person since documents need to be printed in a suitable format for both parties to be able to sign them. Fees and government duties are another factor to be considered in finalizing the loans approval.

(b) Providing a loan tracking mechanism. This mechanism will allow the bank as well as the borrower to track their loan throughout its life. Printing and posting of statements at regular intervals, providing detailed responses to phone enquiries (perhaps through a call centre), and also consideration of a web-based interface to enable the customer to track their loans themselves are potentially all part of this module or subsystem.

Modeling comment

Note that in order to identify the potential revenue from 'this' business, once again an interface to an external database is required. This database need not be external to the organization, but may be external to the system. In either case, it should be treated as an 'external' system to which messages are sent to get the relevant information. When we discuss use cases, we will show how such an 'external' system is a potential actor to which messages are sent.

5.5 Tailoring the OPEN lifecycle

The discussion in Section 5.3 and 5.4 on the problem statement was to make it more understandable. However, the high-level divisions of subsystems may not occur straight away. Another activity that may go on in parallel, or indeed before the architectural work, is the 'tailoring' of the OPEN lifecycle. This tailoring work revolves around one of the first issues that a project following a formal process faces, that is 'to what degree should the process be followed?'. While process purists feel that *everything* described in a process should be followed, coming from a practical angle we feel that it is neither advisable nor necessary to use each and every artefact described in a process. That is one of the main reasons why OPEN was developed as a process *framework*: an environment which can be (and should be) tailored to meet your own specific process requirements exactly. Instantiating a process, based on the overall artefacts of the OPEN process environment, is what is called 'tailoring'. Figure 1.15 in Chapter 1 showed how a typical software engineering process (SEP) is tailored using the lifecycle model, as well as describing the artefacts from the OPEN process environment. An instantiation of such tailoring was called the Web_SEP in Figure 1.15 (others being COMMERCIAL_SEP to indicate SEP for a company called COMMERCIAL Bank, and Small_System_SEP to indicate a cut-down instantiation of OPEN used for small systems development or for case studies in a university course).

This tailoring of a process (Figure 5.6) is a typical question faced by a development team that has been given a combination of loose sheets of paper describing the problem, supported by comments, flyers and perhaps interviews with the potential 'real users'. While a formal requirements gathering process can commence immediately so that we can start collecting information that is flowing into the project, it is also important, at this early stage, to ensure that all major participants in the development, including users, architects, designers and programmers are in agreement with 'how' the development is going to proceed. This includes the decisions on which activities will be undertaken during the development, as well as the tasks and techniques commensurate with these activities that will help ensure accurate and sufficient collection and modeling of requirements. Deliverables may also be selected at this stage and their formats agreed upon.

Some of the factors that help in tailoring the process at this early stage include:

- Understanding of the *programme* architecture – which is the overall architecture of the enterprise and which will be applicable to many projects within the organization. This understanding of the programme or enterprise architecture ensures that only the relevant tasks and techniques are selected for the project. For

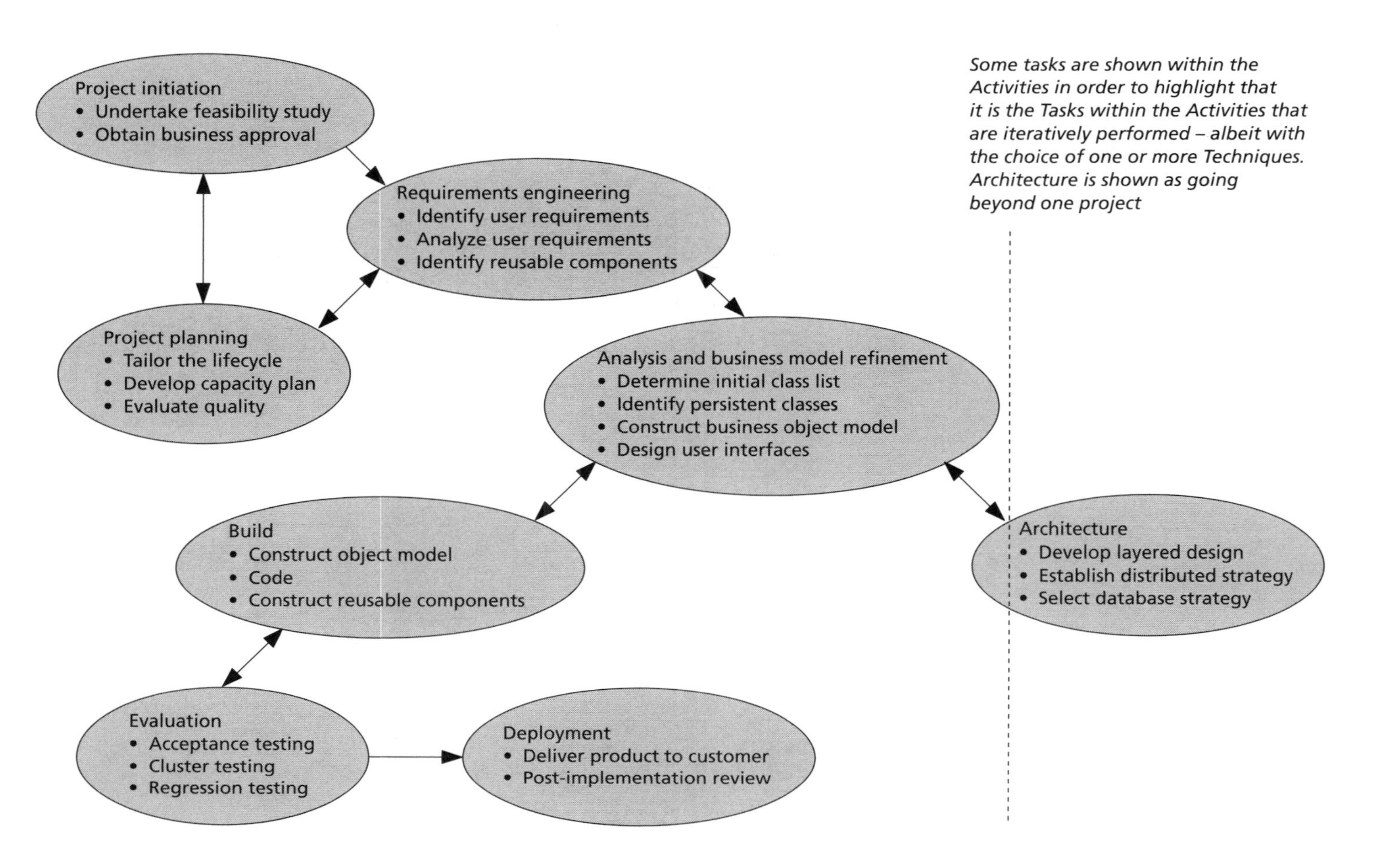

Figure 5.6 An instantiation of the OPEN process for the web-based BLS development

example, if the programme architecture dictates use of a certain database, performing the tasks related to the selection of database becomes irrelevant. Another example would be that the programme dictates use of the Internet, or that the company is itself moving towards an Internet architecture. In that case, the tailored process will contain more tasks, techniques and deliverables related to the usability of the Internet, more security as well as better search facilities on the net.

- Process-based experience – the experience of the person responsible for tailoring, in working in a process-based environment, can be very helpful in the customization process. This is so because the process engineer or project manager is aware of what is available in terms of tasks and techniques within the process and therefore does not spend time *learning* the process, but starts with the tailoring process straight away. In other words, learning the process should be a separate activity from tailoring the process and should not be performed by the same person at the same time. Knowledge of the process (or process environment, as we are calling it in this book) is a pre-condition for the execution of the process-tailoring task.
- Domain knowledge – knowledge of banking or insurance or finance – ensures that the process engineer knows the importance of the Tasks and Techniques relevant to that domain, and would place sufficient importance and weighting on them, as the project unfolds. For example, mathematical formulae might be so important in a financial market modeling project that Tasks and Techniques related to lower-level modeling would be performed first in the project.
- Process maturity needs of the organization – if an organization aims to achieve level 3 on the CMM scale, then it will need a far more rigorous definition of the process than, say, a smaller-sized organization only wishing to adopt the process to ensure that the basic deliverables are defined. In some situations, management may decide that aiming for a higher process maturity is unnecessary and may wish to apply their understanding of the process at a much lower scale. Thus, the important task of tailoring the *Deliverables* of the process (as against simply the Activities–Tasks–Techniques) may also be partly dictated by the maturity needs of the organization. Furthermore, the need to follow the iterative and incremental delivery cycle is also an important requirement for the process-tailoring task.

There are three major aspects in tailoring the OPEN process environment:

- the Activity–Task mapping, describing the selection and weighting of the Activities and corresponding Tasks;
- the Task–Technique mapping, which focuses on the use of certain Techniques to accomplish the Tasks; and
- the Deliverables, alternatively called Work Products, which includes selection and customization of the Deliverables to suit a particular project or domain.

These three aspects of the tailored lifecycle are now presented in the context of the BLS, which is a combination of a WEB_SEP and a BANKING_SEP. Please continue to note that we are not considering the many sociological aspects in this tailoring process. These sociological aspects of the process include issues such as team formation, motivation and morale, skills and training of personnel, and so on. These *do* form an important part of the OPEN process environment, but are outside the scope of this book.

5.5.1 The Activity–Task mapping

Table 5.1 describes a practical Activity–Task mapping for the development of the Bank Loan System. The * ratings indicate the level of importance attached to a certain group of tasks for the corresponding activity (see Table 3.1). This * may either translate in practice into a greater number of iterations of the same group of activities, or result in the activities being performed with more intensity. Thus, effort here translates into time and/or people needed to complete the activities. Both these '*' issues are reflected in a well-construed project plan.

Note that the Activities are executed based on OPEN's 'contract-driven lifecycle'. This means that for each Activity there are a set of pre- and post-conditions. Once these conditions are satisfied, Activities can be executed in any order. However, built into the pre- and post-conditions of the Activities are the safeguards that ensure that Activities are executed in the correct sequence. Furthermore, these Activities (unlike the corresponding phases from the waterfall model) are *not* watertight compartments that have to be completed before the next Activity is started. These Activities are iterative and incremental in nature and, therefore, may be performed more than once during the entire development lifecycle. This iterative nature of the Activities is also reflected in their pre- and post-conditions. Here, we describe the activities and the corresponding grouping of tasks within the activities – with a focus on the requirements modeling and analysis/design aspect of the lifecycle. This is the aspect of the development lifecycle that makes significant use of the UML notation. The deliverables resulting from the requirements modeling and analysis and design feed into the lower-level build iteration, also called coding, which is not of immediate concern to us in our current role of business analyst or system modeler.

5.5.2 Activity: Project initiation

This is the activity that deals with exploring in detail the 'brilliant flash of lightning' that someone in the organization has, which has the potential of becoming a project. Sometimes, circumstances or external factors dictate the initiation of a project (e.g. Y2K, or a competitor's product). This is a fairly high-level activity and deals with the tasks of nominating the project manager and forming the steering committee. These tasks are of relatively less interest to the modeling aspect of the process and hence are only briefly mentioned here.

Table 5.1 A practical Activity–Task Mapping for BLS

Activities–Task groups	Project Initiation	Requirements Engineering	Project Planning 4QA	Analysis and Business Model Refinement	Build	Evaluation	Deployment
Activity Percentage Effort (Suggested)	3%	20%	7%	20%	30%	15%	5%
User interaction and business issues	***	**	**	*			**
Large-scale architectural issues	**	**		*	***		
Project management issues		***	***	**	**	*	**
Distribution issues		***	*	***	***		*
Modeling/building		*	**	**	***	**	
Reuse		**	**	***	***	*	

- Task: Undertake feasibility study. Ensures that a project is not started without proper investigation of the conceptual and technical aspects. This would involve collecting information on similar projects and technologies, corresponding risks, cost estimations, etc. It is worth mentioning that this task becomes easier and more relevant after the first project, since the subsequent projects now have some organization-specific data.
- Task: Obtain business approval. During this task the overall approval of the business is obtained to proceed with the software project. This is a formal okay that not only ensures business support but also ensures business participation in the development process. Once again, it is worth noting that this task may not happen sequentially, but may occur in an iterative manner, being performed alternatively and with varying intensity with a few tasks within the activity of requirements engineering.

Suggested Work Products[3]

- *Feasibility report*
- *Business case/proposal*

5.5.3 Activity: Requirements Engineering

This is a crucial modeling activity in which use cases play an important role. Use case diagrams and the business object diagrams (or package diagrams, as shown earlier) are documented here following the OMG/UML standard. This activity and its corresponding tasks are discussed in greater detail later on in this chapter. Note that this activity is called Requirements Engineering as it encompasses both requirements capture as well as requirements modeling. The relevant tasks for this activity, as decided by the tailoring activity, are:

(from the User Interaction and Business Issues group)

- Task: Identify user requirements – which makes use of the use case diagrams to identify and document the requirements of the system. During this activity of Requirements Engineering, the problem statement may be in the form of a plain English document, results from interviews with the users, and so on. This task identifies all such loosely floating requirements and starts putting them together in the form of use case models.
- Task: Analyze user requirements – which understands the documented requirements and expands them further to encompass GUI specifications (especially for the web application). At this stage, analysis of user requirements is in an initial iteration, perhaps followed by a second iteration of this activity itself. However,

3 As mentioned earlier, Work Products is the OPEN term for what are often known as Deliverables.

it is not uncommon to leave the second and more intense iteration for the Analysis and Business Model Refinement activity.

- Task: Develop Business Object Model – resulting from the analysis of the user requirements, as well as from the architectural understanding of the project. While this model can be documented using the UML notation for objects and classes and their relationships, it need *not* be an object-oriented model in its pure sense.[4] Therefore, a very high-level class diagram that shows the major business entities of the system identified during the task of analyzing user requirements is quite acceptable here.

(from the Reuse group)

- Task: Identify reusable components (patterns and frameworks) – making use of the architectural knowledge of the modelers. Increasingly, this task is also focusing on reusing *use case models* that may have been documented during earlier projects, and that have sufficiently generalized use case diagrams and documentation.
- Task: Manage library of reusable components. This task would come in play if the project is going either to incorporate third-party libraries in its development, or to produce components that will be reused by subsequent projects. Also, the task may be iterated many times during the analysis and design activity.

Suggested Work Products

- *User requirements document (or requirements model)*
- *Task object model*
- *Use case model*
- *Reuse plans*

5.5.4 Activity: Project planning

This activity is performed in two parts: (a) the brief effort up front, to produce estimates related to time and budgets, and the initial effort at producing the cost–benefit analysis, and (b) the detailed project planning, once the project has received the 'go ahead'.

- Task: Tailor the lifecycle. A task we are performing *now*, and the one that has been discussed earlier.

4 We stress here that this comment does NOT undermine the importance of using OPEN-UML for pure OO modeling. This comment merely highlights the fact that at this stage of the lifecycle, when the BOM is being developed, the diagrams that are produced may not be directly 'implementable'.

- Task: Develop capacity plan – dealing with the *non-functional* or technical aspects of (a) the development itself and (b) the solution, i.e. the running of the product.
- Task: Develop security plan – related to security of the development, as well as security and access related to the product

In addition to planning for the project overall, we also need to plan for a number of quality issues. Quality evaluation of the system will, of course, occur somewhat later in the project. However, we do need to think forward to the following tasks related to quality issues.

Quality issues (part of project management)

- Task: Evaluate Quality – by following the various well-known QA techniques such as walkthroughs and inspections.
- Task: Evaluate Usability – to ensure that the software not only does what it is meant to do, but also does it in an elegant and user-friendly fashion.
- Task: Maintain trace between requirements and design – a very difficult task in practice, unless the requirements and changes to the requirements are tightly controlled. This task essentially boils down to maintaining a healthy correlation between the use case diagrams and their documentation with the system-level class and sequence diagrams.
- Task: Perform class, cluster, acceptance and regression testing – which suggests the levels of testing by different personnel. For example, class and cluster testing would be performed by technical roles, possibly involving the writing of test harnesses. Acceptance testing will be primarily the job of the end users; regression testing would involve all participants in the development process.
- Task: Write manuals and other documentation. This task takes on additional meaning in a web-based application, where manuals may not be simply paper-based documentation, but online training and help subsystems.
- Task: Analyze metrics – if they already exist within the organization. If new metrics have been collected, the analysis would take place towards the end of the project.
- Task: Undertake in-process review – to ensure that the process itself remains fine-tuned to reflect the needs of (say) a web-based development.
- Task: Undertake post-implementation review – a task that essentially asks the question 'what went right and what went wrong?'.

Suggested Work Products

- *Documented tailored version of OPEN*
- *Planning documents (e.g. contingency, quality, security planning)*
- *Test plans (initial iteration)*
- *Draft manuals*
- *Draft metrics report*

5.5.5 Activity: Analysis and business model refinement

Analysis is usually the analysis of the requirements model, produced as a result of the Requirements Engineering Activity. Analysis is also involved with the architectural issues of the application development. Needless to say, it may not be performed in the sequence in which it is discussed, but rather in an iterative and incremental fashion, together with the requirements modeling activity.

Modeling/building

- Task: Analyze user requirements. This is a second iteration of the task of analyzing the user requirements. In the first attempt, a given problem statement was being analyzed to determine the requirements, which were then documented (in this case study) by a use case model. During the Analysis and business model refinement Activity, it is the use case model that is being analyzed, resulting in a more finely tuned use case model as well as providing a list of initial key classes.
- Task: Determine initial class list. A list of key business- and system-level classes, and their preliminary relationships is documented here. Many projects which are *not* following use case analysis and documentation perform this task following on from the list of key business entities identified during the earlier activity of Requirements Engineering.
- Task: Identify persistent classes – a task that can go deeper into the database modeling aspect of this activity of analysis and design. Identification of persistent classes can greatly assist the database modeling work, especially if the CASE tools used are able to create initial database schema from the class diagrams themselves. It may be worth noting here, from a strictly practical angle, that a class diagram *without* its *behaviour* or *operations* is reflecting the schema for its corresponding database. This is because the persistent attributes within a class correspond to the columns within a relational table, as is shown for Car objects being stored in Figure 5.7. Note how the various attributes of Car are stored in tables, and corresponding columns within the tables, whereas the Car objects themselves are represented as *rows* within the tables, and identified by their corresponding *keys* or *indexes*. This discussion does not hold true, of course, if you are using an object-oriented database.
- Task: Identify roles. Once more and more classes are identified and their relationships shown on a class diagram (or a few class diagrams, if the overall model is large), it starts becoming obvious that a class is related to many other classes in the system. However, not every facet of a class relates to every other class – rather a subset of the services provided by a class makes sense to one class, and another subset makes sense to some other class. For example, a class Person may relate to two classes, Car and Home. In relationship with the class Car, Person is in the role of (say) Driver, and in relationship with class Home, the same Person is now playing the role of (say) Owner. Thus, the task of identifying the roles ensures that we are not dealing with large and bulky classes, but only with the part of a class exemplified by smaller interfacial *subsets* of services that make semantic sense to the relationship in which they appear.

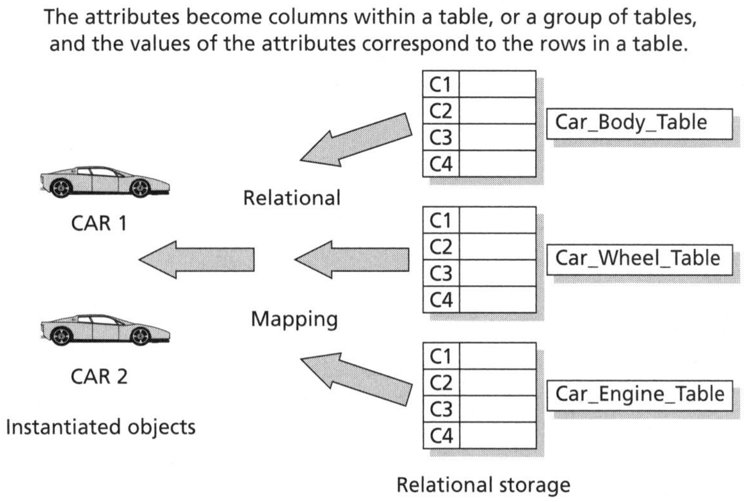

Figure 5.7 Storing objects in a relational database (after Unhelkar. 1999; © CRC Press)

- Task: Refine class list – an iterative task that is performed after further requirements analysis and also further analysis and design. The class list may continue to improve based on incorporation of third-party software, issues related to persistent classes (may also be read as databases), GUI changes, and more understanding of the initial class list itself.
- Task: Develop the Business Object Model (BOM). Using tasks and/or use cases, business processes can be reified and modeled. These objects (in the BOM) are naturally in the business domain and will eventually be translated into system (software) objects as part of the Task: Construct the Object Model. These two tasks will probably overlap as more detail is added and the modeling moves into the software domain – analysis/design and later coding.
- Task: Design user interfaces (especially for the Web) – a task that may not wait to be performed in the sequence in which it is described here. Web-based systems may even start their analysis with this task, since the user interfaces form an excellent starting point for web-based requirements. However, this task may iterate in practice with use case analysis, or use cases may themselves be specialized (stereotyped) to specify web user interfaces.
- Task: Undertake usability design (with navigation diagrams for web usage). Once again this task assumes tremendous importance in a web application, wherein it is not only the quality of the GUI, but also the navigability between the GUI screens that ensures that the user gets their desired output from the system with a minimum of keystrokes within and between interfaces. During this task, it is customary to draw a 'flow-chart like' navigation diagram that indicates the flow of GUI screens as the user navigates through them. Some practitioners use the Activity diagrams of the UML to achieve this purpose.

Suggested Work Products

- *Class diagrams*
- *Inheritance diagrams*
- *CRC cards*
- *Interaction diagrams*
- *Statechart diagrams*

5.5.6 Activity: Build

The Build Activity deals with the final lower-level technical design and the implementation of the system. We discuss this activity in detail, but it is only the modeling and design aspect of this activity that is of importance to us here. The implementation-related tasks within this Build Activity are outside the scope of this book, since they bring in the specific knowledge of languages, their compilers and builders.

- Task: Construct (refine) the Object Model – essentially refining the class, sequence and statechart diagrams, all of which form part of the Business Object Model, into a more software-focused analysis/design, often called the System Object Model or SOM. During this task, using a use-case-driven approach, we make attempts to refine the class diagrams by looking at the sequence diagrams in a fairly detailed manner, as we go through each scenario and document them in the sequence diagrams. Statechart diagrams also provide good help in documenting the changes to the state of an object, and thereby helping in refining the operations performed by the object shown in the statechart diagram.
- Task: Code. This task appears in the Build Activity almost as an anti-climax. It is the most important and elaborate task in which the development team is involved, yet it appears late in the process lifecycle, thereby indicating that the 'assets' generated by the development team are no longer just code, but also include all the other deliverables that we have produced until now, as well as those that will be produced during the rest of the development exercise. However, this exercise of coding is detailed in its own right, and may follow a 'mini-lifecycle' of its own. This task may also be influenced by the issues related to personal software processes (PSP) followed by individual developers, as well as their own skills, knowledge, experience and training. If the activities of Requirements Engineering and Analysis and business model refinement have been documented in detail in a CASE tool, then the CASE tool facilities can be used during the initial iteration of this task to generate skeletal code.
- Task: Construct reusable components – by integrating the code generated by the developers with corresponding third-party classes and components, and then refining the components to ensure reusability. This task assumes more

importance in a component *integration* exercise, wherein we are not simply generating new code, but also trying to 'carve' components out of existing legacy code in a way that will enable these components to be reused in current and future projects.

Suggested Work Products

- *Revised class diagrams*
- *Revised statechart diagrams*
- *Reports on reusable components*
- *Code*
- *Manuals, etc.*

5.5.7 Activity: Evaluation

This activity involves evaluation of the product to ensure that it complies with the requirements specified by the users. Thus this is an activity which involves detailed planning and execution of acceptance and usability testing of the deliverable. It is important to stress the fact that, although this activity appears towards the later part of the process lifecycle, its successful execution depends on meticulous planning right from the activity of project initiation. Thus, in a way, the iterations of this Evaluation Activity become important, with the initial evaluation being conducted almost in parallel with the activity of Requirements Engineering and just after the activity of project initiation. Furthermore, this activity also involves evaluating the *process* aspect of the project – what went right and what went wrong in the execution of the project. A detailed discussion of this activity follows towards the end of this chapter.

Suggested Work Products

- *Design report*
- *Fault report*
- *Test report*
- *Review report*
- *Traceability report*

5.5.8 Activity: Deployment

Deployment is also often called 'use of the system'. This is the installation and deployment of the system to the users. Depending on the type of system being developed, this could be a detailed and time-consuming activity of cutting CDs or creating diskettes for installation purposes, or it may be a simple event of upgrading the system on the production machine and sending a message/email out to the users. The Internet nature of BLS implies that its deployment will follow an 'upgrade' of the web-site of the bank (if it is already being used) or a new web-site followed by promotion of the site. Bank staff will be informed by an email followed by some training to get them off the ground in using the application. End-users (i.e. borrowers) may also be provided with an on-line tutorial on how to access their loan balances by using the Internet.

Suggested Work Products

- *System conversion plan*
- *Conversion cut-over report*
- *Post-implementation review*

5.5.9 Activity: Architecture[5]

In architecting the project, consideration of the overall architecture at a programme level is important. Hence, this is not a project-level activity, but a programme-level activity that spans multiple projects, and is performed at a lower level within a project to ensure that the project complies with (and takes advantage of) the programme architecture and standards.

Large-scale architectural issues

- *Task: Develop layer design.* Layering is a key technique for any software architectural work. This includes layering of the application architecture, or the technical architecture or the infrastructure and network architectures. We are primarily interested in the slicing and layering of the system to accommodate the application and the infrastructure architecture. As shown in Figure 5.8, the primary architectural work deals with slicing the system vertically based on the application's functional requirements and layering it horizontally based on its infrastructural architecture.
- *Task: Establish distributed systems strategy* – a task with growing importance in almost all new applications, but even more so in integrating with an existing architecture. This task focuses the architect's attention on the need to distribute components on an Internet or an intranet architecture so as to take maximum advantage of the various hardware and supporting software components in the context of the physical architecture of the system. Knowledge of existing middlewares and their role in 'integrating a distributed' architecture is important, as shown in Figure 5.9.

5 While Architecture itself does not appear as a formal Activity within the lifecycle as described in previous standard texts on OPEN, it may be treated so for most practical purposes. The alternative is to treat it as a group of tasks that are performed under the Activity of Requirements Engineering and/or Analysis and business model refinement.

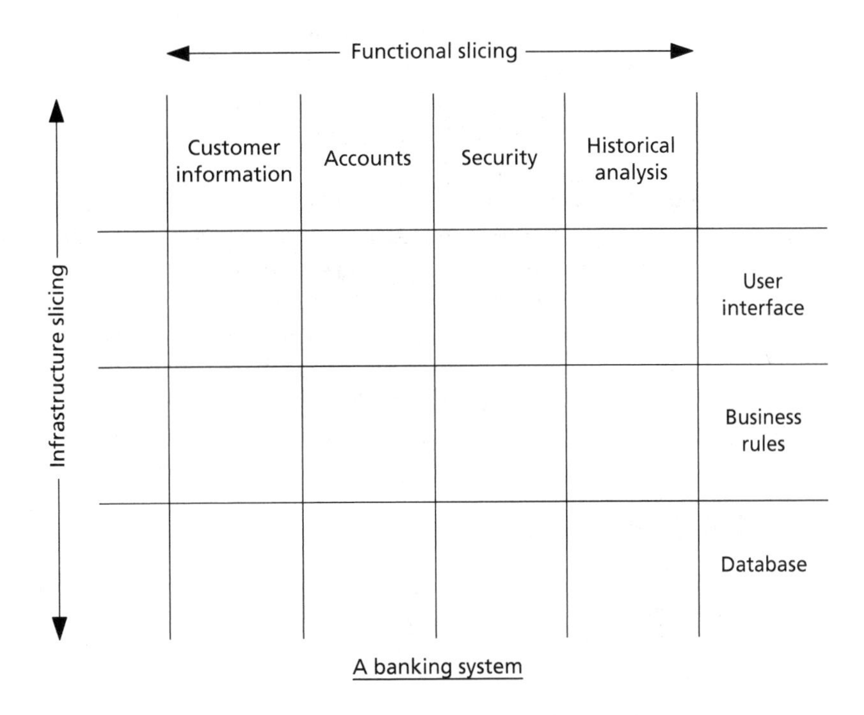

Figure 5.8 Functional-based versus infrastructure-based layering in a software architecture (after Unhelkar, 1999; © CRC Press)

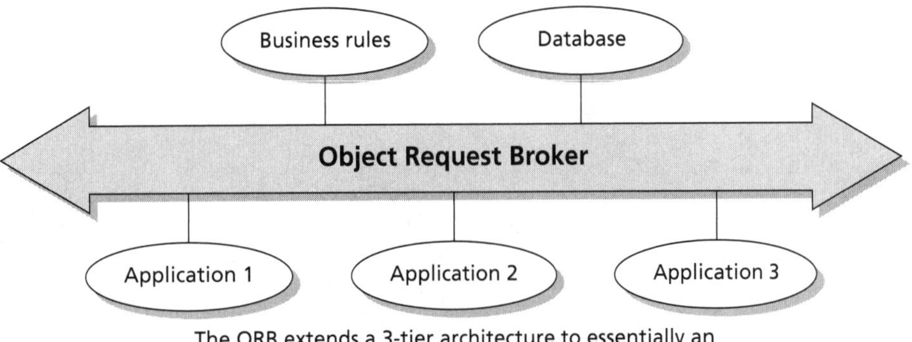

Figure 5.9 The role of middleware in a distributed architecture (after Unhelkar, 1999; © CRC Press)

- *Task: Select database/storage strategy.* This goes into the details of lower-level implementation issues of the persistent classes. These persistent classes were identified in the Task: Identify persistent classes within the modelling/building group of tasks in Analysis/Design Activity.

Modeling comment

It is important to note here that, if parts of the data are already existing in a database, then the architectural tasks will have to be modified to consider the existing architecture of the system and the corresponding database. For the existing 'legacy' system, attempts will have to be made to bring the data and application together – perhaps by means of a 'wrapper' – so that they can be considered as components on their own, and can be used in the integration effort. This attempt of bringing the data and functionality of the 'legacy' application together in order to view them as objects (or components) is shown in Figure 5.10. However, this is not always easy, as legacy code does not lend itself to componentization. Thus, Figure 5.10 shows an ideal situation or a situation we would be aiming for, in our effort to produce an integrated architecture.

Suggested Work Products

- *Layered design*
- *Plan for distribution*
- *Detailed design, etc.*

5.5.10 The Task–Technique mapping

While the Tasks describe *what* needs to be done, they do not describe in detail *how* it is to be done. This is accomplished by Techniques. OPEN contains a large number

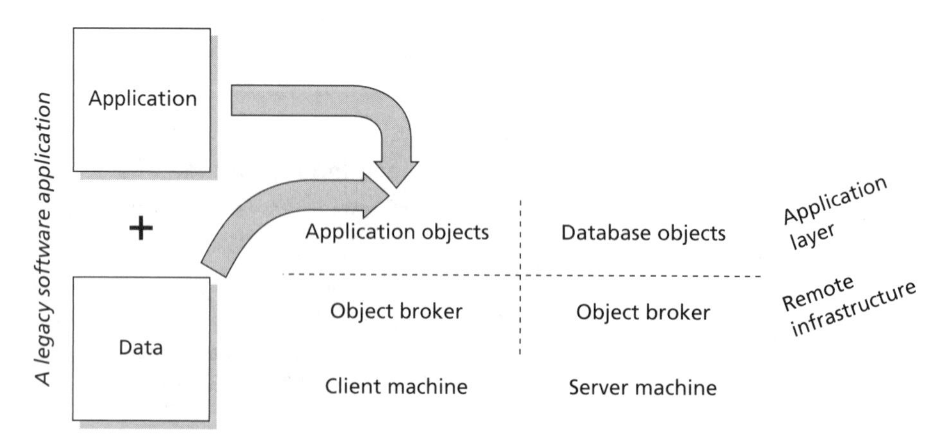

Figure 5.10 Attempting distributed component architecture from a legacy application

of Tasks for each Activity, and each of these Tasks is accomplished by one or more Techniques. It is not possible to list here all the Techniques and provide their mappings (see instead *The OPEN Process Specification*, Graham *et al.*, 1997a). However, we do make an attempt to show the Task and Technique mappings that are relevant to the case study BLS project. It is further worth noting that the Task to Technique mapping is neither a one-to-one mapping nor a one-way mapping. Therefore, although Tasks are related to Techniques, a Technique may be applicable to many Tasks and vice versa. In our current attempt at tailoring the OPEN lifecycle, we look at the various groups of Tasks, as listed in the Activity–Task mapping (shown earlier in Table 5.1), and list the corresponding techniques that will apply to these groups of Tasks (Table 5.2).

5.5.11 A mini project plan

There are a number of approaches to planning a project within the context of the OPEN process environment. Figure 5.11 highlights the two approaches a project manager can take in preparing his or her project plan: (a) an approach based on the deliverables or work packages wherein *iterative* production of the work packages appears in the project plan, and (b) the approach based on Activities–Tasks–Techniques that appear in the project plan – again *iteratively.* Both approaches can produce a plan down to a fine granularity depending on the requirements of the project. However, in the second (behavioural) approach, it may be occasionally possible to leave out the tasks, and go directly to techniques underneath each of the activities. This is because techniques indicate how tasks are to be carried out, and putting them in the project plan directly makes more practical sense than placing the techniques underneath the tasks. Figure 5.11 also highlights the iterative and incremental nature of the project plan by suggesting that whatever the approach chosen, the suggested items within the figure will be repeated more than once in the project plan.

A detailed project plan for the BLS would form part of the project planning activity. However, only a cut-down version of the plan is shown here in Table 5.3, primarily to highlight the sequencing of activities and tasks, as well as their iterative nature. Thus, this project plan is based on the option (b) in Figure 5.11 – a plan that may be called a 'behavioural-driven' project plan. We have not shown some of the standard elements of a project plan such as dates and resources. The project plan results from and is directly influenced by the important task of tailoring the lifecycle.

Once the OPEN lifecycle has been tailored, and the 'project plan' made available, the requirements modeling phase proceeds in detail. In the subsequent major sections, the activities of Requirements Engineering and of Analysis and business model refinement are discussed, with their corresponding deliverables.

Table 5.2 A practical Task–Technique mapping within the BLS lifecycle

Techniques for Task groups	Higher-level Techniques	Lower-level Techniques
User interaction and business issues	Brainstorming; Domain analysis; Interviewing; Roleplay; JAD; Workshops; Cost–benefit analysis	CRC modeling; Throwaway prototyping; Screenpainting
Large-scale architectural issues	DCS classification; Distributed system partitioning and allocation; Granularity; Layering; Pattern recognition Interfacing to RDBMS and legacy code	Implementation of distributed aspect of the system; Application scavenging; Framework creation; Genericity specification;
Project management issues	Business process modeling; Configuration management; Cost estimation; Risk analysis; Team building; Metrics collection; Group problem solving; Roleplay; Lectures; Train the trainer	Library management; Project planning; Gantt charts; Timeboxing; Versioning (product, DBMS); Complexity measurement; Internet and web technology
Distribution issues	Granularity; DCS classification; DCS optimization; Distributed system partitioning and allocation	Implementation of distributed aspects of system; Interfacing to RDBMS and legacy code
Modeling/building	Class internal design – component design; Generalization identification; DBMS product selection modeling; Mapping to RDBMS	Interfacing to RDBMS and legacy code; Implementation of rules, structure, services, distributed aspects; Screen scraping; ER
Reuse	Access analysis; Granularity; Library management CIRT indexing	Revision of inheritance hierarchies; Reuse measurement; Complexity measurement;

Table 5.3 A mini project plan for the BLS (behavioural driven)

Activity	Techniques*	Comments
User interaction and business issues	Interview users 1; Workshops and JAD 1; Domain analysis; Cost–benefit analysis 1; Throwaway prototyping 2; Granularity 1	While not mandatory, this project starts off with interviewing the users and conducting workshops with them. Prototyping is almost a final sketch, to be thrown away. Granularity decisions are made early.
Large-scale architectural issues	Granularity 2; Layering 2; Pattern recognition 2; Framework creation; Interfacing to RDBMS and legacy code 2	The division of the BLS system into its corresponding packages indicates early layering; work on interfaces with existing customer and asset RDBMS also starts here.
Project management issues	Cost estimation 2; Risk analysis 1; Team building 1; Metrics collection; Group problem solving; Roleplay; Library management; Project planning; Timeboxing 1; Versioning 1; Internet and web technology 1	It is impossible to list these project management techniques in any sequence. They are *not* performed in the sequence in which they appear here, but continue in the background throughout the project. Hence, the same techniques will have 1, 2 and 3 numbers throughout, if explicitly stated.
Distribution issues	Distributed system partitioning and allocation; *Implementation of distributed aspects of system 1; Interfacing to RDBMS and legacy code 1;* Risk analysis 2; Team building 2	The two tasks in *italics*, although under the umbrella of distribution issues, will appear later in the lifecycle. Hence, it will be appropriate to create another heading in this plan repeating distribution issues, if desired (not done here).
Modeling/building	Class internal design – component design; Generalization identification; Interfacing to RDBMS and legacy code; Implementation of rules, structure, services, distributed aspects; ER modeling; Mapping to RDBMS; Risk analysis 3; Team building 3	
Reuse	Granularity; Library management; CIRT indexing	Like project management, these techniques will also be repeated throughout the lifecycle, appearing more than once.

* Numbers against Techniques indicate their 'iterations'.

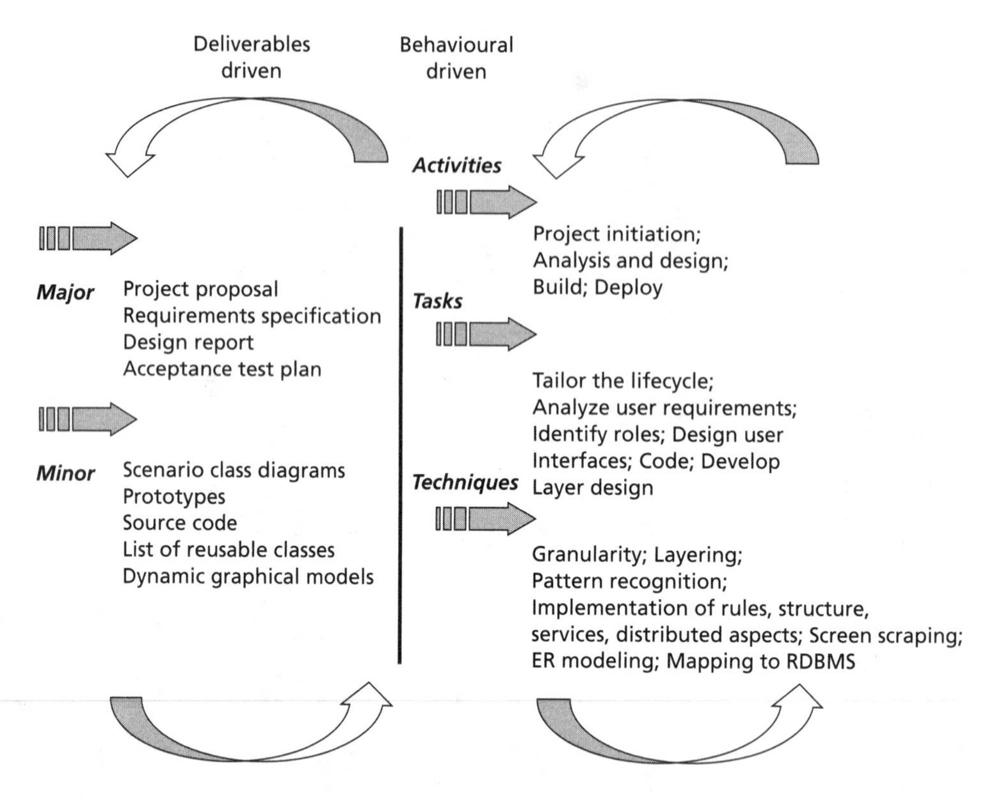

Figure 5.11 Project planning in OPEN – possible approaches which are all iterative and incremental

5.6 Activity: Requirements Engineering

The activity of Requirements Engineering focuses on extracting correct and complete requirements from the end users of the system. It ensures that the users understand what they want, and then formally documents those requirements so that they can be understood and transformed into designs. The primary deliverable resulting from the activity of Requirements Engineering, as stated in the OPEN process, is the user requirements statement. We will call it the requirements model. Because of the choice of techniques made by us in this use-case-driven example, the requirements model for this case study will be essentially a use case model, documented by using the standard UML use case diagrams and sequence diagrams. Note that the requirements model *need not be* a use case model, but can be simply a high-level class diagram (made up of packages) followed by the standard descriptive text. We have chosen to draw the use case diagrams because we want to illustrate the use-case-driven approach. Furthermore, it is worth pointing out that a good requirements model is *not* just a use case model. There are a number of requirements from the business users that are *not* related to how the user is going to use the system. These are the 'Technical user requirements' that range from statements like 'we will have 30% extra users logged-in to the system during every October' through to more technical ones like 'my end users will be running this application on a Windows95™ operating system'. 'Technical user requirements' include operational requirements, performance-related requirements, peak and off-peak loading on the system, user migration requirements and usability issues, to name but a few. We leave the discussion on technical user requirement with a final note that these are *non-functional* or *non-behavioural* requirements, which also come from the users, but which cannot be described by use case diagrams within the requirements model. Description of such requirements is documented in technical user specifications, and is mostly text documented.

We had discussed the relevant tasks related to requirements engineering earlier on, when the activity of Requirements Engineering was outlined. Now we mention some of the relevant techniques that can be used in modeling requirements for the BLS. These are:

- Quality templates. These are the templates used for documenting the process deliverables. The templates for documenting the use cases and actors can also be treated as a part of the creation and use of these templates.
- Blackboarding, storyboarding and brainstorming are all part of the process of extracting and documenting the requirements. Each of these techniques will remain in the back of our minds (from the process viewpoint) as we continue to develop the requirements model here. These techniques will also include discussion on the granularity of requirements, as well as of the design.
- The technique of dialogue design in UI can be either a part of requirements modeling, or part of a separate task. Certainly, *specifying* the UI should be a part of the activity of requirements modeling, but detailed design of the UI, including all its 'bells and whistles', may require specialist skills in GUI design.
- Some of the other techniques which are worth mentioning here are granularity, internet and web technology, package construction, prototyping and workflow analysis. These techniques have all been documented in *The OPEN Toolbox of Techniques*.
- Finally, we mention the major technique used here in engineering our requirements – the technique of use case modeling. Use case modeling includes development and documentation of the use case diagrams, documenting the use cases and scenarios, drawing the sequence diagrams based on the scenarios (specified by the users and documented by the requirements modeler) and refining these diagrams iteratively and incrementally, as well producing other diagrams within the overall requirements model.

5.6.1 A useful view of use cases

Since use case modeling is our preferred technique for the example case study in this chapter, it might be worthwhile to pass a few remarks on the technique (to supplement and extend those in earlier chapters). Needless to say, the use case approach to requirements engineering has probably generated more discussions and debates than the language and database debates. Every conference and journal is replete with discussions of the 'usefulness' or the 'uselessness' of use cases. We feel that, as part of the UML standard, use cases have a role to play in requirements modeling. Because of the ease with which they relate to the end user, and the ease with which they enable the end user to participate in specifying the requirements and assist with the modeling process, we feel that use cases serve a valuable purpose in the earlier activities of the software lifecycle.

Criticism of use cases stems from the fact that they are they are 'general' and not 'object-oriented'. True. Even a casual walkthrough of a use case documentation is enough to convince the reader that the documentation has a 'flow' in it, and that a corresponding pictorial representation of that flow within the use case can be easily accomplished by drawing a 'flow-chart' of the interactions between the actor and the system. However, this 'general' or 'non-rigorous' approach of the use case modeling is extremely valuable in capturing the unstructured way of thinking of a potential user – certainly during the initial stages of a project. Hence, instead of being daunted by the 'unstructured' thinking of the end user, we consider use cases as a 'technique' that relates well to that 'unstructured' thinking. Thus, use cases are the bridge between the 'unstructured' thinking of the end user and the 'organized' thinking of a software engineer. Even a novice in the technique of use cases is immediately able to relate to the 'stickfigure' and the 'ellipse'; and the software engineer can start analyzing the diagrams and documentation and see the classes emerge from this documentation. This 'dual advantage' of use cases perhaps justifies their popularity to a large extent.

The one question that is frequently asked by requirements modelers following the use-case-driven approach is 'how to move from use cases (pure requirements model) to class diagrams (business object model)?'. The answer is not easy. However, this is where a process like OPEN can play a crucial role – in outlining the tasks and techniques, as well as their iterative and incremental usage, in producing the use case diagrams and corresponding class diagrams. Some of the popular alternatives in moving through the techniques of the process are as follows:

(a) As shown by process option (a) in Figure 5.12, the process can start with the use case diagrams and then move on to documenting the sequence diagrams based on the example scenarios provided by the user. Documenting the example scenarios in (blackbox) sequence diagrams helps in identifying missing classes, as well as missing operations within existing classes. Once the major classes have been identified, and their attributes and operations documented, they provide a rich source of information to start modeling the interface (GUI) classes.

(b) Process option (b) in Figure 5.12, on the other hand, depicts the process of analyzing the use cases and identifying a list of candidate classes first. A detailed iteration of identifying these classes provides a backbone for the documentation of the scenarios, which *follow* the major exercise of identifying and listing the candidate classes.

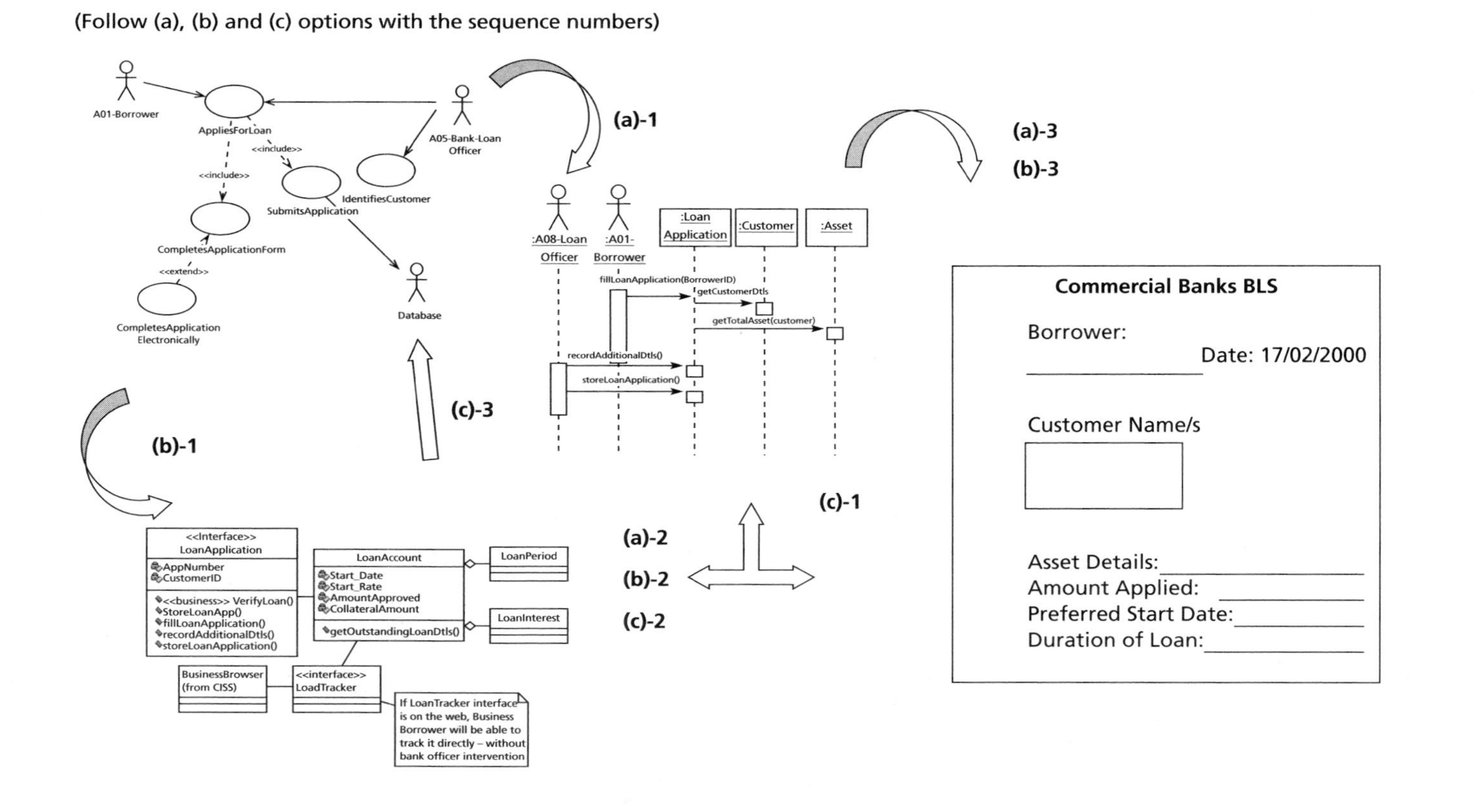

Figure 5.12 Process options in proceeding with use case modeling

(c) Process option (c) is going in the *reverse* to the first two options, and is ideally suited for many web-based developments. These are the situations where the user is able to think initially only in terms of a user interface. In those situations, GUIs should be specified up front, followed by attempts at sequence or class diagrams. Use case diagrams may still be helpful here, because all GUIs have actors and, whenever we have actors, use cases are very helpful.

The role of a process like OPEN continues throughout the lifecycle, guiding and supporting the modelers and managers, architects and testers, designers and developers in tailoring and performing the various activities, tasks and techniques to produce the system. By leveraging from the iterative and incremental nature of the process, it is possible to analyze the use cases and produce an initial class list, which is then used to refine the use case model.

Finally, as mentioned earlier, there are a number of requirements in a project that simply *cannot* be modeled with use cases. These are the technical user requirements. There are also some projects that involve back-office integration, or that deal with sending and receiving of streams of data and/or files. These are the projects that *do not* have a user in its traditional sense. Therefore, there is not much that an 'actor' can do, if such an actor can be identified at all. These are the situations where use case modeling should not be attempted, and perhaps other approaches like the responsibility-driven design discussed in Chapter 4 may be followed. If use case modeling is still attempted, be prepared for use case diagrams *without* any actors on them.[6]

5.6.2 Actors for the BLS

5.6.2.1 Actors and actor diagram for the BLS

Actors interact with the system to derive some measurable benefits. The interactions of the actors with the system are documented in the use cases. Actors are usually users, who are persons extracting information from the system. However, they can also be external systems and devices which are sending messages to and receiving them from the system. Use case modeling starts off with identification of the actors. The first question to ask when starting with use cases is 'who are the actors of the system?' or 'to whom is this system supposed to provide benefits?'. Answers to these questions start providing clues as to the actors of the system. Note that while actors are mostly people, one person can play the role of more than one actor. For example, John can play the role of a Bank Loan Officer, or can represent the actor Bank Manager, or may even be the borrower of a loan from the bank in which he

6 This is not necessarily wrong, as at times such use case diagrams without any actors do serve the purpose of allowing uniform documentation of requirements. However, note that the formal description of the use case diagram in the UML standard indicates that it must have at least one actor.

works. Thus, it is the *role* that John the 'actor' plays which is important for use case modeling – and not John himself.

The actors for the BLS are documented in the actor diagram shown in Figure 5.13. These actors of the Bank Loan System (BLS) are based on our understanding of the problem statement and can be categorized into three major groups. These groups are (a) the borrowers who are going to apply to the bank for a loan and, on being granted the loan, will also use the system for tracking them, (b) the bank staff who are going to use the system to accept and process loan applications, and (c) the administrators, the system and the external database that are used for the management of all loans-related data. While the focus of the borrower group of actors is on the Small-Business-Borrowers, other types of borrowers are also shown as existing (legacy) or potential actors for the system. Furthermore, it is important to note that while the Small-Business-Borrower appears as an actor, it is actually a customer behind the borrower that will be sending and receiving messages to the system.

Figure 5.13 pictorially shows various actors and their groups. From a modeling point of view, this is only a supporting diagram, rather than a main one. The first job of the actor hierarchy is to assist in clarifying the roles of the various users of the system. In our example, we have identified the actors A01-Borrower and A05-Bank-Loan-Officer as the *Abstract* actors. The *concrete* or *real* actors are A02-Personal-Borrower, A03-Small-Business-Borrower and A04-Large-Corporate-Borrower, all belonging to the *type* A01-Borrower. Remaining *real* actors from the bank's side are: A06-Customer-Information-Officer, A07-Securities&Assets-Officer and A08-Loan-Officer-SmallBusiness. There are also two more actors shown which are not representative of the people who will use the system. A09-Database is an

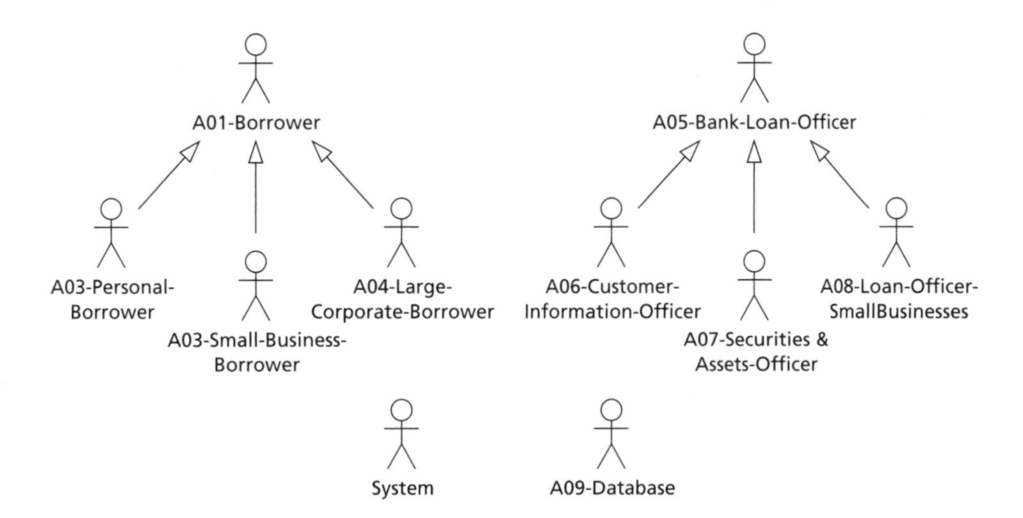

Figure 5.13 Actor diagram for the BLS example, illustrating hierarchies between actors. Each actor name is prefixed by the letter A to indicate actor and a simple numbering system in order to facilitate quick and abbreviated reference (e.g. A03) to elements of this diagram.

actor that is *external* to the BLS. Messages are sent to and received from it through a predetermined interface. System also occasionally appears as an actor. However, appearance of the system actor is a debatable issue as, eventually, it is what we are developing that is the system and that system is not a separate 'concrete' actor on its own. Having the system as an actor may help in documentation of the use cases.

Modeling comment

Abstracting an actor to a higher level, even if it does not represent a real person, is sometimes advisory. This is the situation when, if you have not done the abstraction, you may find that the use case diagram itself starts to look like a spider's web – with effectively all actors interacting with all use cases. Hence, even if abstract actors are unreal (and hence non-implementable), they play a major role in reducing the complexity of a use case diagram. Similarly, use cases can also be abstracted to a higher level in order to reduce the complexity and enhance the understandability of the diagrams.

Modeling comment

An additional point to note from a practical modeling viewpoint is that all formal standard UML documentation for the use case approach specifically states that actors are not a part of the system. In practice, however, many of the actors may need corresponding storage space in the system. Thus, many of the actors will have their 'shadows' in the system. Although this will alarm the 'purists', all practitioners of use cases should look out for actors whose 'shadow' needs to appear in the system, and cater for that situation when it happens. For example, while A03-Small-Business-Borrower is an actor sending messages to the BLS, there will also be a need to store many attributes and behaviour related to this actor. That will need a corresponding persistent class, or a group of classes. These are the 'shadows' of the actor, yet are fully-fledged classes in their own right. One additional small problem that this leads to in documenting the use case diagrams and the corresponding class diagrams in a CASE tool is that the Actor-names and the corresponding class-names will have to be different. A suggestion here is to judiciously use prefixes and suffixes to differentiate the actor from the corresponding class. For example, in our actor diagram, we have prefixed all actors with an 'A' followed by a short numbering scheme. This will ensure that there is no clash between the actors and corresponding classes in the class diagram that may have similar names but without the 'A' prefix.

5.6.2.2 *Actor descriptions*

Actors, shown in the actor diagram, also have an underlying description which describes the actors and helps in understanding their role in the system. In our case study, we will not document all the actors here. We show only a couple of illustrative examples in order to demonstrate how actors are documented. The template we use for such documentation is also important and a sample version of such a template is provided here. In most projects, this template gets 'fine tuned' to suit the needs of the project and the organization. The sample actor documentation follows the description of the template in the next section.

Before proceeding with the documentation of actor, it is worth mentioning the

Table 5.4 Actor/goal/priority table (after Cockburn, 2000; © AWL)

Actor	Task-level goal	Priority
A03-Small-Business-Borrower	Provide information related to their assets	1
A03-Small-Business-Borrower	Assist in calculation of the net asset value available as collateral	2
A07-Securities&Assets-Officer	Calculate the net asset of the borrowers	1
A07-Securities&Assets-Officer	Calculate the collateral by balancing the net assets with the loan amount requested	2
A07-Securities&Assets-Officer	Store asset details in the database	2

increasingly popular association of 'goals' of the use case with the 'actor'. First proposed by Cockburn as an 'actor–goal' model, this pairing indicates the benefits or 'goals' achieved by the actor from the system, as documented in the use case. Furthermore, since there are several goals achieved by an actor and, potentially, there are several actors within a use case, it is worthwhile listing the actor–goal pairs as well as providing a list of priorities for the same. A table documenting such a list of actor–goal pairs and their priorities for the BLS system is shown in Table 5.4.

Process comment

Please note that although Table 5.4 shows a list of actor–goal pairs and their priorities, we are currently, within our process, at the stage of identifying and documenting the actors. It is only after a few of these actors have been used in documenting the use cases that a table such as shown in Table 5.4 will be properly constructed.

5.6.2.3 *Template for documenting actor*

Actor Thumbnail

<Name of the actor and, optionally, a number>

Actor Type & Stereotype

<Describes the type of actor. This can include whether it is a primary or secondary actor, person or external system or device etc. The type of actor may be described in general or it may be a formal stereotype.[7] Occasionally, an actor is made 'abstract' in order to reduce the clutter and complexity on the diagram>

7 Such as «person» or «external system».

Actor Description

<Few lines describing the actor and what he/she/it does>

Actor Relationships

<Thumbnails of relevant use cases and/or other actors with whom this actor is interacting. If there is an inheritance hierarchy, thumbnails of generalized/specialized actors can be noted here>

Interface Specifications

<Since, by definition, the actor has to interact with the system, we note here the details of the interface through which the actor performs this interaction. This will be a list of the number and name of GUI specifications related with this actor – including specifications of web interfaces. For external systems and devices, it may be a description of the interface that may not be graphic>

Author & History

<Original author and modifiers of this actor description>

Reference Material

<Relevant references, as well as sources>

5.6.2.4 Sample actor documentation

Actor Thumbnail

Actor: A01-Borrower

Actor Type & Stereotype

Abstract actor representing any Borrower; «CISS»

Actor Description

The Actor: Borrower is the 'entity' that applies for and receives a Loan from the bank. This actor is made up of two or more Customers, who come together as a Borrower to acquire the Loan. Thus, this actor is not a person, but a group of persons, acting in unison.

Modeling comment

When an application form has to be filled, one of the two or more customers might fill out the form, but it will be signed by all Customers who are party to the borrowing.

Actor Relationships

Three different types of concrete actors are derived from this actor:
A02-Personal-Borrower
A03-Small-Business-Borrower
A04-Large-Corporate-Borrower

Interface Specifications

UI010_Loan_Application_Form
UI320_Web_Loan_Tracker

Author & History

Mark Douce

Reference Material

Rules related to Borrowers can be seen on the Bank's intranet, and are being documented in file \\loans\BLSBorr.doc

Actor Thumbnail

Actor: A08-Loan-Officer-SmallBusiness

Actor Type & Stereotype

Primary Actor; «LASS»

Actor Description

This actor is the loans officer of the bank responsible for receiving the loan applications, cross-checking on the assets offered as collateral with the help of other actor(s), and approving the loan. Finally, this actor disburses the loan and also helps the borrower in tracking the loan

Actor Relationships

Inherits from A05-Bank-Loan-Officer
Deals with A07-Securities-Officer in getting customer assets valued for collateral

Interface Specifications

UI010_Loan_Application_Form
UI320_Web_Loan_Tracker

Author & History

Levi Martinovich and David Hazlewood

Reference Material

Rules under which the A08-Loans-Officer-SmallBusiness deals with the application are all derived from the Bank's Loan manual, which is also reflected in the use case documentation: \\loans\LoanRules.doc

Actor Thumbnail

Actor: Database

Actor Type & Stereotype

External system, not a person; «DB»

Actor Description

The external database receives and stores all the data sent to it by the BLS. It also handles all queries on the assets and customer-related data stored in it

Actor Relationships

Deals with the BLS in order to store data and reply to queries

Interface Specifications

None

Author & History

Levi Martinovich and David Hazlewood

Reference Material

Database documentation is stored in file \\loans\BLSDB.doc

5.6.3 Use case diagrams for the BLS

Once we have identified and described as many actors as possible within the system, we start with the process of creating use case diagrams.[8] Use case diagrams put the actors and the use cases together to show how the actors interact with the system. Note that it is not unusual to discover new actors during the process of creating use case diagrams. Thus, a *mini*-iteration between the actors and the use case diagrams takes place during this early stage of the Requirements Engineering life-cycle.

We had presented, in Chapter 3, some of the *process* steps in use case modeling. Here, we consider some important and practical issues during the creation of use case diagrams as they appear in a requirements model. These issues are:

- Get the *granularity* of the use cases right. This is one of the most important consideration in diagramming and documenting with use cases. Too few use cases, and everything will be reduced to the earlier ways of documenting the problem statement with too much text and not enough pictorial representation. Too fine a granularity and the requirements model will be nothing but a large number of 'bubbles and arrows'. No precise rules exist for getting the granularity right. However, we can apply some guidelines. For example, if the problem statement is already in the shape of a large textual document, it may *not* be necessary to convert it into a large number of use cases. Instead, we may use more *abstract* use cases to represent pictorially at a high level what is required of the system. This would also be the approach to *component integration* exercises, wherein the development work deals with integrating newly created components with the existing legacy code or, more importantly, attempts to *componentize* legacy code itself. These situations require coarse granular use cases. Compared with the coarse granular approach, when we are starting a system from scratch, and we want to elicit more user involvement, we may go for a large number of initial use cases (which would then be changing, as we proceed with the subsequent iterations of the activity of requirements engineering). This would be a fine-granular use case diagram(s), with most of the development work focused on 'greenfield' development.
- Documenting the use cases using a precise and commonly agreed format. Use cases can be documented in a number of different ways. Although a few headings in the use case documentation are common, each group of users tends to use their own flavour. Many times this is justified. For example, a use case dealing with user interfaces may be different from one that deals with storage

8 From a *process* viewpoint, it might be worth mentioning here that identifying the actors *first* and *then* identifying the use cases (by asking questions to the actors such as 'what will you do with the system?' and 'what will you derive from the system?') is our preferred approach. It is always possible to identify some use cases first and then use them to identify the actors, but that goes against the philosophy of putting the 'user' at the centre of modeling. In practice, though, this discussion only indicates the *starting point* of the process, with the creation of the final use case diagrams complete with their actors and use cases being an iterative process.

and retrieval of data. However, every project *must* have a commonly agreed template from which all use cases are documented in order to ensure consistency and easier readability of the use cases, as well as ensuring that some important headings relevant to the problem domain or the organization are not missed out.

- In practice, an actor may interact indirectly (secondarily) with more use cases than it is essential to show on the use case diagram. Novice practitioners of the use case approach find that if they draw a line between an actor and a use case even if the actor is only remotely related to the use case, then that results in a myriad of lines connecting all actors to all use cases. What is important to remember in drawing a use case diagram is that it is a pictorial representation used to clarify the *major* relationship between actors and the use cases. It is *not* meant to be a syntactically precise diagram.[9] Without such an understanding, as mentioned earlier, the use case diagram may start looking like a spider's web, and may be too complicated to read. Judicious use of abstractions of both actors and use cases can greatly assist in reducing the complexity of use case diagrams. In other words, think of a use case diagram as a *context* diagram or a *topological* diagram, rather than a detailed and precise *design* diagram.
- During the early stages of adopting the use case modeling approach, many modelers tend to draw the use case diagrams as a *flow*. This is almost certainly an error with people proficient in Data Flow Diagramming techniques, wherein the DFD is meant to depict the flow of data. As against a DFD, a use case diagram is a *static* diagramming tool, and is *not* meant to depict the flow within the requirements – for that we use sequence diagrams. Hence it is important to keep the static nature of use case diagrams in mind and avoid depicting and reading them as a flow.
- Use case relationships. Because use case diagrams are not syntactic diagrams, they leave open to discussion the precise nature of relationships between use cases. UML 1.3 describes three relationships, include, extend and generalize. Of these three, we focus only on include and extend as the two most practical relationships between use cases. Our practical experience suggests a simple rule of thumb on which relationship to use: if use case 'B' is mandatory for the execution[10] of use case 'A', then 'A «include» B'; and if 'A' is a complete use case which can be executed independently, but has a special case which is shown in 'B', then 'B «extend» A'.
- Use cases without actors. These are the situations where a back-end interface for a large system is being modeled to enable it to interface with the database, or where EDI applications are only sending and receiving data without much user intervention, or data conversion projects, etc. In such situations, use case diagrams may not add much value. However, if they are still desired then we may

9 No code generation is possible from a use case diagram.

10 Execution is not used here as in a 'program execution' but, instead, more like following the steps within the use case text.

end up with situations where there is a use case diagram without actors. Such a diagram would still have the advantage of abstracting repeatable requirements and enabling them to be reused (in addition to overall being better organized) through the use case relationships. The format of the use case documentation can also help.

The use case diagrams depicted in the following sections (Figures 5.14 to 5.16) relate to the overall major business process within the BLS. This business process encompasses the sub-processes within the three major subsystems or components identified as CISS, SASS and LASS. However, this 'clean' componentization is not always easily achievable in practice – hence we should not be too concerned if the major processes within our requirements model do not directly correspond one-to-one with components or subsystems identified by us.

The diagram for the major subsystems within the BLS (shown in Figure 5.5, the BLS package diagram) is *exploded* further into a set of use case diagrams. These use case diagrams represent the *lower level* processes going on within the BLS, and may be called the key process areas of the business processes. The primary business processes within the BLS are identified as follows:

(a) Application for loan by the customer – which includes the customers providing their existing details to the bank (and if they do not already have a saving or cheque or credit account with the bank, then opening such an account in order to become customers of the bank), forming a group of two or more customers and becoming a 'borrowing entity' or a small business borrower and making the application for a loan as that entity.

(b) Maintaining the details of the customers and their assets (which already occurs in the bank), and relating this information back to the loan application to determine the value of the customers to the bank, and valuing their assets to ensure they cover the requirements for the collateral.

(c) Once all details related to the application are ratified, then the loan can be disbursed.

(d) Once the loan is disbursed, to track it and to allow the borrower to track it themselves on the web.

Extensive workshops and brainstorming will lead to many more business processes that we assume exist in practical situations. These business processes include (a) existing business processes that need to be *re-engineered* due to changes in technology or changes initiated by technology, and (b) new business processes resulting from newer requirements. An example of an existing process in the BLS is identifying an existing customer; a new process example would be creating a borrower using a group of customers. Having identified these processes, we now make an attempt to document some of the aforementioned key business processes in their corresponding textual use case diagrams.

5.6.3.1 *Use case diagram for Applying for Loan*

The use case diagram called 'Applying for Loan' (Figure 5.14) is relevant to the process of a potential borrower making the loan application. In its simplest form, this use case diagram has one main use case 'AppliesForLoan', and the actor involved is A01-Borrower. The A01-Borrower is purposefully selected (as against the small business borrower) to capture the process of applying for any kind of loan in this bank. There can be a few small details that are different when the small business borrower makes an application but, for the most part, the process of applying for loans is the same. Furthermore, it is worth noting that we have not differentiated between a potential borrower (a group of two or more customers of the bank) and a real borrower (i.e. a borrower whose application has been accepted and loan disbursed, by the bank). In practice, if this difference is important, then we will have to show two separate actors called potential borrower and borrower.

While 'AppliesForLoan' «include»s 'CompletesApplicationForm', which is a straightforward inclusion of one use case into another, completion of the application form electronically[11] is an *optional* extension which may not always be executed when the loan application is made. Hence, we have «extend»ed the use case 'CompletesApplicationForm' with the 'CompletesApplicationElectronically' use case. After the application forms have been completed by the A01-Borrower, they are submitted for processing by the A05-Bank-Loan-Officer. These forms are

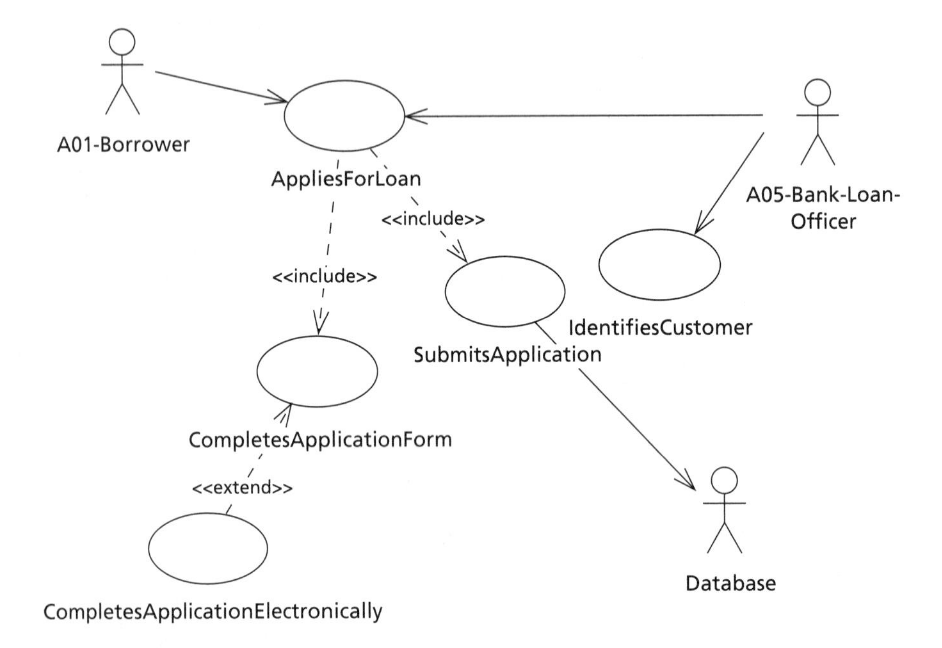

Figure 5.14 Use case diagram for 'Applying for Loan'

11 Perhaps by completing it within the bank's premises where some workstations have been set up, or by completing the form from the bank's website, and then posting it electronically.

sent to the database for storage in the form of a message – hence the 'SubmitsApplication' use case is shown with a directional arrow going towards the database actor. (All these details are given in the accompanying textual use case.)

Finally, note that the A05-Bank-Loan-Officer actor, who is interacting with the system in order to identify the customer, does not need to interact with the A01-Borrower or even with the process of applying for loan, in order to carry out the identification of customer – documented through a series of interactions in the 'IdentifiesCustomer' use case. This use case 'IdentifiesCustomer' identifies the individual customers who together form the 'borrower' entity, and have made application for loans. This is done because, although the borrower makes the application, it is the assets and other details of individual customers that will be of interest to the bank loan officer in identifying the potential value of the customer.

Process comment

Creation of this use case diagram appears here sequentially, as a part of the Requirements Engineering activity. However, it does not reach completion at this stage, and it is usually necessary to iterate a few times between this and other use case diagrams, as well as the class and sequence diagrams, before a complete and correct version of this diagram is arrived at. Furthermore, note that the diagram is not meant to depict the flow of the business process. Instead, it is a topological diagram showing the static organization of the process of applying for a loan. Finally, the entire diagram, and the use cases inside, is named from the point of view of the A01-Borrower. For example, the diagram itself is called 'applying' for loan rather than 'receiving' loan application – which would have been from the bank's perspective, rather than from the customer's (actor's) perspective.

5.6.3.2 Use case diagram for Verifying and Valuing Assets

The use case diagram *Verifying and Valuing Assets* depicted in Figure 5.15 deals with the process of verifying the correctness of the assets described by the A03-Small-Business-Borrower in the loan application form, and its subsequent valuation against the market value of the assets. For example, a customer may declare an asset of $300,000 for his house, whose market value may be $400,000. The bank is interested in the *real* or market value of the house, and particularly so if the value has *dropped* due to whatever reasons.

The use case 'CalculatesNetAsset' includes 'IdentifyAssets' which identifies the assets as available on the bank's database. If not found, the asset descriptions are used in creating the asset descriptions within the bank. The stated value of the assets by the customers (in the role of potential borrowers) is compared with the market value of the assets. These details, either pulled from the bank's database and/or physically recorded by the A07-Securities&Assets-Officer[12] are recorded in the loans database through a series of interactions documented in 'RecordDetails'

12 For example, a A07-Securities&Assets-Officer may physically visit a street address of a house which has been put up as an asset.

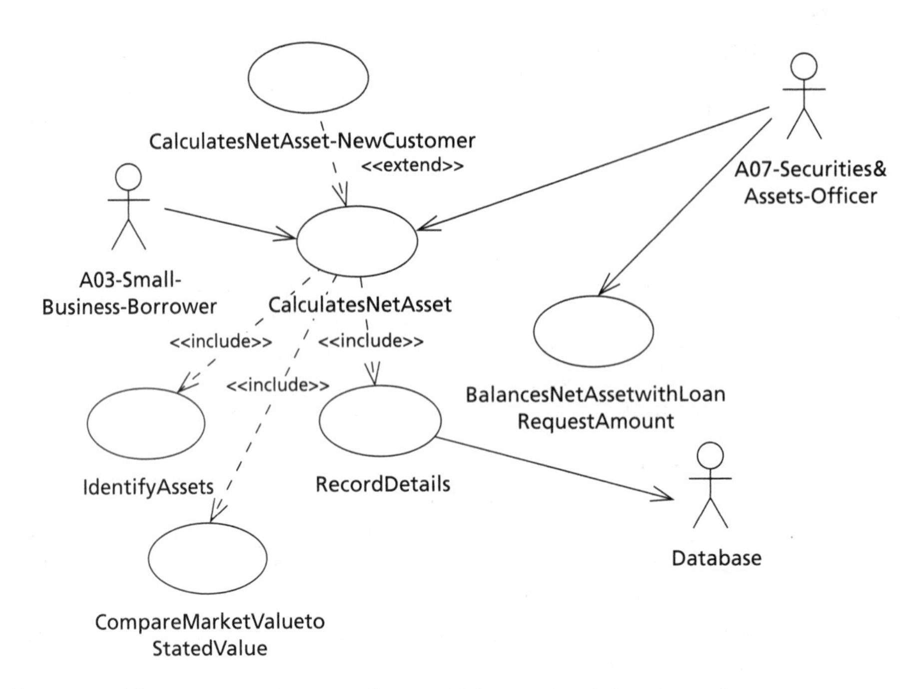

Figure 5.15 Use case diagram for 'Verifying and Valuing Assets'

use case. However, the process thus far has dealt only with the facts related to recording all details related to the assets of all customers appearing as borrowers. Indeed, some of these assets may have already been used as collateral elsewhere, or may not be worth using as collateral. Furthermore, even if an asset were worth a certain amount, depending on the type of asset, the bank would have rules to allow only a certain percentage of the value of the asset to be used as collateral. For example, the bank may have a rule which says that the loan value can be up to 70% of the value of the collateral, if that collateral is a property, but only 60% if it is a blue chip equity, and even less if it is an ordinary equity. This detailed application of various business rules, and in various permutations and combinations of assets, their market values, groups of customers appearing as borrowers, and the value of the customers to the bank, will all dictate the value of the loan. This process is documented in the use case 'BalancesNetAssetwithLoanRequestAmount'. While this entire process is a normal flow of event for all existing customers of the bank who are trying to become borrowers, there might be exceptional cases where the person walking into the bank for a loan is not yet a customer (in the sense of having no other debit accounts with the bank). In that case, the value of the customer to the bank will depend on other factors like the collateral offered, the need for someone else to guarantee the loan and the potential future business the bank can do with the person in the role of a borrower. These specialized interactions of the A07-Securities&Assets-Officer with the system are documented in the specialised use case 'CalculatesNetAsset-NewCustomer'.

5.6.3.3 *Use case diagram for Loans Disbursement*

We have shown the business process of disbursal of loan, which may require some legal involvement from the parties involved in disbursing and receiving the loan. Figure 5.16, the use case diagram for Loans Disbursement, also highlights the use of the «extend» stereotype relationship in a simple way. 'DisburseLoan' is a use case that reads from the A08-Loan-Officer-SmallBusiness's viewpoint, since in this use case diagram the primary actor is the Loans officer of the bank. The A03-Small-Business-Borrower is going to *receive* the loan that is disbursed by the loans officer and hence that actor is *passive* in this diagram.

5.6.4 Sample use case documentation

Not all use cases can be documented during this exercise. This is because once the concept of documenting is explained and demonstrated, it should be relatively easy for practitioners to carry out further documentation of the use cases without major difficulties. The use cases documented here belong to the security subsystem group. The remaining two groups are left as exercises for the readers to try out – based on the template provided in the next section. This template further expands the simplified template discussed earlier in Figure 2.43.

5.6.4.1 *Template for documenting use cases*

Use Case Thumbnail

<Number and name of the use case and, if necessary, a version number> Note, though, that the status towards the end of the template can also be used to indicate the version of the use case

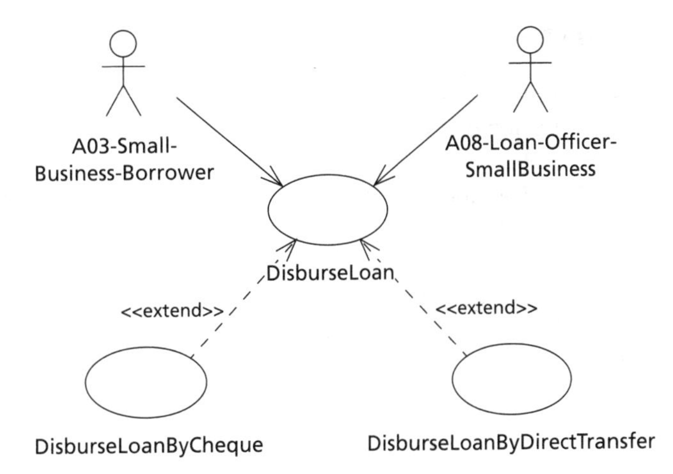

Figure 5.16 Use case diagram for 'Loans Disbursement'

Use Case Description

<A short one or two line description of the use case>

Stereotype and Package

<Description of the stereotype and the package to which this use case belongs>

Preconditions

<Conditions that must be satisfied before this use case can begin – may include a list of other use cases>

Postconditions

<Conditions that must be met at the end of this use case>

Actors

<A list of the actors involved in this use case>

Goals

<Goals that the actors will achieve in interacting with the system, as documented in this use case>

Use Case Relationships

<Thumbnails of other use cases that are included, extended and inherited>

Use Case Text

1.0 <description of step>
2.0 <description of step> (A1, E1, E2)
3.0 <description of step> (A2, E3)
INCLUDES <Thumbnail of use case/s Included>
EXTENDS <Thumbnail of use case/s Extended>

Alternative Courses

<A1>

Exceptions

<E1>

Constraints

<special constraints/limitations in executing the use case>

User Interface Specifications

<Number and name of UI specifications related with this use case, including web-screen specifications>

Metrics

<Measurements related to this use case – if relevant to the programme; also, perhaps, complexity factor>

Priority

<The importance of the functionality described by this use case – High/Medium/Low>

Status

<The state of completeness of the documentation of this use case – Initial/Major/Final>

Author & History

<Original author and modifiers of this use case>

Reference Material

<Relevant references, as well as sources>

5.6.4.2 Documentation for use case IdentifyAssets

Use Case Thumbnail

UC100-IdentifyAssets (version 0.9)

Use Case Description

This use case describes the process of identifying the assets of each of the individual customers that together make up the borrower, so that they can be used by the securities and assets officer of the bank in order to calculate the collateral value of the assets for the purpose of granting loan to the borrower.[13]

13 Note that some of the assets may have been registered by the individual customers even before they decide to become borrowers, while doing other business with the bank. (Also note that this note is 'not' a part of the use case documentation.)

Stereotype and Package

«Entity»; SASS

Preconditions

Asset details must be provided by the customers (potential borrowers at this stage) before any classification and verification process can start. The A07-Securities&Assets-Officer should already have such data in hard form (the actual loan application form) and/or soft copy at hand.

Postconditions

None

Actors

A03-Small-Business-Borrower
A07-Securities&Assets-Officer
A09-Database

Goals

A03-Small-Business-Borrower – to provide information related to their Asset; to assist in calculation of the net asset value available as collateral.
A07-Securities&Assets-Officer – to calculate the net asset of the borrowers; to calculate the collateral by balancing the net assets with the loan amount requested; to store all details in the database.
A09-Database – to store the asset details.

Use Case Relationships

CalculateNetAssets «include»UC100-IdentifyAssets
Further details in use case diagram *Verifying and Valuing Assets.*

Use Case Text

1. A03-Small-Business-Borrower provides details of assets to be offered as collateral.
2. A07-Securities&Assets-Officer records identification details of the assets.
3. A07-Securities&Assets-Officer queries the system if the assets already exist in the system (Alternative 1).
4. System notes details of assets not already recorded in the system.
5. System prompts for asset name and other details.

6. A07-Securities&Assets-Officer records name and other details of the asset.
7. Asset details are sent as a 'contract' or 'string' to the A09-Database.

Alternative Courses

Alternative 1

1. Asset already exists in the system (as made available by the borrower as existing customers of the bank).
2. System provides names and other asset details.
3. A07-Securities&AssetsOfficer verifies the name and other details of the asset with A03-Small-Business-Borrower – and updates the relevant changed details.
4. Asset details are sent as a 'contract' or 'string' to the A09-Database.

Constraints

None

User Interface Specifications

UI150_RecordAssetDetails

Metrics

None

Priority

High

Status

Major

Author & History

Bhuvan Unhelkar

Reference Material

Details of the system recording assets provided for other purposes to the bank. Assets database stored in ASSET.DB as a part of overall database.

5.6.4.3 Use case for AppliesForLoan

Use Case Thumbnail

UC150-AppliesForLoan

Use Case Description

This use case documents the details of the potential borrower making an application for loan from the bank. This use case is written in a *generic* fashion – it shows how *all* types of borrowers can apply for loans, and how a bank's officer can take action.

Stereotype and Package

«Entity»; LASS

Preconditions

Borrower is a valid group of two or more customers if the application is by a small business borrower.

Postconditions

None

Actors

A01-Borrower
A05-Bank-Loan-Officer
A09-Database

Goals

A01-Borrower – make an application for loan.
A05-Bank-Loan-Officer – identify valid customer; accept and store application for loan.
A09-Database – store application details.

Use Case Relationships

UC210-AppliesForLoan «include» UC250-CompletesApplicationForm
UC210-AppliesForLoan «include» UC270-SubmitsApplication

Use Case Text

1. A01-Borrower approaches the bank for a loan.
2. A05-Bank-Loan-Officer identifies the customers that make up the A01-Borrower.
3. A01-Borrower provide details requested by A05-Bank-Loan-Officer on their existing business (accounts with the bank).
4. A01-Borrower completes the application form UC230-CompletesApplicationForm.
5. A05-Bank-Loan-Officer does initial checks and submits the form to the database.

Alternative Courses

None

Constraints

None

User Interface Specifications

UI350-Bank-Loan-Officer-Login
UI360-BorrowerInternet-Login

Metrics

Medium Complexity use case (current estimate two person-weeks for development)[14]

Priority

Medium

Status

Major

14 This metric is based on a rule of thumb arising out of the authors' (BU) practical experience. Roughly speaking, a simple use case takes one person-week, one with medium complexity takes two person-weeks and a complex use case takes four person-weeks for full development. This includes the time spent in analysis and design, but does not include the final coding effort. If, however, detailed metrics are being used for class specifications during the analysis and design activity, then this metric is either considered redundant or merely used as a cross-check against other metrics.

Author & History

Bhuvan Unhelkar

Reference Material

Interviews with users, loan approval procedure details document.

5.7 Activity: Analysis and business model refinement

The activity of Analysis and business model refinement *iterates* with that of Requirements Engineering. Therefore, neither of the two activities is completed in isolation, and neither is sequential. An initial iteration of Requirements Engineering will produce a sufficiently detailed use case model to help in producing an initial version of an object model that contains business-level objects. Together with the interaction diagrams (in our case, sequence diagrams), the class diagrams make up the Business Object Model.

5.7.1 Business Object Model (BOM)

Just as we had a suite of techniques to choose from in creating the requirements model, so also we have a list of techniques to choose during the creation of the BOM. Many of these techniques are also applicable at a lower level, during the creation of a class diagram close to implementation. Some of the techniques worth mentioning here (and which have been described in earlier chapters) are:

- Aggregation, association, inheritance: these describe some of the various possible relationships between classes. Relationship modeling is the common name for these techniques, and indicates the modeling process of class relationships. Aggregation deals with composition of a class, and Association with a 'loose' relationship between two classes; both these relationships translate to client–server within object-oriented programming languages. Inheritance is the third relationship between two classes. All these relationships are used in creating a business-level object (class) diagram.
- Class internal design, class naming, design templates: these techniques deal with the precise definition of class name, the attributes, their types and initial values and operations, their parameters and their return values. The class naming standards can be derived from the local organization standards; class design templates can be used if classes have to be documented in plain text, as against a CASE tool.

- Design patterns, generalization identification, generalization for reuse, pattern recognition: some of these techniques relate to architectural work, wherein decisions related to reuse (and therefore related to patterns) are taken. However, the techniques also relate to class-level designs.
- Component integration patterns: although not described in the OPEN literature until now, these patterns capture the essence of *integrating* components with the existing applications – an aspect quite important in BLS wherein customer-related details are already existing in an application of the bank.
- Layering, partitioning and allocation: these are all architectural techniques, playing a role in more than one activity of OPEN. These techniques are pure architectural techniques yet they can be used along with the techniques related to patterns described earlier.
- Granularity: just as it is important to get the granularity of use cases right, so it is important to get the level of granularity right within the class diagrams. That implies getting the class *size* right, or getting the right number of attributes and operations within a class. In other words, 'granularity' of design means 'for a given functionality, class sizes can be ascertained as *small* or *large* – and smaller sized classes will need *a greater number* of classes to satisfy the same functionality that, if it were satisfied by larger sized classes, will need fewer classes'. This is shown in Figure 5.17. If the organization has a reuse strategy then it is easier to ascertain the granularity of classes during the earlier projects. Coarse granular classes (whose size is large) are less reusable and, if they are reused, they carry lot of unnecessary functionality called 'baggage'. Finer granular systems, on the other hand, need more up-front effort, but are more reusable over a number of projects.

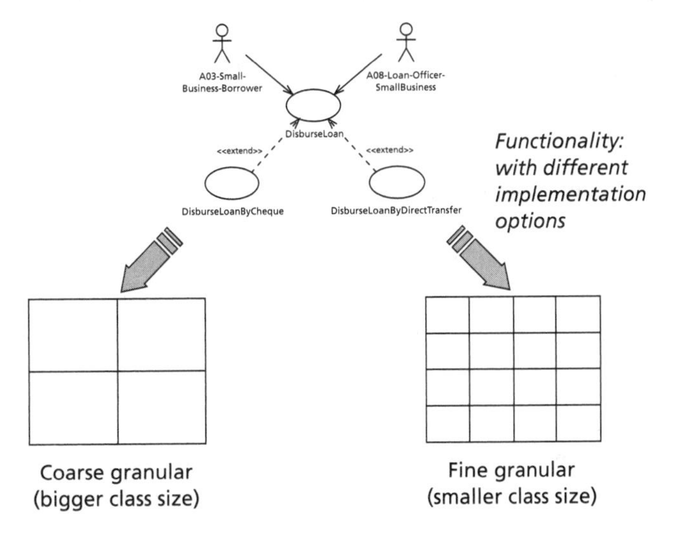

Figure 5.17 Two extreme granularities for an object-oriented design

- Interaction modeling, state modeling: these techniques deal with the dynamic aspect of the BOM. They show what is happening in *memory,* and are documenting a 'snapshot' of the system as it is being executed. The interaction model contains the sequence and collaboration diagrams, and the state model contains the statechart diagrams.

Thus, the OPEN process describes a number of techniques and deliverables that go on to make up the BOM deliverable. As mentioned earlier, this deliverable is produced by examining the requirements model (primarily the use case diagrams and the use case descriptions) for candidate business objects. Analyzing the use cases not only reveals the candidate business objects, but also provides details of the high-level subsystems and components. Thus, in addition to the knowledge of requirements modeling, the BOM can also benefit by the architectural knowledge, which is the information related to high-level grouping of the business objects. Instead of starting with business objects, which might be at a lower level, we can start with components or packages, which are at the right level for business analysis and creation of the first diagram in the BOM.

A BOM would contain a package diagram at the highest level, followed by one or more class diagrams, which may also be at a high level. The main purpose of this first iteration of BOM creation is to show the key business objects (which are also called key business entities as, at that stage, the modeler cannot be sure whether these entities will actually become objects or remain just entities) and their relationships. Furthermore, the BOM, at this stage, plays the crucial role of showing where the new objects will be *integrated* with the existing objects. The 'how' of the integration is left up to a later iteration. In fact, it should not worry the modeler if the diagrams within the BOM are *non*-implementable, since implementation is not the purpose of the BOM. It is only when the diagrams are refined further during the final iteration of the analysis and design that they will reach a state where they can be implemented.

5.7.2 Business object definitions

The high-level packages identified during requirements engineering activity were the BLS and its corresponding three subsystems acronymed CISS, SASS and LASS, as shown in Figure 5.5. These packages, as shown in the main class diagram for the system, together with the use case diagrams, form the starting point of the business object model. Some of the classes, which represent the key business abstractions, are described here using a class template. Note that if a CASE tool is employed in documenting the requirements, then the class descriptions may not be documented in great detail in a template but, instead, in the model created within the CASE tool itself.

Process comment

The process issue in arriving at the business class definitions is 'whether the class definitions are spelled out first or whether the key classes and their relationships are arrived at first'. Without having some idea of the potential classes, it will not make sense to start putting them together in a class diagram. Hence, OPEN recommends identification of the key business classes first, followed by corresponding class diagrams. The process will, of course, be an iterative one, wherein the earlier identified classes will change their attributes and operations depending on the relationships drawn out for them within the class diagrams. In reading the following class descriptions, the reader may want to refer to the subsequent class diagrams appearing in Figures 5.18–5.21.

5.7.2.1 Suggested class template

«Stereotype» Name	A one-word name for the class (two words are joined); the name is prefixed by the optional stereotype. Stereotype would indicate, for example, whether this class deals with interface, persistence or control
Derivation	Parent class(es) of this class; also, whether this is an abstract class
Description	A one to two line description of the class
Attributes	A list of all attributes of the class. The attributes here are merely listed at analysis stage. During detailed design, their types, initial values and access control are also specified
Responsibilities	The main responsibilities of this class. There are number of ways these responsibilities are identified. These ways include drawing the sequence diagrams or undertaking Class–Responsibility–Collaboration workshops
Business Rules	If this class (key business entity) has special business rules that are not easily listed under responsibilities, they may be documented here. An example would be rules related to interest calculation, or for Goods and Services Tax, etc., which need to be specified for a class, but which do not form a separate responsibility on their own
Complexity	Simple/Medium/Complex: this complexity is used in order to ascertain some class-related metrics

Modeling comment

Will this class remain a class, or will it become a component? Furthermore, if this class belongs to a package, how do we document that here? Well, using a recognized CASE tool will help in documenting a class properly. For example, a class will appear within a Package within a CASE tool diagram, removing the specific need to show its Package within this documentation. The class-to-component mapping can also be handled by the CASE tool. Thus, not all aspects of a class can be documented at this stage without the use of a CASE tool. The documentation here is most valuable for high-level classes, which we prefer to call key business entities as discovered by analyzing the use cases. Detailed class design should be done 'within' a CASE tool as far as possible. Detailed design in a good CASE tool may also be used to 'generate code'.

Using the above template, we describe some (and not all) key business entities of the BLS and its corresponding subsystems.

5.7.2.2 *Customer*

«Stereotype» Name	«entity» Customer Belongs to the CISS subsystem or package
Derivation	None
Description	Provides all details of a Customer of the bank, who wants to apply for Loan
Attributes	Customer Identification Account Identification (of all accounts belonging to this customer) Other information related to Customer
Responsibilities	Maintain Customer details Provide Customer profile
Business Rules	Create Customer profile based on following rules: Very Important: Customers with 20+ years with the bank, or total current debit accounts greater than $250,000, or seeking more than $250,000 in business loans Important: Customers with 10+ years with the bank or total current debit accounts greater than $100,000, or seeking more than $100,000 in business loans
Complexity	Complex

Modeling comment

This Customer class is one of the most interesting classes in this system. Although stereotyped as an «entity» class, this class has an important role of integrating the CISS functionality with the existing system storing Customer data. The job of this class is twofold: (a) to provide for all the business rules specified here by doing the appropriate calculations and flagging the Customer into his or her degree of importance to the bank, and (b) the more important job of retrieving the details of the Customer from the bank's current database of Customer, which may not be copied across to the BLS, but may continue to be stored in the existing (perhaps legacy) system. Thus, both major responsibilities of this class need integration with the existing system. This class may have to deal with another class called (say) CustomerDB that deals with the storage and retrieval of data only. Furthermore, note that although the bank has many 'types' of Customers, because this class is representing the 'legacy' side of the system, we have not shown a class hierarchy representing all those types of customers.

5.7.2.3 *Borrower*

«Stereotype» Name	«Entity, CISS» Borrower
Derivation	None, Abstract
Description	This class represents any person or company that is borrowing money from the bank
Attributes	Borrower Identification Borrower Name Customer Identification List (made up of all Customers who have formed the borrowing entity; would be a single Customer if the Borrower is a PersonalBorrower)
Responsibilities	Create a Borrowing entity based on the details of the type of Borrower Maintain details of the Borrower
Business Rules	The Borrower has to be made up of existing Customer(s) of the bank. Changing list of Customers brings in legal issues, and is currently out of scope of this release
Complexity	Simple

Modeling comment

The interesting comment here would be that the bank already has some sort of borrowing facilities, currently being used by 'personal borrowers'. These are individuals who need loans for a car or a boat or an overseas holiday. The chart shows how various types of borrowers are related to each other through this abstract class Borrower. This is a typical integration situation, wherein some key business entities already exist, while others are formed anew. The ones that exist may not be existing in the shape and form they appear in the class diagrams for the new system. The situation will become even more complicated if (say) the existing module, represented by PersonalBorrower, is in a 'legacy' language like C or COBOL, and the new modules (say) SmallBusinessBorrower, are written in VisualBasic or C++.

5.7.2.4 *SmallBusinessBorrower*

«Stereotype» Name	«Entity, CISS» SmallBusinessBorrower
Derivation	Borrower, BusinessBorrower
Description	This class deals with the special situation of a providing loan for small businesses, and is the new addition to the bank's repertoire of 'Borrowing Entities'
Attributes	BusinessNumber
Responsibilities	Maintain common business details
Business Rules	Has to be a registered business – checked by the existence of BusinessNumber
Complexity	Simple

Modeling comment

A SmallBusinessBorrower is a special case of BusinessBorrower, which is a special case of Borrower. The SmallBusinessBorrower, by rules of the bank, has to be made up of two or more Customers. The SmallBusinessBorrower is thus a relatively simple class which derives its needs for maintaining a list of Customers from the facilities offered by the

Borrower class which itself is made up of a collection of Customers. Change to the list is most unlikely, as the loan is provided based on who the borrowing customers are, and those customers cannot be changed. In case a change occurs (say if one of the borrowers wants to quit business), special rules will apply that will close the current loan and start a new borrower.

5.7.2.5 Account

«Stereotype» Name	«Entity» Account
Derivation	None, Abstract
Description	This is an abstract class Account, providing the basis for all types of accounts within the bank, including all debit as well as Loan accounts. This class existed in the bank even before the BLS was implemented
Attributes	AccountIdentification CustomerIdentification
Responsibilities	Maintain basic details of Account
Business Rules	None
Complexity	Simple

Modeling comment

This class represents all types of Account within the bank and hence continues to represent its legacy counterpart, which would exist in the form of an AccountsDatabase. This would also be true of the DebitAccount class and its subsequent derivatives. The CreditAccount side of the derivation is the one that is of further interest to us in this modeling exercise since the LoanAccount is a type of CreditAccount. Furthermore, note that the Customer and the Account class represent a bidirectional relationship as each class has the ID of the other class.

5.7.2.6 LoanAccount

«Stereotype» Name	«Entity» LoanAccount
Derivation	Account, CreditAccount
Description	This is the new account that specifically deals with the Loans provided to Borrowers. Currently, this class is dealing by default with the SmallBusinessBorrower
Attributes	StartDate StartRate AmountApproved CollateralAmount
Responsibilities	Retrieve details from the LoanApplication and store them along with the status of the loan Maintain all details of the LoanAccount Provide all relevant information for tracking the Loan
Business Rules	See LoanRules.DOC document[15]
Complexity	Complex

15 For an extremely complex class such as this LoanAccount class, which forms a major part of the design of the system, the business rules are most likely to be a fairly comprehensive document rather than just a few lines. In such a case, it is always advisable to refer to the document, rather than list all the business rules in the class specification.

5.7.2.7 Asset

«Stereotype» Name	«Entity, SASS» Asset
Derivation	None
Description	This Asset class has all details of the assets of the customer
Attributes	AssetIdentification CustomerIdentification AssetValue
Responsibilities	Maintain details of the Assets of the customer Provide information on the market value of the asset Provide information on how the Assets can be used as a Collateral for loan
Business Rules	Full, part, and joint ownership of Assets should be specified
Complexity	Complex

Modeling comment

The assets themselves are not a new 'thing' to be stored in the system. Customers might be providing details of their assets for personal borrowing and so on. What is important here is the manner in which the Asset class is representing the current module dealing with assets and how it is further developed into various types of assets that will now be offered to the bank for collateral. In situations where a higher-level class represents some existing functionality of the system, and new classes have been added underneath it, there is a very good chance of significant repetition of attributes and functionality in the lower-level classes. For example, the Asset class itself might currently be maintaining details of some assets already in the system. Through newer classes such as Property and FinancialInstruments, some functionality of the basic Asset class might get repeated.

5.7.2.8 Collateral

«Stereotype» Name	«Entity, SASS» Collateral
Derivation	None
Description	This class has all the details related to the Assets, as used in a Collateral for a loan
Attributes	AssetIdentification – an array of a list of Assets that are used together in making a collateral for loan. If only one asset is offered, then only a single ID appears here LoanIdentification CollateralValue
Responsibilities	Ascertain Collateral value based on Assets offered
Business Rules	Collateral value is 70% of the value of Assets offered One asset can be used for more than one collateral, but the value of the asset has to be reduced by its previous use in a collateral
Complexity	Complex

5.7.2.9 FamilyHome

«Stereotype» Name	«Entity» FamilyHome
Derivation	Property, Asset
Description	Family Home is a class representing the use of family home as a type of Asset to be used for Collateral in securing the Loan
Attributes	MortgageAmount
Responsibilities	Ascertain the 'collateral' value of the home, by reducing from the MarketValue of the home, the MortgageAmount
Business Rules	
Complexity	Medium

5.7.2.10 LoanApplication

«Stereotype» Name	«Interface» LoanApplication
Derivation	COMM_FORM[16]
Description	This is the LoanApplication GUI class that is responsible for capturing loan application information
Attributes	AppNumber CustomerID(s) Amount Duration
Responsibilities	Accepting and storing loan application details Part-verification of loan application Make provision for additional details to be recorded in loan application
Business Rules	Only bank customers can apply for loans;
Complexity	Medium

16 This is a generic form from which all forms of GUIs of Commercial Bank are derived (this note is 'not' part of the class documentation).

5.7.2.11 LoanInterest

«Stereotype» Name	«Database» LoanInterest
Derivation	None
Description	This LoanInterest class is made up of a set of SQL statements that would retrieve interest rates based on a number of conditions
Attributes	RateType Rate StartDate EndDate InterestAmount
Responsibilities	Calculate interests for a given block of days (period) and store the calculated interest to provide figures for total interest to be charged, and to provide historical information
Business Rules	See Loaninterest.doc and Loaninterest.xls documents
Complexity	Medium

5.7.2.12 *MarketValue*

«Stereotype» Name	«Entity» MarketValue
Derivation	None
Description	The MarketValue class deals with calculating the 'real' or market value of the asset that is offered as collateral
Attributes	AssetIdentification AssetStatedValue AssetMarketValue
Responsibilities	Calculate the market value of the asset, based on current and historical data
Business Rules	See market value database documentation
Complexity	Complex

Having described the various classes (key business entities), we will put them together in class diagrams. Relevant descriptions of the class diagrams are also provided. Note that, as shown in Figure 5.12 (process options), we have choices in following the process. What is shown here is just one example of how we proceed from classes to class diagrams. It is possible that in practice we may draw the class diagrams first, and then document some of the classes, before iteratively upgrading the class diagrams.

5.7.3 Class diagram for Customer Information Subsystem

Figure 5.18 shows the main class diagram for the CISS. This class diagram shows the Borrower class has Customer as members. The SmallBusinessBorrower class is of importance to us here, and it is a class derived from BusinessBorrower which, in turn, is derived from Borrower. The PersonalBorrower class shows only the context in which an individual Borrower is treated by the system – there is no associated software development work being performed by this class. An instantiation of the Customer class will 'have' additional objects derived from the classes Name, Address and PhoneDetails. In this case, one acceptable way of modeling the relationship between Customer and Address, between Customer and Phone Details and between Customer and Name would be to use an existential dependency. Since one of the possible interpretations of UML's black diamond is that of existential

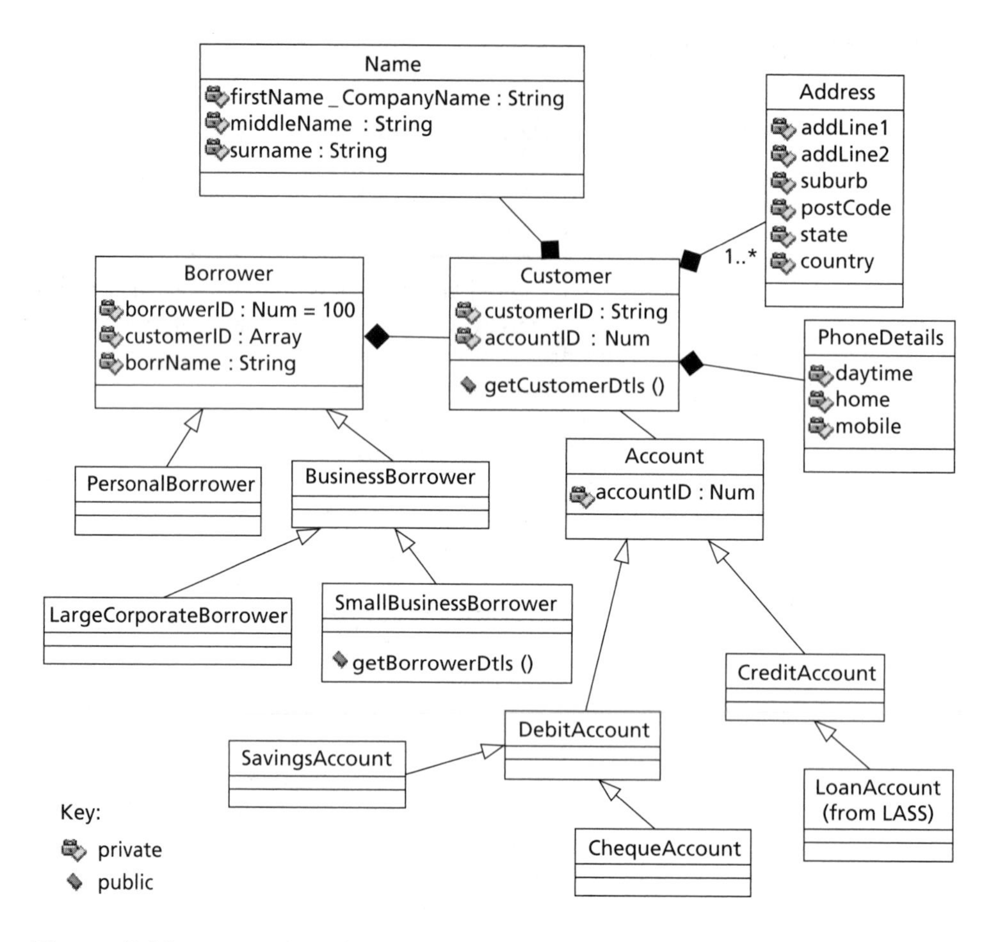

Figure 5.18 Class diagram for 'Customer Information' Subsystem. Here the black diamond symbol (UML 'composition') is used to mean existential dependency.

dependency (see Chapter 3 and, in particular, Figure 3.24), we will use that notation here. Customer can have multiple Addresses, but at least one address is a must. An association relationship (bidirectional by default) is shown between Customer and Account. The Account class has its own hierarchy with DebitAccount and CreditAccount classes derived from it.

Modeling comment

Three major static or design-time components emerge in this diagram. They are the Borrower, the Customer and the Account. While these three 'components' are shown in the same diagram here, in practice each of them may occupy a class diagram on their own. Furthermore, it is important to note how some classes within the diagram – like the PersonalBorrower and the DebitAccount – represent modules 'already existing' in the system. This representation of key business entities in a class diagram, even if they are not implemented in this iteration, is an important aspect of component integration.

At a more technical level, note how LoanAccount is derived from Account, and since Account has an association relationship with Customer, LoanAccount will have an association relationship with Customer. However, it is not the direct relationship we desire between LoanAccount and Customer. Instead, what we want is a LoanAccount and Borrower relationship. However, that creates a problem with the current relationship we have shown between LoanAccount as a derived class of Account. As mentioned before, however, in practice, this group of classes shown in Figure 5.18 will actually start becoming Packages or Components in their own right. Thus, the candidate components here are Account, Customer and Borrower. Furthermore, note that a separate diagram to show only the inheritance relationship is occasionally drawn and, in fact, encouraged in OPEN for complex class diagrams. This is called an inheritance diagram and it brings together in one location all classes in the hierarchy. This means that extraneous subclasses and superclasses can be removed from the class diagram itself. An independent inheritance diagram also highlights the depth of the hierarchy. Although creating hierarchies by small increments is easy at the design stage, it can result in very deep hierarchies. The deeper the hierarchy, the harder the code is to debug, understand and maintain. Hierarchies deeper than about 3 start to become difficult to read in the code and, as a general guideline, we recommend you never design hierarchies deeper than seven (excluding the language-level superclasses).

Process comment

Does this detailed class diagram with so many classes shown on it come first, and then the classes get grouped into packages? Or do the packages come first? When the business domain is new, and there is not much domain expertise, then it is not easy to come up with correct packages to start with. In that case, we are following the bottom-up approach to design. This is what is happening with the classes in Figure 5.18. However, we did come up with the very high-level packages in Figure 5.5. Thus, the process is our case study is a combination of top-down and bottom-up, colloquially called middle-out.

5.7.4 Class diagram for Security Asset Subsystem

This SASS class diagram in Figure 5.19 primarily shows the Asset component. It also shows the relationship between the Customer class drawn from the CISS package and the Asset class belonging to the SASS package itself. Although in day-to-day business parlance we say a 'customer *has* an asset', which sounds as if it would translate into an aggregation relationship, in this diagram we show customer and asset in a relatively *loose* relationship – with no whole/part relationship – which is association. Therefore, for a customer we may or may not have an instantiation of asset. However, once an asset is instantiated, it has to have a market value, indicated by the aggregate MarketValue class.

Modeling comment

Note that the MarketValue class, which is shown as a part of Asset, could have been represented by an attribute or a group of attributes within the Asset class. However, we

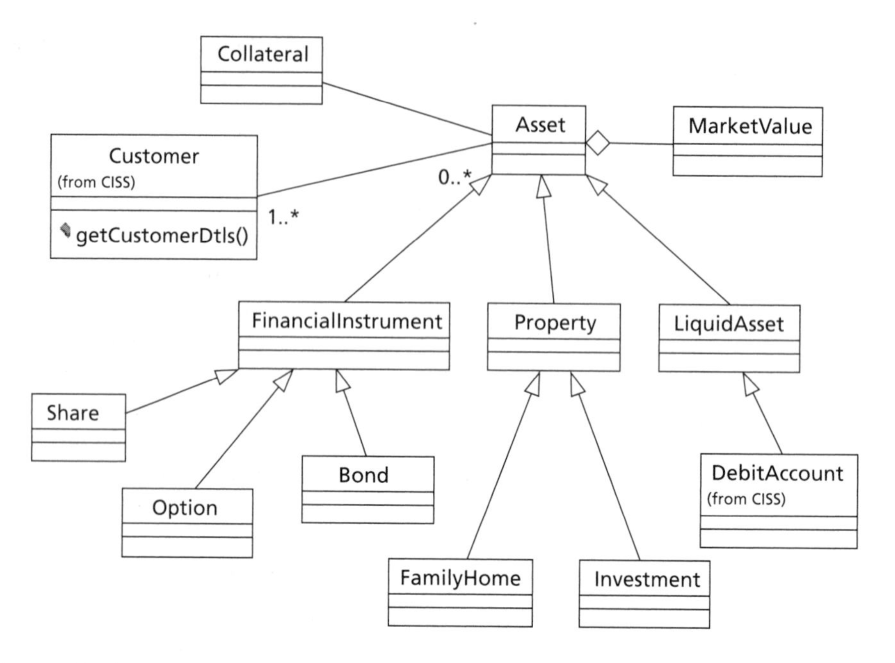

Figure 5.19 Class diagram for 'Security Assets' Subsystem

expect the MarketValue class to expand in the future, with more independent responsibilities assigned to it. These responsibilities may include, in addition to valuing the asset's current market value, creating graphs and charts that 'predict' the growth in the market value of the asset, and so on. This suggests an autonomous class might be a more appropriate model than an attribute.

Also note how the DebitAccount has multiple inheritance, although that is not evident by looking at just one diagram. Indeed, this underlines the suggestion in OPEN that a separate and consolidated diagram for each inheritance hierarchy may be of value – although the diagram itself has not been suggested in the standard UML. A DebitAccount class represents the savings and cheque accounts owned by the Customer. This account will have some cash in it, which is a type of LiquidAsset. Therefore, DebitAccount is both – it IS_A_TYPE_OF Account, as well as IS_A_TYPE_OF Asset – a model that would clearly be unimplementable in languages like SmallTalk or Simula. C++ and Eiffel are languages in which this design could be 'directly' implemented. In other programming languages, these diagrams serve the purpose of providing 'business information', which is then translated into different types of implementations.

5.7.5 Class diagram for Loan Applications Subsystem

While in the previous two class diagrams we have shown classes and their relationships, in this LASS main class diagram in Figure 5.20 we are also trying to show some of the descriptions of the classes as entered within a CASE tool. In earlier sections, we had started with the template for a class and completed the template with all details of the class. We use those details recorded for each class in order to complete the descriptions of the classes here. These descriptions primarily include the attributes and operations of the classes.

Figure 5.20 shows the association between LoanAccount and LoanApplication. The LoanApplication contains all details related to the 'potential loan' but it is only after the application goes through the approval process that it becomes a LoanAccount. LoanAccount has two major parts to it – the LoanPeriod and the LoanInterest. Assuming that an existential dependency is an appropriate description of this relationship, we again use the black diamond to signify this. Out of these two classes, the LoanInterest is particularly important and rapidly changing, depending on the economic situation and, of course, the rules under which the loan has been taken.

LoanApplication is shown to have the attributes AppNumber and CustomerID. This class also has a list of operations like fillLoanApplication() and storeLoanApplication(). Similarly LoanAccount has a list of attributes and operations, of which some are shown here in Figure 5.20.

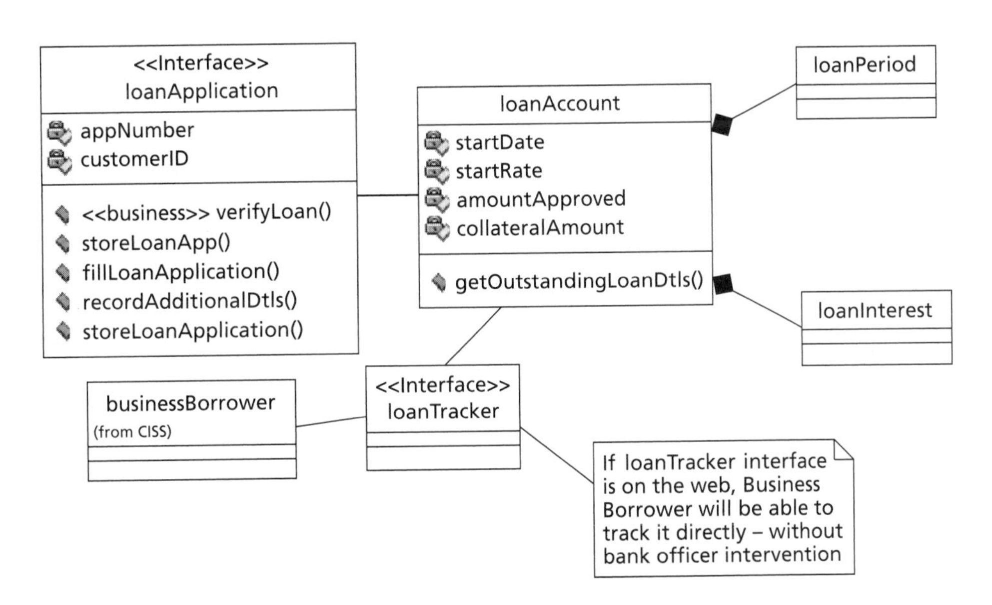

Figure 5.20 Class Diagram for 'Loan Applications' Subsystem. The black diamond again represents existential dependency – consistently with Figure 5.18.

An «interface»[17] stereotyped class called LoanTracker is shown here to indicate that that is the form that a customer in the role of a SmallBusinessBorrower may use, presumably from a web interface, in order to automatically track the loans. This LoanTracker interface would provide all details related to the loan, including the outstanding amount, the interest charged, the remaining period of the loan and so on.

Modeling comment

Note how it is difficult to show in this 'static' class diagram the process of LoanApplication becoming a LoanAccount. A number of business rules, which would have been specified in the class descriptions, would be applied by the LoanApplication class, or another class (not shown by us) called LoanRules. The 'dynamic' aspect of sending and receiving of messages cannot be shown in a class diagram but, instead, will be shown using sequence diagrams.

Another important point to be noted is the relationship between LoanAccount and the two corresponding classes LoanPeriod and LoanInterest, assumed before to be existential dependencies. In practice, all three classes will have to be persistent, and therefore stored in corresponding relational tables. More often than not, these three classes may be stored in a common table, which would not be a 'normalized' table. However, the reason why the three classes are kept separate is 'behavioural' rather than 'structural'. Thus, as far as data storage is concerned, the classes need not be separate, yet, as far as their behaviour is concerned, they have to be separate.

5.7.6 Class diagram for Business Loan System

Figure 5.21 is the main class diagram from the Business Loan System (BLS), linking Borrowers to Customers to Loan. It plays the role of showing how the important classes in the three other packages are *linked* to each other. Hence, all classes shown on this diagram are brought from the three packages or subsystems outside this BLS package. However, the BLS package is shown in the main package diagram as *dependent* on the other three packages. However, there will be some more classes in BLS which are not shown here. The classes in the diagram are showing association relationship, as what we show here is some relationship between the three classes from the three corresponding packages – we do not refine the relationship between the three classes at this stage (and we may do so in future only if it is necessary).

17 This may also be called a «boundary» stereotype.

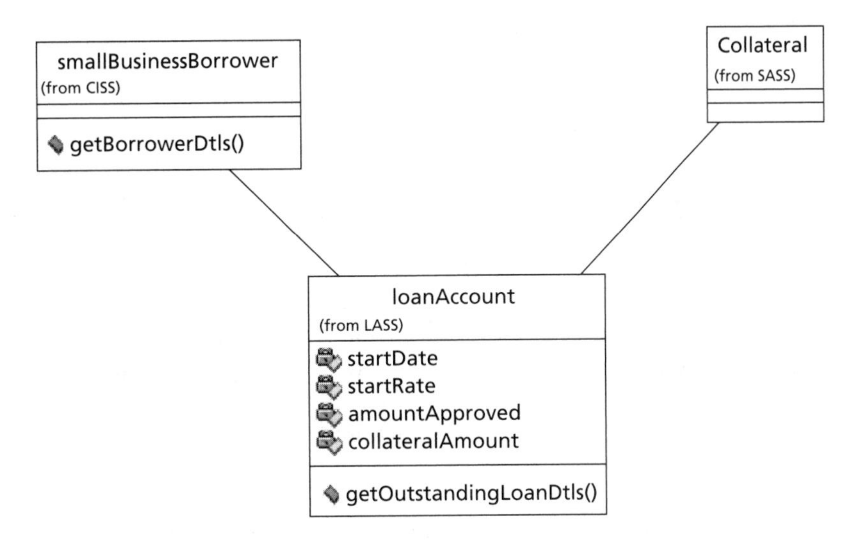

Figure 5.21 Class diagram for 'Business Loan System' (linking Borrower to Customer to Loan)

5.7.7 Sequence diagram for applying for small business loan

The sequence diagram shown in Figure 5.22 depicts the sequence of application for small business loan. It starts off with the actor A01-Borrower, who makes an application for loan by filling out the loan application form using the operation fillsLoanApplication(BorrowerID). The LoanApplication is the «interface» object

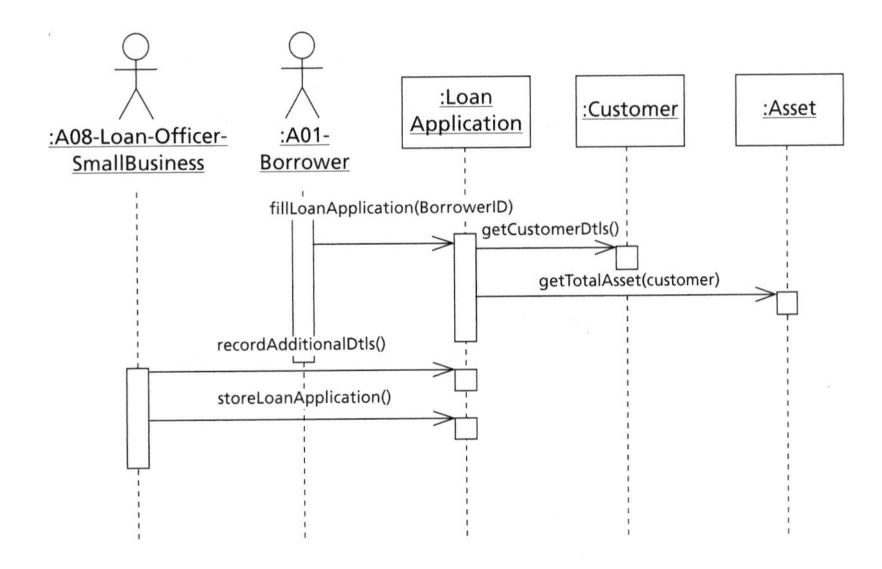

Figure 5.22 Sequence diagram for 'Applying for Small Business Loan'

that is shown on the screen to any type of Borrower. Instead of showing the actor A03-Small-Business-Borrower, we have shown A01-Borrower because the sequence of applying for a loan for any type of actor who is going to fill out an application form does not change. However, if the requirements modeler finds that the sequences of applying for loans do change, and that it is essential to show only the small business borrower, then the actor performing the operation of filling loan application would be a A03-Small-Business-Borrower. Having completed the application form, the next message shown in Figure 5.22 is retrieving the Customer details. This is an important '*integration*' message, in the sense that this message retrieves the details of the Customer which are already stored by the Bank somewhere else. Depending on the number of Customers applying for the loan (under the name of one Borrower), the system will *iteratively* retrieve the details – once for each of the Customers. Once the Customer details are established, the next (again *iterative*) task performed by the system is going to the Asset database and retrieving the Asset details of the Customer. This, of course, is necessary only for any type of BusinessBorrower (see class diagram in Figure 5.18) since, for PersonalBorrowers, it is not essential to show Assets. Finally, the sequences of recording additional details on the loan application and storing the loan application details are shown here as operations performed by the A08-Loans-Officer-SmallBusiness. These operations will have to further send messages down to the database level, in order to successfully store the loan application details – a part of the sequence not shown in this diagram.

Modeling comment

It is worth noting that sequence diagrams are not necessarily complete. They depict the most important or the most complex sequences, and are an excellent mechanism to view pictorially the messages, their recipient objects and the corresponding sequences in which messages are received. If attempts are made to document everything in these sequence diagrams then they tend to 'blow up' and become complicated and unwieldy themselves. Judicious use of notes and scripts is suggested in order to reduce the complexity of the sequence diagrams themselves while they try to depict a complex sequence of events within the system.

Modeling comment

An important question, raised again and again during initial discussions on sequence diagrams, is 'can we show two actors in the diagram, one sending a message to another?'. A simple answer is 'yes'. A typical situation is where a Customer is standing across the counter and withdrawing cash – given by the Teller. In that scenario, the Customer is 'not' directly dealing with the system, but the Teller is. How is that sequence of events to be shown in a sequence diagram? The Customer, in that scenario, does appear as a 'secondary' actor, who is handing over a request to the Teller to withdraw cash, and plays no further role in directly interacting with the software system. In practice, it becomes a two-part exercise, with the first attempt at sequence diagramming showing the actor:Customer sending a message to actor:Teller; when the same diagram is refined, it will be the class:Customer that will come into play. This is because when the actor:Teller starts interacting with the system, the system will be asking for lots of details related to the actor:Customer which will have been stored in the 'shadow' of this actor in a corresponding class:Customer. In the sequence diagram shown in Figure 5.22, we have also shown two actors but not interacting directly with each other. This is so because we are showing a sequence in which any actor A01-Borrower makes application for Loan.

5.7.8 Sequence diagram for loan tracking by the small business borrower using the Internet

Figure 5.23 shows a part of the sequence used by the actor A03-Small-Business-Borrower in order to access their LoanAccount. Note that, in this sequence diagram, the small business borrower is the direct user of the system – logging on to the system via the Internet. While the logging procedure itself is not shown in this sequence diagram, the sequence shows the search criteria being recorded by the actor on the SearchLoanForm object, the details of the borrower being retrieved from the SmallBusinessBorrower object followed by the details of the loan from the LoanAccount. These loan details are displayed on the SearchLoanForm itself in this diagram.

Modeling comment

Note that this sequence diagram shows the small business borrower directly accessing the loan details. However, if the small business borrower were to walk up to the bank and enquire about their loan balance in a traditional way, then the sequence diagram

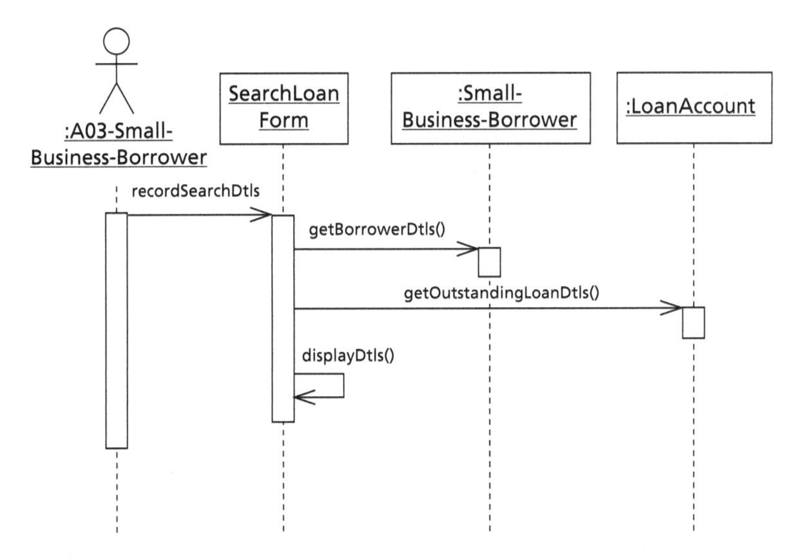

Figure 5.23 Sequence diagram for 'Loan Tracking by Borrower' using the Internet

would have the bank's loan officer as a primary actor sending and receiving messages from the system. Also note that if the bank was printing statements of all loans to be mailed to the borrowers the next day (a typical overnight batch job), the sequence diagram would change considerably, and either would show the bank officer initiating the printing or, more significantly, may not show an actor at all (as would be the case if a batch job is scheduled to start automatically every first or last day of the month).

5.7.9 Statechart diagram showing some states of LoanAccount

OPEN recommends statechart diagrams, like sequence diagrams, be drawn only for the most important and the most complex changes to the states of an object. Drawing statechart diagrams for all possible states of all objects will not add value to the overall requirements model. Figure 5.24 shows a statechart diagram for

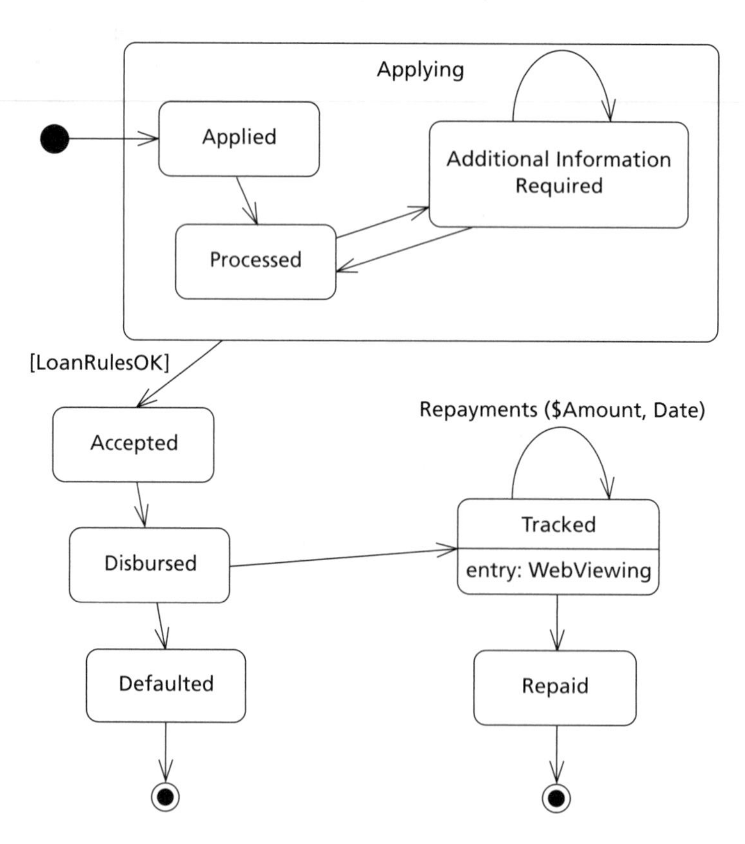

Figure 5.24 Statechart diagram showing some states of the LoanAccount class

some of the states of the LoanAccount object. The initial state is shown as a nested state, with 'Applying' being the higher-level state for the LoanAccount object. When the LoanAccount object is in this 'Applying' state, it could be in any of the three sub-states. These sub-states are 'Applied' for the loan through the completion of the LoanApplication form and the 'Processed' state wherein the loan application has been processed and therefore the LoanAccount object is in the processed state.

If additional information were sought on the loan application, then the LoanAccount object would move to the 'Additional Information Required' state and once the required information provided by the borrower, revert back to 'Processed'. Once all information is available and all the LoanRules have been satisfied, the state of the LoanAccount moves from 'Applying' to 'Accepted'. On acceptance of the loan application by the bank, the applicants will be informed of that decision and the loan amount handed over to them, with the LoanAccount object changing its state to 'Disbursed'. After the loan is disbursed, the LoanAccount object lends itself to tracking. The manner in which the loan is tracked (e.g. phone queries, printed statements, Internet) is not shown on this statechart diagram. The tracking of the loan continues while the repayments are made. Finally, the loan is repaid. The other alternative state is from 'Disbursed' to 'Defaulted'.

Modeling comment

This statechart diagram, like the sequence diagram, shows a part of the changes in the states of LoanAccount object. For example, it does not show what happens if the loan has been rejected. One way of interpreting this situation is that once the loan is rejected the bank is not interested in what happens to the LoanAccount. This statechart diagram also indicates that as soon as the LoanApplication is made, the system opens a LoanAccount object and starts tracking the process of applying for a loan through the states of the LoanAccount. This is quite feasible as this approach focuses on the LoanAccount itself, and treats the LoanApplication as more of an 'interface' object with the responsibility of interfacing with the applicants, and retrieving their loan application details. With this approach, no business logic is kept in the LoanApplication object but, instead, with the LoanAccount.

Another very interesting observation to be noted from the database modeling viewpoint is that the states of a persistent object, more often than not, represent the values of 'flags' stored with those persistent objects in a relational table. For example, objects belonging to class LoanAccount and stored in a table would have a flag 'attribute' that would store a value indicating the state of the object. Occasionally, good requirements modelers who are able to extract this requirement of the various states of an object may end up specifying them in a tabular form, rather than draw a statechart diagram. For example, the various states of the LoanAccount object, shown in Figure 5.24, could be represented as shown in Table 5.5.

Table 5.5 Table representing the various states of a LoanAccount object, and the corresponding values of a Flag

State description	Values of a 2-digit Flag	
Applying	0	
Applied		1
Processed		5
Information required		2
Accepted	2	
Disbursed	3	
Tracked	5	
Repaid	9	
Defaulted	8	

5.8 User interface specification (Activity: Requirements Engineering)

User interfaces play a crucial role in a web-based application. This is because of the need to *limit* the use of the 'richness' within a user interface. GUI specifications and design for a web-based application are more complicated and challenging, because there is a need to provide detailed and comprehensive information within a concise space and time. Furthermore, navigation within a web-based application is a vital challenge, since not all of the needs of the user can be satisfied on the web and, even if they are, they need lot of work in the navigational aspect of the user interface design. More often than not, users tend to get 'lost' within the complex multitude of screens if they are not provided with support for where they are in terms of navigation. Furthermore, user interfaces also provide an interesting starting point for requirements modeling. From a 'process viewpoint', user interfaces, especially through the prototyping mechanism, can provide, and have provided, a very good starting point for requirements modeling (as against use case diagramming or class diagramming, as shown in Figure 5.12).

5.8.1 User interface – aspects

The major groups of user interfaces are:

(a) the standard front-end user interfaces which provide information to, and gather information from, the user – these user interfaces not only have the informative aspect, but also need the 'bells and whistles';

(b) the administrative user interfaces which deal with helping the system and database administrators to manage the system;

(c) the prototypical aspect of the user interfaces, which are meant for brainstorming and workshops wherein they provide the basis for discussions as well as a mechanism to extract complete and correct requirements from the users.

Some of the issues that we need to consider in the 'user interface' aspects of the lifecycle are:

- Specifications – these are the specifications of the user interfaces, and these specifications could be documented during the requirements engineering activity
- Design – these are lower-level designs of the user interfaces and these designs benefit greatly from the skills of a graphics artist, in addition to the technical and functional skills needed
- Testing – user interface testing provides interesting challenges in terms of functional as well as stress and volume testing, and special testing tools will be needed at this stage; furthermore, usability testing is also required in the GUIs
- Incorporation of third-party graphics – requires proper understanding of the third-party packages, due consideration to the licensing arrangements and so on
- Navigability between user interfaces – as users jump rapidly from screen to screen, especially in a web environment. The goal here is to provide maximum information to the end user with minimum navigation between screens.

5.8.2 UI010_Loan_Application_Form

Figure 5.25 shows a sketch of the GUI that will be used in order to capture details of the loan application. These details include the name of the potential Borrower (which, as we know, would be a legal entity comprising two or more Customers for a small business loan). The name of the potential borrower is followed by list of customers making up the 'Borrowing Entity', details of the Assets offered as loan Collateral, amount of loan applied for, duration of loan and a preferred starting date for the loan. This form is at an early stage of design and therefore does not show many more details related to the loan application, such as details of the loans officer involved in the application, the process of reaching this GUI (perhaps from a login screen) and the standard features of Help, Cancel and OK. While not being a

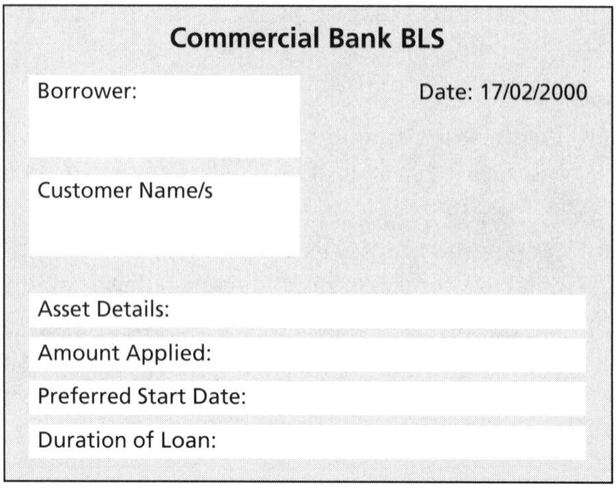

Commercial Bank BLS
Borrower:
Date: 17/02/2000
Customer Name/s
Asset Details:
Amount Applied:
Preferred Start Date:
Duration of Loan:

Figure 5.25 GUI design for UI010_Loan_Application_Form

full design, this screen can be instrumental in extracting correct and complete requirements from the users, as well as playing a crucial role in the navigation and other usability issues from an early stage of the lifecycle.

5.8.3 UI320_Web-Loan_Tracker

Figure 5.26 depicts a GUI that is used by the borrower in automatically tracking the loan on the Internet. While this screen itself is not exhibiting any new design concept, from the process viewpoint it is important to have this screen. Navigability to

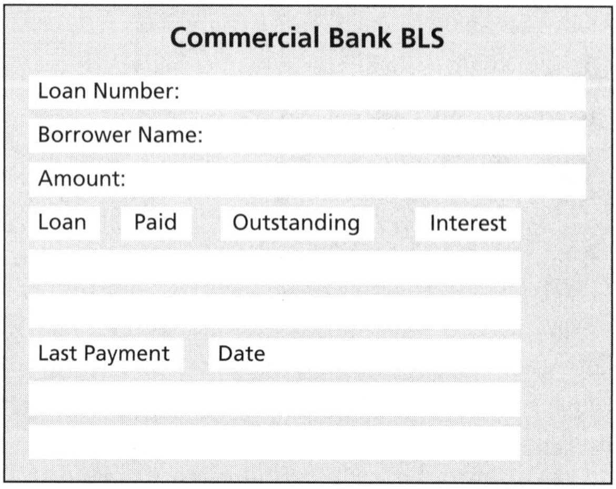

Commercial Bank BLS
Loan Number:
Borrower Name:
Amount:
Loan
Paid
Outstanding
Interest
Last Payment
Date

Figure 5.26 GUI design for UI320_Web-Loan_Tracker

the screen, the process of reaching the screen on the Internet, the security issues related to accessing the loan data, and the frequency of access (and therefore the speed of access) are all important parts of the process of modeling the GUI requirements.

5.9 Testing (Activity: Evaluation)

The OPEN process environment ensures that testing is not left as a last-minute activity within the process but, instead, is integrated in the entire contract-driven lifecycle by means of various tasks and techniques that appear with the activities of Requirements Engineering, Analysis and business model refinement as well as Build. The final acceptance testing performed by the end users is the only testing that happens towards the end of the lifecycle. Once again, as is the case with every artefact in OPEN, even this last end-user testing is done iteratively and incrementally. In practice, the testing activity is 'embedded' through all other activities within the OPEN lifecycle, and it ensures that testing and quality are planned and executed as an integral part of the other activities of the lifecycle. The major areas of testing that are worth discussing, albeit briefly here, are as follows:

- Test planning, including creation of test plans, test designs and the test cases as well as sorting out the test environment, test database and the resources needed for testing
- The architecture of testing, that describes the iterations of testing and the types of testing carried out
- The various testing approaches and the right approach or combination thereof, especially when component integration is being tested
- Risks associated with testing.

5.9.1 Test planning

Test planning is a task undertaken earlier in the lifecycle of the project. The planning process for testing can be made a part of the overall project planning process or it may be kept as an independent task. In either case, test planning includes the 'when' and the 'who' of creation of test cases, the resources that will conduct the actual testing, the test environment creation, and issues related to *integration* testing. The test plan itself can be envisaged as a textual document describing the strategic and logistic details of testing, including the scope and intensity of testing, the resources required for the tests, the risks associated with testing, management of a separate physical testing location, creation of a test environment that has the combination of existing legacy and newly integrated components, creation of test-beds in test databases, management of test databases including their backups and versions, recording and analyzing of results, network administration, scheduling of test

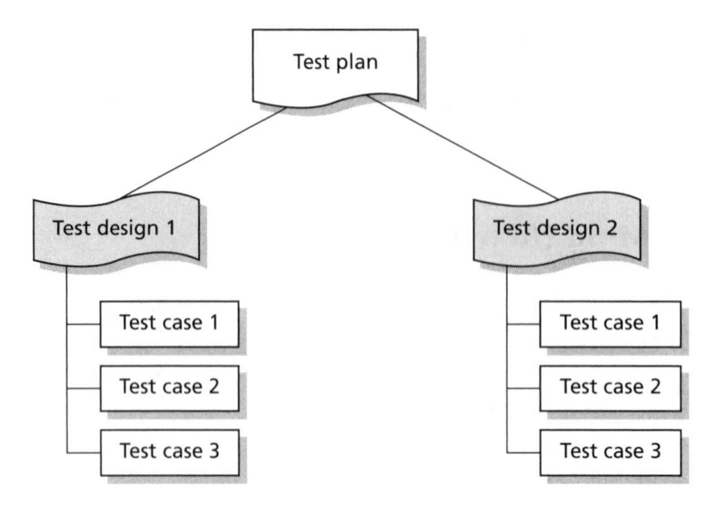

Figure 5.27 An appropriate organization for test designs/test cases (after Unhelkar, 1999; © CRC Press)

cases and so on. In addition to this high-level document which may include a 'test project plan', details of each of the test cases and how they are put together in test designs may be mentioned only briefly in the first iteration of test planning. As shown in Figure 5.27, the test plan includes description of test designs which, in turn, have test cases.

Process comment

It is worth mentioning that if the project is following the use-case-driven approach, then the text descriptions, as documented within the use cases, provide a very good starting point for functional test case designs. Each step within the text description, wherein an actor is interacting with the system, is a potential test case. The non-functional aspect of testing (e.g. performance and load testing) is derived from the 'technical user specifications'. These documents (namely technical user specifications and use case documentation) may not be available at an early stage of the lifecycle. However, provision for the use of these documents in the test design and test case creation should be made.

5.9.2 Testing architecture

The testing architecture in Figure 5.28 is a high-level view of the various types of tests and where they fit in with respect to each other. This architecture is influenced by the overall test planning process. For example, unit tests are extremely important at an individual programmer level and therefore need programming resources, whereas integration testing is important from the *component integration* viewpoint, requiring some organizational work of getting legacy and new components together *before* the actual testing can begin.

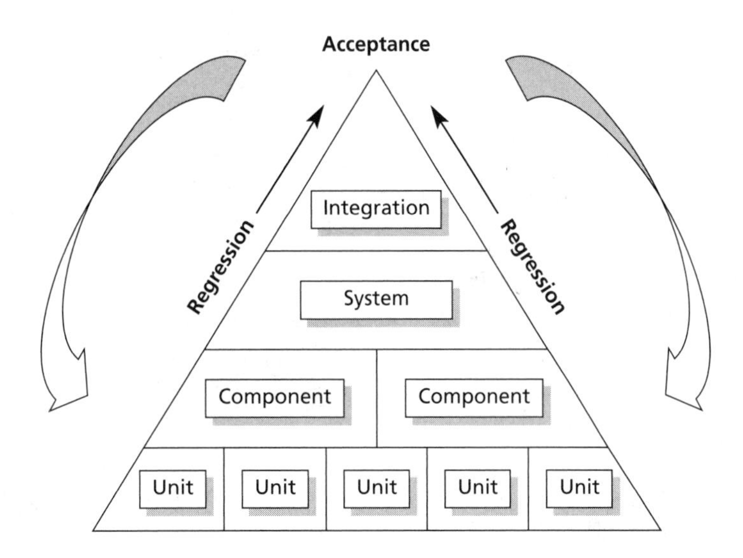

Figure 5.28 Testing architecture (after Unhelkar. 1999; © CRC Press)

Furthermore, the testing architecture also helps in organizing the *iterations* or *cycles* within testing. Testing is carried out in cycles to take major advantage of the results of earlier cycles of testing. Test cycles accumulate the experience and the data resulting from the execution of the tests, thereby ensuring that the first broad-brush cycle provides input to the next detailed cycle or iteration of testing. Scheduling of test cycles, therefore, becomes important and should be done in such a manner that the results from a particular module or the execution of a particular module positively influence the next cycle of testing. This also results in *reuse* of test cases and test results from earlier cycles of testing.

5.9.3 Testing approaches

Testing approaches, as a part of the overall testing strategy, provide an understanding of the various ways in which software can be tested. Each testing approach can be considered as an OPEN *Technique* in the context of planning an appropriate test strategy. While each individual test technique has distinctive merit and is theoretically sound, in practice we use a *combination* of these approaches to arrive at a good testing strategy. Figure 5.29 describes the various possible testing approaches that can be used in testing components. These are:

- The black–white box testing deals with the openness or closedness of the code and design of the components
- The manual–automated testing indicating the type of people and usage of tools in testing components

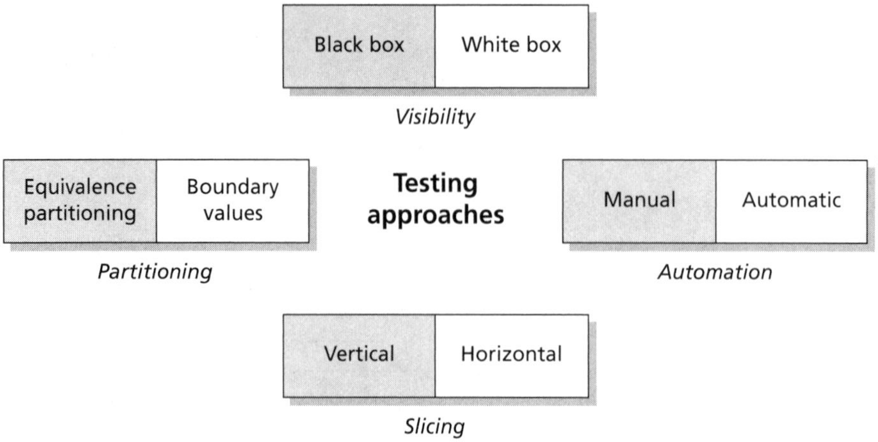

Figure 5.29 Testing approaches incorporated into a good testing architecture (after Unhelkar, 1999; © CRC Press)

- The vertical–horizontal slicing indicates how the system made up of the components is to be divided for testing
- The equivalence partitioning and boundary values indicate how the test data are to be sampled for testing.

5.9.4 Risks in testing

To close the discussion on testing, we highlight some of the common examples of risks in the testing process, especially those that deal with testing integrated components.

- Lack of specialist testing staff – especially those that deal with integration issues. Testing normal new object-oriented development is relatively easy compared with testing the development that deals with existing legacy applications. Some of the principles of good object-oriented software development such as encapsulation will *not* be adhered to in *component integration*, requiring specialist testing skills.
- Unavailability of suitable test environment. It will be essential to create a separate environment to test the system, but an environment will include both the legacy aspect as well as the new aspect of development. Creation of this environment and its maintenance is a testing overhead that needs to be considered during test planning. If a suitable test environment is not created early in the testing cycle, then it will be a significant risk to the project.
- Discovery of major errors in the later cycles of testing. We plan for regression tests to ensure that the errors detected in the earlier cycle are fixed, and that those fixes have not created problems elsewhere in the new system or, more

importantly, in the legacy system with which the new components are being integrated. Significant risks are associated in the assumption that no major problems will be discovered during the later cycles of regression tests.

- Unavailability of test data. If suitable test data are not available for creation of the test database, then we cannot guarantee sufficient and thorough testing. Design and creation of data are vital elements of test planning, without which the testing of the system is at a considerable risk. Furthermore, creation of the *right* amount of test data (not too much, not too little) is an important part of the test manager's role and should be arrived at correctly.
- Distributed components need to be tested over a 'real-life' network. Unavailability of such networks, or their inability to simulate real-life situations, would lead to inaccurate performance and load tests.
- Sufficient hardware in terms of machines, memory and communications should be available for testing.

Summary of Key Points

- In this chapter, we have described a detailed case study for a Business Loans System (BLS).
- We have discussed and demonstrated the 'tailoring' of OPEN to suit the problem at hand.
- We have discussed relevant Activities, Tasks, Techniques and Work Products as application to this 'instantiation of OPEN (Figure 5.6).
- We have highlighted, from a practical perspective, the importance as well as the iterative and incremental nature of Activities and Tasks (Table 5.1) and the corresponding Techniques (Table 5.2).
- We have used use case diagrams, use case textual descriptions, class diagrams, sequence diagrams and state chart diagrams to document the BLS.
- We have discussed the extremely important activity of evaluation (Testing) with its practical approach.

References

Ambler, S.W., 1999, Persistence modeling in the UML, *Software Development*, August 1999.

Brachman, R.J., 1985, 'I lied about the trees' or, defaults and definitions in knowledge representation, *The AI Magazine*, **6**(3), 80–93.

Cockburn, A., 1997a, Goals and use cases, *J. Obj.-Oriented Prog.*, **10**(5), 35–40.

Cockburn, A., 1997b, Using goal-based use cases, *J. Obj.-Oriented Prog.*, **10**(7), 56–62.

Cockburn, A., 1999, The impact of object orientation on application development, *IBM Systems Journal retrospective 'Turning points in computing'*, **39**(2/3), 308–332.

Cockburn, A., 2000, *Writing Effective Use Cases*, Addison-Wesley (in preparation).

Constantine, L.L., 1997, The case for essential use cases, *Object Magazine*, **7**(3), 72-70.

Constantine, L.L. and Lockwood, L.A.D., 1999, *Software for Use: A Practical Guide to the Models and Methods of Usage-Centered Design*, Addison-Wesley, Reading, MA, USA.

Firesmith, D.G., 1999, Use case modeling guidelines, in *Procs. TOOLS 30* (eds. D. Firesmith, R. Riehle, G. Pour and B. Meyer), IEEE Computer Society Press, 184–19.

Firesmith, D.G. and Henderson-Sellers, B., 1999, Improvements to the OPEN process metamodel, *JOOP/ROAD*, **12**(7), 30–35.

Firesmith, D., Henderson-Sellers, B. and Graham, I., 1997, *OPEN Modeling Language (OML) Reference Manual,* SIGS Books, New York, USA, 271pp and 1998 Cambridge University Press, New York, USA, 271 pp.

Gamma, E., Helm, R., Johnson, R. and Vlissides, J., 1995, *Design Patterns. Elements of Reusable Object-Oriented Software*, Addison-Wesley, Reading, MA, USA, 395pp.

Graham, I., Henderson-Sellers, B. and Younessi, H., 1997a, *The OPEN Process Specification*, Addison-Wesley, UK, 314 pp.

Graham, I.M., Bischof, J. and Henderson-Sellers, B., 1997b, Associations considered a bad thing, *J. Obj.-Oriented Programming*, **9**(9), 41–48.

Henderson-Sellers, B., 1996, *Object-Oriented Metrics. Measures of Complexity*, Prentice Hall, Englewood Cliffs, NJ, 234 pp.

Henderson-Sellers, B., 1998a, Towards the formalization of relationships for object modelling, *TOOLS 25* (eds. C. Mingins, R. Duke and B. Meyer), IEEE Computer Society, Los Alamitos, CA, 267–284.

Henderson-Sellers, B., 1998b, OO diagram connectivity, *JOOP/ROAD*, **11**(7), 60–68.

Henderson-Sellers, B. and Barbier, F., 1999, Black and white diamonds, *«UML»'99 – The Unified Modeling Language. Beyond the Standard* (eds. R. France and B. Rumpe), Lecture Notes in Computer Science 1723, Springer-Verlag, Berlin, 550–565.

Henderson-Sellers, B., Simons, A.J.H. and Younessi, H., 1998, *The OPEN Toolbox of Techniques*, Addison-Wesley, UK, 426 pp + CD.

Henderson-Sellers, B., Atkinson, C. and Firesmith, D.G., 1999, Viewing the OML as a variant of the UML, in *«UML»'99 –The Unified Modeling Language. Beyond the Standard* (eds. R. France and B. Rumpe), Lecture Notes in Computer Science 1723, Springer-Verlag, Berlin, 49–66.

Jaaksi, A., 1997, Our cases with use cases, *J. Obj.-Oriented Prog.*, **10**(9), 58–65.

Jacobson, I., 1999, Interview with Ivar Jacobson (by Adriano Comai), http://www.analisi-disegno.com/uml/JacobsonInterview.html.

Jacobson, I., Christerson, M., Jonsson, P. and Overgaard, G., 1992, *Object-Oriented Software Engineering: A Use Case Driven Approach*, Addison Wesley, 524 pp.

Jacobson, I., Griss, M. and Jonsson, P., 1997, *Software Reuse. Architecture, Process and*

Organization for Business Success, Addison Wesley Longman/ACM Press, Reading/New York, USA, 497 pp.

Jacobson, I., Booch, G. and Rumbaugh, J., 1999, *The Unified Software Development Process*, Addison Wesley Longman, Reading, MA, 463 pp.

Kilov, H. and Ross, J., 1994, *Information Modeling. An Object-Oriented Approach*, Prentice Hall, Englewood Cliffs, NJ, 268 pp.

Korson, T., 1998, The misuse of use cases (managing requirements), *Object Magazine*, **8**(3), 18–20.

Kruchten, P., 1999, *The Rational Unified Process. An Introduction,* Addison Wesley Longman, Reading, MA, 255 pp.

Lilly, S., 1999, Use case pitfalls: top 10 problems from real projects using use cases, in *Procs. TOOLS 30* (ed. D. Firesmith, R. Riehle, G. Pour and B. Meyer), IEEE Computer Society Press, 174–183.

OMG, 1997, *UML Notation. Version 1.1, 15 September 1997*, OMG document ad/97-08-05 (unpublished).

OMG, 1999a, *OMG Unified Modeling Language Specification, Version 1.3, June 1999*, OMG document 99-06-09 (unpublished).

OMG, 1999b, *Analysis & Design Platform Task Force. UML 2.0. Request for Information, Version 1.0, 25 August 1999*, OMG document ad/99-08-08 (unpublished).

Reenskaug, T., Wold, P. and Lehne, O.A., 1996, *Working with Objects. The OOram Software Engineering Manual*, Manning, Greenwich, CT, 366 pp.

Rumbaugh, J., 1994, Getting started: using use cases to capture requirements, *J. Obj.-Oriented Prog.*, **7**(5), 8–12.

Rumbaugh, J., 1998, Depending on collaborations: dependencies as contextual associations, *J. Obj.-Oriented Prog.*, **11**(4), 5, 8–9.

Rumbaugh, J., Jacobson, I. and Booch, G., 1999, *The Unified Modeling Language Reference Manual,* Addison-Wesley, Reading, MA, 550 pp.

Unhelkar, B., 1999, *After the Y2K Fireworks. Business and Technology Strategies*, CRC Press, Boca Raton, FL, 421 pp.

Wirfs-Brock, R., Wilkerson, B. and Wiener, L., 1990, *Designing Object-Oriented Software,* Prentice Hall, Englewood Cliffs, NJ, 368 pp.

Bibliography

I. OPEN books

Firesmith, D.G., and Henderson-Sellers, B., 2000, *The OPEN Process Framework. An Introduction*, Addison-Wesley (in preparation).

Firesmith, D., Henderson-Sellers, B. and Graham, I., 1997, *OPEN Modeling Language (OML) Reference Manual*, SIGS Books, New York, USA, 271 pp.: also 1998 Cambridge University Press, New York, 271 pp.

Firesmith, D.G., Hendley, G., Krutsch, S. and Stowe, M., 1998, *Documenting A Complete Java Application Using OPEN*, Addison-Wesley, Harlow, UK, 404 pp. + CD.

Graham, I., Henderson-Sellers, B. and Younessi, H., 1997, *The OPEN Process Specification*, Addison-Wesley, Harlow, UK, 314 pp.

Henderson-Sellers, B., Simons, A.J.H. and Younessi, H., 1998, *The OPEN Toolbox of Techniques*, Addison-Wesley, Harlow, UK, 426 pp + CD.

II. UML books/articles

American Programmer, 1997, Special issue on UML, **10**(3).

Booch, G., Rumbaugh, J. and Jacobson, I., 1999, *The Unified Modeling Language User Guide*, Addison-Wesley, Reading, MA, 482 pp.

Fowler, M. and Scott, K., 1997, *UML Distilled. Applying the Standard Object Modeling Language*, Addison-Wesley, Reading, MA, 179 pp.

Meyer, B., 1997, UML: the positive spin, *American Programmer*, **10**(3), 37–41.

OMG, 1999, *UML Notation. Version 1.3, June 1999*, OMG document 99-06-09 (unpublished).

Proceedings of *«UML»'99* (ed. J. Bézivin *et al.*), 1998, Springer-Verlag.

Proceedings of *«UML»'99* (ed. R. France and B. Rumpe), 1999, Springer-Verlag.

Quatrani, T., 1998, *Visual Modelling with Rational Rose and UML*, Addison-Wesley, Reading, MA, USA, 222 pp.

Si Alhir, S., 1998, *UML in a Nutshell*, O'Reilly & Associates, Cambridge, MA.

Warmer, J. and Kleppe, A., 1999, *The Object Constraint Language. Precise Modeling with UML*, Addison-Wesley, Reading, MA, 112 pp.

III. Useful websites

http://www.open.org.au
http://www.cetus-links.org
http://www.rational.com
http://www.omg.org
http://www.foruse.com
http://members.aol.com/acockburn
http://www.myriadsl.com.au

IV. Other valuable material

Ambler, S.W., 1999, Enhancing the Unified Process, *Software Development*, **7**(10), 33–39.

Baudoin, C. and Hollowell, G., 1996, *Realizing the Object-Oriented Lifecycle*, Prentice Hall, NJ, 508 pp.

Constantine, L.L. and Henderson-Sellers, B., 1995, Notation matters: Part 1 – framing the issues; Part 2 – applying the principles, *Report on Object Analysis and Design*, **2**(3), 25–29 and **2**(4), 20–23.

Constantine, L.L. and Lockwood, L.A.D., 1994, Fitting practices to the people, *American Programmer*, **7**(12), 21–27.

Daniels, J., 1997, Object method: beyond the notations, *Object Expert*, **2**(2), 36–40.

Firesmith, D.G., 1995, Use cases: the pros and cons, *Report on Object Analysis and Design*, **2**(2), 2–6.

Firesmith, D.G. and Henderson-Sellers, B., 1998, Upgrading OML to Version 1.1: Part 1. Referential relationships, *JOOP/ROAD*, **11**(3), 48–57.

Goldberg, A. and Rubin, K.S., 1995, *Succeeding with Objects. Decision Frameworks for Project Management*, Addison-Wesley, Reading, MA, 542 pp.

Graham, I.M., 1995, A non-procedural process model for object-oriented software development, *Report on Object Analysis and Design*, **1**(5), 10–11.

Henderson-Sellers, B., 1995, Who needs an OO methodology anyway?, *J. Obj.-Oriented Programming*, **8**(6), 6–8.

Henderson-Sellers, B. and Barbier, F., 1999, What is this thing called aggregation?, in *TOOLS29* (eds. R. Mitchell, A.C. Wills, J. Bosch and B. Meyer), IEEE Computer Society Press, 216–230.

Henderson-Sellers, B. and Firesmith, D.G., 1998, Upgrading OML to Version 1.1: Part 2 – Additional concepts and notations, *JOOP/ROAD*, **11**(5), 61–67.

Henderson-Sellers, B. and Mellor, S.J., 1999 Tailoring process-focussed OO methods, *JOOP/ROAD*, **12**(4), 40–44, 59.

Pfleeger, S.L., 1991, *Software Engineering. The Production of Quality Software* (2nd ed.), Macmillan, New York, 517 pp.

Rawsthorne, D., 1999, Using use cases, *C++ Report*, **11**(7), 54–57.

V. CASE and drawing tools

We used the following CASE tools for drawing figures in this book:
Simply Objects (www.adaptive-arts.com)
Paradigm Plus (www.cai.com) then follow links to Products and then to Platinum
Rose (www.rational.com)

Appendix: OPEN in a Process Tool

Process and tools

In this book we initially considered the theory of the OPEN process together with the UML. Later on, in Chapters 4 and 5, we applied the theoretical discussions to a couple of case studies. We tried to show these case studies as practical real-life situations. We also used some CASE tools to create the UML designs, in those case studies. Here, in this appendix, we attempt to demonstrate the use of a *process tool* in applying the OPEN process. Thus, this tool is *not* an alternative to the tools used to create and document the UML designs but, instead, a complement to it in real projects.

In practical (and especially large) projects, it is not only important to use the rigours of a proven process – such as OPEN – but it is equally important to ensure that the entire project team is fully aware of what is going on in the project. Which deliverables are being produced, what is their status, who is working on them and, eventually, what is the status of the project? These are some of the questions a *process-centric* project should be able to provide the answers to at all times. This is where tools related to a process come into their own.

Process tools help in configuring the process. In case of OPEN, it is the *instantiation* of the OPEN lifecycle that is facilitated by the use of a process tool. Furthermore, by capturing the instantiation data again and again within a tool, the subsequent instantiation and tailoring of the process become much faster. Finally, as OPEN continues to be used in many projects, it is important to capture the lessons learnt during each of the projects. These lessons are stored in a process tool resulting in a suite of knowledge specific to an organization or a domain. Instantiation of the process would be a much faster process itself, as it will now be supported by a body of knowledge captured within the process tool. An attempt is made here to instantiate OPEN with Process Continuum™. A few screen shots are shown in the figures in this appendix in order to demonstrate the process of instantiation of OPEN. An actual practical process instantiation would be an iterative and incremental process spread over a few days and, perhaps, over a few projects. In order to start demonstrating the instantiation, we quickly reconsider the major artefacts of the OPEN process. These are the artefacts that are mapped to the 'elements' provided by a process tool.

The OPEN artefacts for a tool

We have already seen how OPEN is made of various process-elements or artefacts, which can be put together in order to create an instance of OPEN. These are:

- Activities: These are reusable chunks of 'units of process' or 'Kernels' that can be plugged in and iterated through the project lifecycle.

- Activity–Task mapping: This is effectively a work breakdown structure that describes the Activities and the Tasks within the activities that need to be performed by the project team.
- Work Products: These are well-defined Deliverables, forming the input and outputs to the activities.
- Roles: These are the roles played by people in order to perform the activities and tasks. These are a set of clear definition of responsibilities of the role within the activities that must be completed.
- Techniques: These are a suite of industry-standard as well as custom-developed techniques that can be used depending on the type of projects, business requirements and so on. Physical execution of many of these techniques requires the use of the modeling CASE tools (such as Paradigm Plus™, Rational ROSE™ and Simply Objects™) as used for the diagrams in the earlier chapters.

If we are able to incorporate these artefacts within a process tool, then that tool will be able to help us implement OPEN in a practical environment. It is worth noting here that the use of such a process tool is *not* mandatory for the use of OPEN. OPEN is a discipline that can provide benefits anyway – the use of a tool can only enhance its benefits, especially in a larger IT environment.

Process Continuum™

Platinuum Process Continuum™ from Computer Associates is a *process-tool* that readily lends itself to configuration with OPEN. Process Continuum claims to provide a holistic approach to process-based project management. This tool enables the capturing of processes in an electronic form, thereby making these processes 'active'. These active or live processes or 'units of processes' or 'kernels' can then be electronically published within the organization through (say) a suite of HTML pages. This configured process can also be used by the Project Engineer component of Process Continuum to develop project plans which would closely reflect the estimates based on industry-standard metrics. Furthermore, the time-sheeting component within Process Continuum can also be used, if needed, to capture some of the productivity metrics which can again be published electronically within the organization.

A simple exercise to configure Process Continuum for the OPEN process environment is described below.

To start with, Process Continuum's Launch Pad provides the ability to crate the main artefacts of the process. In our exercise, we have created the following artefacts for an instantiation of OPEN:

1. Templates
2. Kernels
3. Techniques
4. Products
5. Tools

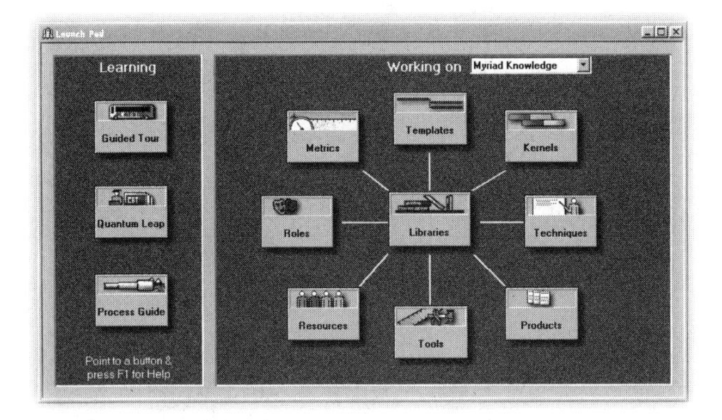

Figure A1 Instantiating a process in Process Continuum™

6. Resources
7. Roles
8. Metrics

This would result in a suite of libraries which together represent the entire process knowledge of the organization. Figure A1 shows such a launch pad with 'Myriad Knowledge' being created for an organization called Myriad.

Figure A2 depicts the creation of a Work Breakdown Structure within Process Continuum. Each of the kernels within this WBS represents an Activity within OPEN. Underneath each Activity is a suite of Tasks that have to be executed in order to accomplish the Activities. For each Activity and Task in the browser window on the left-hand side in Figure A2, there is a corresponding series of descriptions including templates, rules, techniques, library, inputs, predecessors, description and so on. These descriptions fully document the Activities as well as the Tasks of

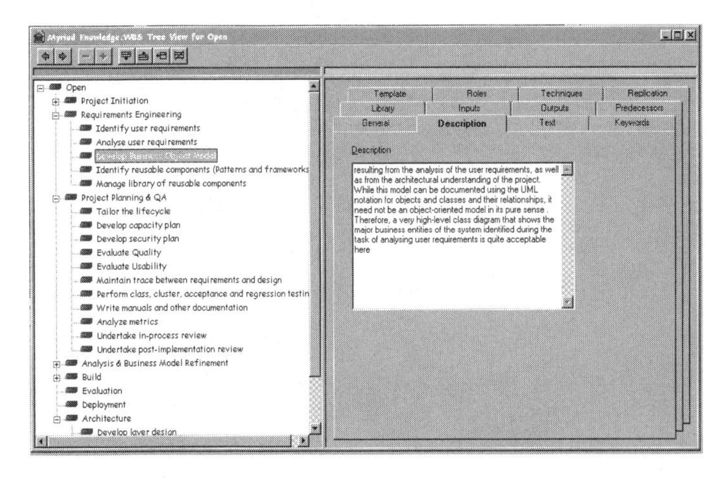

Figure A2 A typical work breakdown structure corresponding to the Activities ('kernels') within OPEN

OPEN within Process Continuum. It is possible to *iterate* within these Activities and Tasks as needed by providing a corresponding description for the Activity and Task.

Figure A3 shows the mapping of the Activity of Requirements Engineering of OPEN within Process Continuum. On the left-hand browser in Figure A3, we also see the description of the Activity as well as the definition of Outputs. The Activity of Requirements Engineering is shown with its corresponding five tasks. A click on any of these Tasks will lead to further description of the Task. Similarly, the Activity of project initiation with its corresponding description is shown in Figure A4.

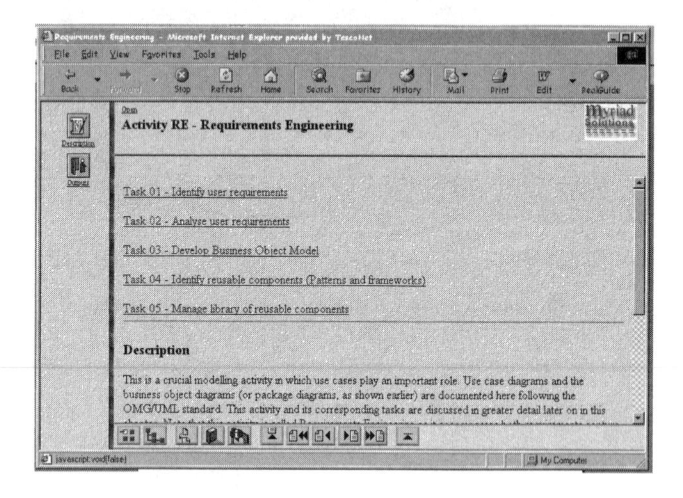

Figure A3 The OPEN Activity of Requirements Engineering configured within Process Continuum™

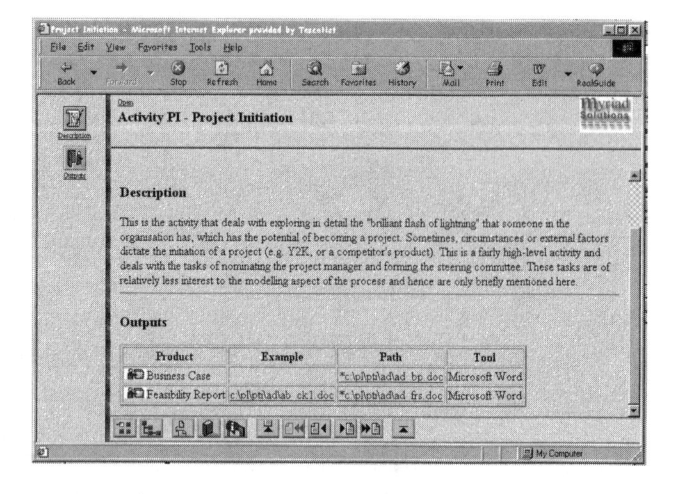

Figure A4 The OPEN Activity of project initiation configured within Process Continuum™

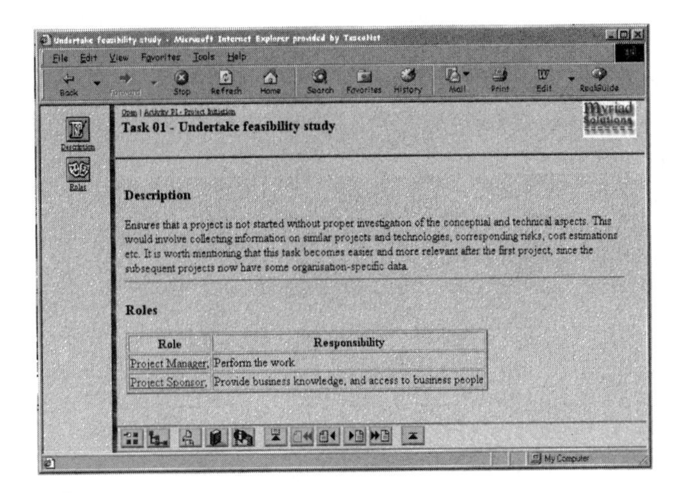

Figure A5 The OPEN Task of Undertake Feasibility Study for the Activity of project initiation configured within Process Continuum™

Finally, Figure A5 shows a part of the detailed description of the Task: Undertake Feasibility Study, which is a part of the Activity of project initiation. This figure also shows the roles involved in carrying out the Task: Undertake Feasibility Study, and their corresponding responsibilities.

Extending the exercise shown in this example will lead to complete documentation of the OPEN process within Process Continuum. This documentation will provide the suite of *process knowledge* so essential in creating different process instances within the organization.

Acknowledgements

We specifically wish to record our thanks to David Hazlewood of Myriad Solutions, Inc. (www.myriadsl.com) in helping us configure parts of OPEN within Process Continuum. Thanks are also due to Computer Associates in Sydney for enabling us to use a copy of Process Continuum for this purpose. Process Continuum™ is the trademark of Computer Associates.

Index